GARDENING
with
CLIMBERS

GARDENING
∼ *with* ∼
CLIMBERS

Christopher Grey-Wilson

&

Victoria Matthews

TIMBER PRESS
Portland, Oregon

First published in 1997 by
HarperCollins*Publishers* London

Editorial Director: Polly Powell
Project Editor: Carole McGlynn
Designer: Amzie Viladot Lorente
Indexer: Susan Bosanko

Published in North America by
Timber Press, Inc.
The Haseltine Building
133 S.W. Second Avenue, Suite 450
Portland, Oregon 97204, U.S.A.

A CIP catalog record for this book is available
from the Library of Congress

ISBN 0-88192-399-0

Text set in Perpetua and Gill Sans Light

Colour reproduction by Saxon Photolitho, Norwich, UK
Printed and bound by LEGO S.p.A., Vincenza, Italy

Acknowledgments
The publishers thank the following for their kind
permission to reproduce the photographs in this book:

Gillian Beckett pages 17 (top right), 25 (bottom), 36, 42, 45, 56, 51 (left and right), 42 (right), 54, 55, 62, 65 (top and bottom), 69 (right), 71 (top), 83 (middle), 86 (top right), 88, 90, 96, 97, 124, 127 (left), 139, 143 (bottom); **The Garden Picture Library** pages 3 (Lynn Brotchie), 6–7 (Mayer/Le Scarf), 32–3 (Nigel Temple), 61 (Sunniva Harte), 86 (Linda Burgess), 120–1, 123; **John Glover** pages 1, 9 (top left), 14 (top and bottom), 15 (left),17 (bottom right), 18 (right), 24, 34, 35 (left and right), 37, 38, 53, 57 (left and right), 58–9, 61 (right), 66–7, 71 (bottom), 82, 83 (top), 91, 93, 100 (bottom), 130; **Chris Grey-Wilson** pages 10–11, 11 (top and bottom), 15 (right), 22, 23 (left and right), 39, 41, 48 (left and right), 50 (left and right), 56, 60, 63 (top and bottom), 64 (top left and bottom), 69 (left), 70 (left and right), 72, 73 (left, top right and bottom right), 74 (left), 75, 76 (bottom), 77, 78 (left and right), 79 (right), 80, 81, 83 (bottom), 84–85, 86 (bottom right), 98, 99, 100 (top), 115 (left and right), 122 (bottom), 123 (top and bottom right), 127 (right), 131 (right), 133, 134 (left and right), 135 (top and bottom), 136, 137, 138, 140, 141 (top and bottom), 142, 143 (top), 148 (bottom), 149, 150 (left), 152, 154 (top); **Harpur Garden Library** pages 8, 9 (bottom right), 18 (left), 19, 20 (right), 21 (bottom), 25 (top), 27 (right), 28, 68, 104 (top and bottom), 106, 111, 117, 122 (top), 147 (all Jerry Harpur), page 105 (Marcus Harper); **Victoria Matthews** pages 20 (left)26, 27 (left), 43, 44, 47, 64 (top right), 74 (right), 76 (top), 79 (left), 92 (bottom right), 101, 102–3, 107 (left and right), 108, 109, 112, 113 (top and bottom), 114, 116 (top, bottom left and right), 118, 119 (top, bottom left and right), 131 (left), 132 (top and bottom), 144–5, 146 (top right), 148 (bottom), 150 (right), 153, 154 (bottom), 155, 156 (left and right), 157 (left and right) 158; **Graham Strong** pages 9 (top right), 16, 17 (left), 87.

Contents

the World
of Climbers

Introduction

An archway draped in sweet-smelling honeysuckle or a wall clothed with clematis or dripping blue wisteria are features much admired in temperate gardens. In tropical and subtropical gardens, more vibrant colours are set against the lushness of foliage: a tree enshrouded in rampant purple bougainvillea, for example, or an arbour yellow with allamanda or a wall cloaked with orange pyrostegia. All these vertical surfaces provide a wonderful environment against which to grow an exciting range of garden plants: the climbers.

There is a large number of fine climbing plants that can be grown in our gardens and the choice can often seem perplexing. Choosing the right climbers for the garden can be both an exciting and a pleasurable experience; their infinite variety of form, colour, scent and foliage provide plenty for the gardener to enjoy. Climbers certainly add a new dimension to gardening. Carefully chosen and sited, they can be an integral part of the overall garden design and can make important vertical focal points. Growing climbers on their own can produce interesting effects but, used in combination with other plants, and especially when associated with trees and shrubs, climbers can greatly enhance the garden, adding interest for many months of the year. Some climbers can even be used for their ground cover effect.

Walls and fences offer the most obvious support for climbers. The walls of houses and other buildings are often high enough to provide the perfect environment for some of the more rampant climbers. Unsightly walls and fences can be concealed perfectly below a shroud of clambering stems and foliage, enlivened at the right season by a show of flowers or fruits, or an eye-catching blaze of autumn leaf-tints. Yet there are many other structures that can support climbers, from trellis and arches to pergolas, obelisks and arbours. A stout wooden post or a tripod of stakes set up in

(Left) A trellis arch dripping with roses in summer casts inviting shade over the entrance to a garden 'room'.

(Right) Vitis coignetiae provides brilliant autumn hues and luxuriant enough foliage to cover a wall or fence completely.

the garden can become a focal point, created especially for climbers. More natural effects can be produced by allowing climbers to clamber up trees and large shrubs. The luxuriant effect of trees and climbers need not be confined to gardens in warm climates; in cooler regions a tree festooned with a vigorous form of *Clematis montana* or *Hydrangea petiolaris* can produce a more exotic effect.

Walls and fences offer not only support but also protection for climbers. In cooler gardens, the warmth and protection afforded by a sheltered wall can enable the gardener to grow less hardy climbers that would never survive in the more open parts of the garden. In addition, walls and fences can provide various different aspects for climbers, furnishing suitable places for those that relish full sun as well as for those that prefer partial or deep shade.

Climbers need not be confined to the open garden. More and more gardens today have large glasshouses or conservatories that are ideal for growing climbers in. Furthermore, in cooler regions the use of such buildings allows a greater scope for introducing subtropical and even tropical climbers into 'the garden'; some of these require only a minimum of heat to allow them to survive the winter.

There is a number of different types of climbers. Some are annuals, which need to be grown from seed each season; they are excellent for producing a quick and effective cover, especially for temporary sites and, as most can be readily grown from seed, they are generally inexpensive to acquire. Others are herbaceous perennial climbers that die down each year to a permanent base, producing new shoots again each spring. The largest number, however, are woody, with a permanent framework of branches that are in essence climbing shrubs; in fact many climbers, like the honeysuckles, have shrubby, non-climbing cousins. Their framework branches may be slight and relatively lightweight or they may be more massive, developing in time hefty trunks and branches with a considerable volume and weight. All types of climbers have a place in the garden. Many prefer full sun or half-shade, but do not be discouraged by that dull wall or fence in heavy shade, for there are climbers that thrive there too.

(*Above*) Large-flowered clematis make a perfect companion for summer-flowering shrubs.

(*Left*) The exquisite foliage effects of *Actinidia kolomikta* are just as rewarding as flowers. Here it is offset by *Elaeagnus pungens* 'Variegata'.

Climbers in the Wild

Climbing plants are found growing wild in many parts of the world from cool temperate regions to the tropics and sub-tropics, although it is in the latter environments that they are most prolific. Walk into almost any forest or jungle in these steamy regions and you will quickly notice the climbers and lianas clambering high into the canopy, their tracery of stems often covering considerable distances. In the mountain forests and shrubberies of cooler regions climbers are also an important part of the natural associations of plants. Climbers have evolved to fill an important niche: by using other plants (or sometimes rocks) for support, they are able to reach upwards towards the light and to occupy places where few other plants can compete successfully with them.

Most climbers are fast-growing, producing long, thin and whip-like growths that seek support long before the leaves unfurl and the stems thicken; thus they are secure before the stems become too weighty and unmanageable. It is in the nature of many climbers to bloom at the top of the plant leaving below large expanses of bare or leafy stems, the flowers adorning the shoots that have reached the canopy of trees or shrubs.

Tropical regions have provided us with some really colourful and magnificent climbers. From South America come golden yellow *Allamanda cathartica*, many species of *Philodendron*, the familiar bougainvilleas with their often jazzy tones, and the brilliant flame vine (*Pyrostegia venusta*). The Caribbean has given us *Ipomoea horsfalliae*, fragrant queen of the night (*Selenicereus grandiflorus*), as well as silver chalice (*Solandra grandiflora*) and Gabriel's trumpet (*S. longiflora*) with their gigantic blooms. Australia has contributed bower plant (*Pandorea jasminoides*) and the rex begonia vine (*Cissus discolor*).

South Africa is a country richly endowed with a large and diverse flora and has provided us with the well-known Cape

leadwort (*Plumbago auriculata*), with its heads of blue flowers, and the orange Cape honeysuckle (*Tecomaria capensis*) which is not a true honeysuckle but a plant belonging to the family Bignoniaceae, which also contains *Campsis* and *Eccremocarpus*. From Madagascar comes stephanotis with its strongly perfumed, white waxy flowers. India is the home of *Jasminum sambac*, and the spectacular blue-mauve sky flower (*Thunbergia grandiflora*) and its cousin *T. mysorensis*. South-East Asia is another area rich in climbing species including king's jasmine (*Jasminum rex*) from Thailand and

Cambodia, the golden pothos (*Epipremnum aureum*) from the Solomon Islands and the legendary jade vine (*Strongylodon macrobotrys*) from the Philippines, whose hanging racemes of turquoise-green flowers have to be seen to be believed.

But there are also numerous exciting climbers from cooler regions. The southern Andes of South America have contributed the mutisias with their big, brightly coloured daisy flowers, as well as *Solanum crispum* and *S. valdiviense*. China has given us many actinidias, *Clematis* and species of *Ampelopsis* and *Rosa*, and from Japan come

(Left) *Rosa longicuspis* clambers through a pine in N.W. Yunnan; it is one of several vigorous climbing rose species from western China.

(Above) *Bougainvillea* hails from Brazil.

(Right) *Clematis tibetana* subsp. *vernayi* tumbles down a valley in Nepal.

some of the beautiful species and cultivars of *Wisteria*. It was the sight of these beautiful plants growing in their native lands which convinced the early plant-explorers and botanists that they should be brought back and introduced into gardens so that we can all enjoy them.

Many different species of clematis are to be found in both the northern and southern hemispheres where they are typically plants of woodland, scrub or hedgerows, beautiful in flower but many also attractive in the autumn when their trailing growths are adorned with fluffy seedheads.

The old man's beard (*Clematis vitalba*), is widespread along hedgerows and in woodlands throughout southern Britain and much of southern and central Europe. In the same places you might well find another familiar climber, the sweet-scented common honeysuckle (*Lonicera periclymenum*), which twines its shoots up all manner of trees as well as shrubs.

There are undoubtedly many other exciting climbers yet to be introduced from the wild. Recent expeditions to China, for instance, have collected seed of several new clematis species.

Climbing Techniques

Plants climb by various means. In the less sophisticated types the stems simply scramble, producing a network of branches that clamber through and up the branches of other plants. This may be aided by the presence of hooked spines and prickles that literally serve to pull the plant up through its host. But many are more refined and attach themselves in a more secure manner. Many climbers have twining stems that wrap themselves around suitable supports, clinging tightly as they develop; twiners always twine in one direction, either clockwise or anti-clockwise, and this is specific to a particular species.

Some climbers have clinging tendrils that literally grab onto a support as the stems lengthen; the coiling action of the tendrils often bring the stems in close and securely to their host support. Tendrils can develop from various parts of the plant but are usually a modification of the leaf, or the stems themselves, and they may be simple or branched. In some plants the tendrils (usually branched) end in an adhesive pad which sticks firmly to the support. In yet another type, particularly clematis, there are no tendrils but it is the leaf stalks, or petioles, that coil around the support.

A smaller number of climbers produce a mass of short adventitious roots from the stem surface adjacent to the potential support (the best is one with a rough surface such as an old brick wall); once attached, these cling with a limpet-like grip to their support, whether it be a tree trunk or cliff-face.

The different methods by which plants climb are illustrated *(right)*, showing the varied means of attaching themselves to their supports.

a Aerial roots

b Twining stems

c Coiling petioles

d Adhesive pads

e Leaf tendrils

f Stem tendrils

g Hooked thorns

Choosing Climbing Plants

Selecting plants can be great fun. With climbers it is especially important to consider subjects and sites before acquiring the plants. Many climbers can be vigorous and will soon outgrow their allotted position, even with a careful regime of pruning, so it is important to consider the space available. Climbers for walls and fences will require suitable support in the manner of trellis or wires and it is easier to put these in place before any planting is undertaken *(see page 22)*. On old buildings in particular it may be unwise to plant one of the self-clinging types of climber in case it does harm to the walls, especially to old mortar.

Aesthetic ·considerations include the colour of leaves and flowers and whether these go well with the support – be it a wall of grey stone or of red brick, or even a wooden fence; whether they complement neighbouring plants; the season of flowering and for how long it is in bloom; and whether or not the plant is evergreen or deciduous. There is little point in trying to cover an unsightly structure with a deciduous climber!

Your final choice of plants is obviously a personal one but try to choose a climber that will thrive in your particular locality. If in doubt, much valuable information can be gleaned by visiting local gardens or parks and seeing what does well in your own area, taking into consideration that soil types can sometimes change radically over quite a short distance. Walking or driving around your neighbourhood and seeing what people are growing can be very informative.

It goes without saying that you should choose only vigorous and healthy young plants. It is always satisfying to go to a large and reputable nursery or garden centre and to choose the plants for yourself, ensuring that you get healthy specimens and exactly what you want. Reject any plants that show any sign of pest or dieback, or those that are obviously old and pot-bound.

When choosing suitable climbers, bear in mind the following criteria; some of these will be elaborated in later sections but they are worth considering here:

(Above left) Hydrangea petiolaris clings unaided to walls and fences.

(Left) Choose flowering climbers (here clematis, *Actinidia kolomikta* with *Geranium psilostemon*) whose colours go with each other and the wall.

SIZE

The eventual size of the plant (use the directory entries in this book to determine the dimensions of different climbers).

BULK

The eventual bulk of the climber: some extensive climbers can be moderately light-weight but others, for instance wisteria and bougainvillea, can become very bulky and heavy in time. They will need strong and long-lasting supports.

MAINTENANCE

How much maintenance will the climber require? If a lot of attention is required to prune and tie in shoots, then the position should be readily accessible without having to clamber across other plants to reach it. Climbers which require regular pruning in order to perform well are generally unsuitable for growing up trees where access can, at the least, be awkward.

THE FRAMEWORK

If the structure on which the climber is to grow requires regular maintenance (painting a fence, for instance) then it is unwise to plant a climber which needs a permanent framework and better to choose one which has a temporary framework, such as one of the many herbaceous climbers which will die down to the ground level at the end of each season.

(Below left) The golden hop (*Humulus lupulus* 'Aureus') is a perfect choice for this trellis, which needs regular painting, as it dies down each year.

(Below) Spectacular flowers adorn the fragile herbaceous climber, *Tropaeoleum tricolorum*, early in the spring. The wall stores heat and will give extra protection.

Associating Climbers in the Garden

Working out plant associations can be a lifetime occupation – gardening books are full of different possibilities for all sorts of plants. What may suit one garden or gardener may not suit another and personal preferences for colours, forms and textures are very individual. Combinations of plants can be carefully planned but often the best associations happen by chance. Climbing plants can be happily combined with various trees and shrubs, or indeed with other climbers. The prime consideration, apart from the more aesthetic ones of colour and texture, is that of vigour. Many climbers are quite rampant and can easily overwhelm neighbouring plants, besides which their weight has been known to bring down old walls and even quite large trees.

PARTNERS FOR CLEMATIS

Certain combinations of climbers go extremely well together: climbing roses and clematis (especially the large-flowered cultivars and the viticella types) will harmonize very well, whether they are planned to flower at the same time or to follow on. Where rose and clematis require pruning at the same time, then the association seems to work best and is the easier to maintain; mixing the more rampant forms of *Clematis montana*, which requires little or no pruning, with climbing roses which have to be kept under control is impractical.

Clematis and honeysuckles associate well together, the various combinations of colour and the added bonus of scent from the latter can create delightful partnerships. Try, for instance, mixing *Clematis* 'Mrs Cholmondeley' (wisteria-blue), or 'Lady Northcliffe' (lavender-blue) with *Lonicera × tellmaniana* (glowing yellow), which will all flower in the early summer.

Climbers such as *Akebia*, *Celastrus*, *Sinofranchetia* and the robust forms of

Left: The deep pink of *Clematis* 'Madame Julia Correvon' is enhanced by the pink-flowered astilbe and the purple-leaved *Acer palmatum*. The clematis has been allowed to ramble over these lower-growing plants, rather than being trained up a support.

Right: *Clematis montana* var. *rubens* makes a lovely companion for the large-leaved ivy on a fence, its yellow centre matching the golden variegation of the ivy.

Clematis montana and *C. viticella* can be allowed to romp up a large tree and can be left entirely to themselves if desired. Trees that are scarcely noticed when they are not in flower or fruit can, when they are draped with climbers, provide a focal point in the garden at different seasons of the year.

Shrubs can provide excellent support for climbers. Many gardeners think that clematis, for example, look more natural and pleasing when allowed to tangle with shrubs as they do in the wild. The best type of shrub for this is one with a fairly open

branch system, otherwise the association of shrub and climber can look altogether too congested. Care needs to be taken that the climber does not smother its shrubby partner; the two must always work together, in harmony.

Clematis viticella cultivars such as 'Royal Velours' and 'Ville de Lyon', which can be pruned hard back in the early spring, make fine partners for shrubs like *Euonymus* 'Red Cascade' or *Corylus avellana* 'Purpurea', whose show of autumn colour and attractive fruits follows the summer display of clematis flowers.

Above: Roses and clematis make a classic partnership. Here, *Clematis* 'Etoile Violette' is planted with *Rosa soulicana*, flowering at the same time.

Left: *Vitis* 'Brant' is a superb example of a climber which needs no partner, especially when seen in its autumn glory.

CLIMBERS ALONE

Many of the boldest climbers work splendidly on their own in the garden and need no companions – in fact, fussy interplanting can spoil their effectiveness. Wisterias, with their twisting branches and streamers of pea-flowers, the climbing hydrangea with its lacecap heads of creamy blooms, the expansive foliage of vigorous *Vitis coignetiae* with its startling autumn colours or the prettily white- and pink-splashed leaves of *Actinidia kolomikta* need no enhancing and make their mark unaided in the garden.

CLIMBERS ON STRUCTURES

Arbours and arches can often be tricky to plant or at least to plant in such a way as to achieve a perfect balance. They can be draped with a single species or cultivar, but an association of different plants can often be more alluring. Try planting the rose 'New Dawn' (pink, early summer) on one side of an arch and *Clematis* 'Jackmanii Superba' (purple, early summer) on the other, or *Jasminum officinale* (white, scented in summer) and *Clematis macropetala* 'Maidwell Hall' (deep blue, spring, but

fruiting in summer with the jasmine in flower). For foliage interest, try planting the golden-leaved hop (*Humulus lupulus* 'Aureus') with one of the gold-variegated ivies or with a small-flowered herbaceous clematis such as 'Madame Correvon' or 'Etoile Violette'.

In a tropical climate, you might try planting *Allamanda* with a bougainvillea, in either an apricot- or a blue/purple-flowered form. There are countless other possibilities, the important consideration being to match the vigour of the climbers chosen to partner each other.

Hardiness, Soils and Planting

(Left) Vitis vinifera 'Purpurea' and wisteria are both hardy with the protection of a wall.

(Right) In temperate climates, conservatories furnish an ideal environment for a host of tender plants, here including the climbing *Plumbago auriculata*.

(Left) Self-clinging *Parthenocissus tricuspidata* is a superb deciduous climber where space allows. Keep it well watered during the summer.

Hardiness is a critical consideration where climbers are concerned. It is pointless spending money on plants if they are simply never going to survive in the open garden, even when given the protection of walls or fences. However, even in cool, temperate gardens it is surprising just how many different types of climber can be grown, so that there is always a wide choice of subjects. In tropical and subtropical gardens hardiness is less important but drought and heat may be critical; many temperate-latitude plants will not grow in the sultry conditions of such gardens. Those with a yearning to grow some of the more tender subjects in cooler regions should consider the use of a heated conservatory.

A word of warning: hardiness should always be ascertained with some caution. A plant may be hardy in a warm, sheltered corner of the garden but not in a more exposed part of it; the same plant may prove hardier on dry, light soils than on heavy, damp clay.

THE SOIL

As with all plants, climbers need soils that are properly prepared. Planting into soil without adequate preparation will often lead to a lack of vigour in plants and even death. Bear in mind that soils close to walls and fences, or those at the base of trees, are generally dry and impoverished. They need to be dug over to a good depth, 45–60cm (18–24in), removing any weeds, large rocks or other debris. If necessary fresh soil can be brought in to fill the hole, especially if the existing soil is very heavy clay or is badly compacted. Plenty of well-rotted manure or compost added to the soil is very beneficial (especially to light sandy soils), as are dressings of organic fertilizers such as bonemeal. All this can be thoroughly mixed in and the area firmed down (not too heavily) before planting.

Acid soils can be modified by adding lime if required, but limy soils cannot be readily converted to a soil suitable for acid-loving climbers. Acid soil pockets *can* be created but this generally involves building special compartments from which calcium can be excluded and obtaining suitable acid soil; this can be both costly and time-consuming and it is generally better to concentrate on

the wide range of climbers suitable for your own average soil conditions.

PLANTING CLIMBERS

Container-grown plants can be planted at almost any time of the year. For fully hardy types of climber, any month will do unless the weather is inclement; however, tender and half-hardy types are better planted in the spring or early summer to ensure they get a good start and are well established by the following winter. Climbers planted during the summer months will need to be well watered in, with repeated watering through dry, hot periods. It may also be necessary to shield plants from hot sun until they have become established: this is usually indicated by renewed growth.

In cooler regions it is generally wiser to plant evergreen subjects in late winter or early spring, although some gardeners advocate getting the plants established before winter by planting them in the early autumn. Once frosts have arrived, it is better to protect container evergreens in a sheltered place, planting them out the following year once the frosts have finished.

Conditions very close to the base of walls, fences or trees do not offer ideal planting places for climbers, despite the protection which such places afford, because rainfall will have difficulty reaching them. You must also allow enough room for the developing stems and branches of the climber, which may grow very thick in time. In summer, walls may become very hot and this can damage the base of plants placed too close to the wall. On the other hand, if plants are placed too far away from walls or fences then they begin to lose the valuable protection offered by these structures; if they are too far way from the base of trees or pergolas, then it is more difficult to train in the young shoots to climb their chosen supports. It is best to compromise: generally speaking, a distance of 15–30cm (6–12in) away from the support will suffice, depending on the plant's expected vigour.

Dig out an adequate-sized hole for the plant's roots, without cramping them. The entwined roots of container-grown specimens can be teased out to some extent and this will help the plants to establish more quickly and to ensure that the roots grow out properly into the surrounding soil. It is always wise to plant at the same depth the plant was originally at, with the exception of clematis which can be planted deeper to encourage strong growth from below ground level.

Once planted, climbers should be firmed in and watered well. Mulches placed around the base of newly planted climbers can be beneficial in helping to prevent drying out, especially during hot, dry spells.

Where no suitable soil is available close to walls, climbers can be very successfully grown in large tubs which can become a decorative features in themselves. Any standard potting compost can be used: choose a suitable one for acid-loving plants. Tubs should never be allowed to dry out.

Walls and Structures for Climbers

Structural supports for climbing plants must be well secured and structurally sound so they can adequately bear the weight of the proposed plant or plants. Nothing is more frustrating than having a climber collapse in full flower because the support was insufficient to bear the weight or was not properly secured. In addition, unsound supports can be danger-ous. Supports must also take into account possible storms and gales.

Some climbers need no additional sup-port other than a wall or fence as they cling by themselves unaided. However, for others something more substantial is required.

(Above) A system of wires allows the rose 'Kew Rambler' to be securely fixed to an old brick wall.

(Right) A pergola planted with a selection of different climbers becomes an integral part of the garden's design.

WALLS

The walls of buildings provide one of the most rewarding places in the garden on which to grow a variety of different climbers. Climbers can soften the harsh exterior of many modern buildings and complement the graceful exteriors of some of the older ones. Where old or historic buildings are concerned, care must be taken that climbers do not hide the architectural details of the building; carefully chosen, the one can enhance the other. It can be a great delight to look out of a window through a frame of flowery climbers, or to have the perfume of climbers like honeysuckle or stephanotis drifting into the house.

Walls are most valuable for the protection that they provide. Close to a house the temperature in winter and summer will certainly be higher than in the more exposed parts of the garden. This gives a valuable opportunity to grow some of the more tender climbers, especially if the wall is well protected, extending the range of plants that can be grown in the open garden. Walls of different aspect will suit different climbers. Shaded walls are as valuable as sunny ones: this is especially so in tropical and subtropical gardens where shaded walls are at a premium, providing a cooler envi-ronment for certain climbers that seek shade rather than blazing sunshine.

A lot has been written in the past about the adverse effect of climbers on the walls of buildings. They destroy the mortar, pull off the plaster and damage the framework of windows and doors, and many people worry unduly about this. The fact is that the majority do very little damage and may even help to protect the building. Self-clinging climbers can, however, damage old soft mortar or strip off pebbledash, so this needs to be taken into account when choosing suitable plants. Stout thorns can scratch paintwork, especially in windy regions but this need not be a problem if the climbers are carefully trained and pruned. The roots of climbers are rarely large and extensive enough to cause damage to the foundations of buildings. Exceptions are seen in some of the very vigorous and woody climbers grown in the tropics and subtropics, but in such favoured gardens they can be grown well away from buildings in any case.

WOODEN STRUCTURES

All wooden garden structures should be made from properly preserved timber, otherwise it will quickly rot in the soil and the effort of construction may be lost in just a few years. There is no reason why a pergola or arch strongly constructed with preserved timbers should not last a lifetime. Existing timber can be treated with a suitable preservative but remember that creosote can badly damage plants, often long after it has been applied, while some other preservatives are safe once they have dried (in a matter of hours usually). Today, pressure-treated preserved timbers are readily available. For large structures it is best to anchor the posts in concrete. Alternatively, special metal post holders, that are widely available, can be driven into the ground in the desired positions.

Today various manufacturers catalogue a whole range of different pre-manufactured, self-assembly pergolas, arches, arbours and so on; these may be made of preserved timbers, rust-proof metal or metal coated with plastic (black in most instances) and these make it easy and quick to construct suitable supports for climbers. For the more ambitious there is always the fun of designing and constructing your own unique structures.

Remember that the structures should be an integral part of the overall design of the garden: try to visualize what they will look like when clothed with climbers. **Arches** can lead you into a part of the garden, along a pathway or down a flight of steps onto the lawn. A series of arches can take one deep into the garden, revealing different vistas as each is passed, like entering different rooms in the house. **Pergolas** have a tunnel effect, taking one's eye down to a distant feature. **Trellis** can provide a break, separating different parts of the garden, the flower garden from the vegetables or fruit, for instance. **Colonnades** can create a similar effect but less formally, while also making a delightful backdrop to the herbaceous border: colonnades festooned with climbing and rambling roses can marry very happily with bush roses, extending the panorama of blooms high in the air.

Poles planted with a specimen climber can make a strategic statement in the border, a focal point amongst other lower plants. A series planted in a row can make a more formal statement. **Obelisks, tripods and quadropods** have a similar effect and are more suitable for some of the bulkier climbers. An informal wigwam of peasticks was much favoured by the cottage gardener, being cheap and easy to construct; they can make a delightful feature when planted with some of the annual climbers, such as

(Above) A pergola draped with tender *Pyrostegia venusta* provides welcome shade as well as colour.

delightfully scented sweet peas or glowing orange *Eccremocarpus*. A circle of canes 2–3m (6½–10ft) tall can have a similar effect, although these are more rigid and formal and can be used to bring some vegetables, such as the many sorts of climbing bean, into the flower garden.

(Right) An arbour festooned with climbing roses provides an idyllic place to sit, and the air will be perfumed with their lovely scent.

Providing Support

(Above) Wire netting provides unobtrusive support for delicate annual climbers, such as sweet peas.

S ome of the popular larger climbers, such as wisteria and bougainvillea, can become very bulky and heavy in time and will need adequate, robust supports. Apart from the self-adhering climbers, like ivy, most climbers will need some form of support. When allowed to grow amongst shrubs or other plants the climbers can find their own support, the only training necessary may be to guide the shoots more or less in the required direction. The informality of allowing climbers to find their own way through other plants appeals greatly to many gardeners, but perhaps not those with tidy and well disciplined minds!

Grown on walls, fences or pergolas, most climbers will require some form of support, otherwise they will never make it to the top. Make sure the proposed support is adequate to carry the weight of the plant, assess how long the support will last (some climbers will be in place for many years), and whether it can be readily attached to wall and fence and properly secured without harming the wall (especially those of old or historic buildings).

For annual and herbaceous climbers, **canes or branches** (peasticks) can be used and these can look quite decorative in themselves. Many lightweight woody climbers can be trained up simple **trellis** secured to the wall but, for the bulkier types, a more elaborate and robust system of **heavy-gauge wires**, **bolts and strainers** will prove necessary. Most garden centres supply a range of different types of trellis (some collapsible and easy to transport) and different brackets and fixings for securing wires or wooden battens to walls and fences, or indeed pergolas, pillars and tripods.

Trellis can be stained various colours to blend in with wall or fence (or however it is used). It can look unpleasing if not blended in and the effect of the climber can be marred by unsightly trellis, so it is always a good idea to spend a little time getting it right before the climbers are installed. Both trellis and wires should be fixed away from the wall (by some 5cm/2in), to allow plenty of space for the developing stems.

Even chainlink fencing or chicken wire can look attractive with flowery climbers clambering over – indeed, this is a suitable form of support for annual climbers such as sweet peas or canary creeper (*Tropaeolum peregrinum*).

FIXING THE SUPPORTS

The correct fixing of climbers is of great importance and careful consideration needs to be given to how the plant will be fixed to its support. It cannot be emphasised strongly enough that the fixings must be up to the job and their sturdiness must be adequate to bear the weight of the plant, sometimes for many years. It can be very frustrating to go into the garden and find that the fixings have snapped under the weight of the climber and the whole plant lies forlorn on the ground. At that stage it is very difficult to re-attach the plant and the year's blooms may well be spoilt. Of course self-clinging climbers need no special help and can be left to their own devices apart from perhaps training growth in the generally desired direction and removing unwanted shoots. Twiners require only vertical wires or battens to climb up. A few horizontal struts, at intervals, will prevent the young stems from slipping down as can often happen, especially in windy or very wet weather.

Galvanized wire of different strengths and thicknesses (10–14 gauge) can be very effective and will blend into walls and fences extremely well without disfiguring them, as do some forms of trellis and wire mesh. They can be attached by means of **galvanized bolts** (screw eyes or vine eyes), 7.5–10cm (3–4in) long; these need to be properly drilled into wood or brickwork and set apart at a distance of about 1.5–2m (5–6½ft). The horizontal wires need to be about 50cm (20in) apart with the lowest about 30cm (12in) from the ground. Vertical wires can be spaced at a similar distance if desired. Short lengths of wire (say up to 3m/10ft) can be strained sufficiently by hand but longer lengths will

(Above) Clematis montana 'Tetrarose' covers a wooden fence with the aid of supporting wires.

require extra assistance, otherwise the wires will be too loose. This can be accomplished by purchasing adjustable **straining bolts or eye bolts** (various types are available): the wires are tightened by hand as much as possible, then the final tightening is achieved by screwing up the adjustable bolt. Each length of wire will require one straining bolt. Eyelet holed metal pins (or small screw eyes) can be used to hold the wires between the end vine eyes and are very quick and easy to install; these are simply strong, pointed narrow wedges of metal which are driven into the support and have a hole in the broad end to take the wire. Fixing these wires in place can be time-consuming but it is well worth the effort.

For lighter-weight climbers, garden centres supply various types of **wall nails, pins** or **eyes**, useful for fixing individual stems or short lengths of wire or string. Depending on the make, they can be either knocked directly into wood, brick or other material, or screwed in (walls will need to have rawl plugs or anchors drilled in first).

TYING STEMS INTO SUPPORTS

Various types of **string** are available. Soft string should be used for young growths as they can be easily damaged. Over-tightening should always be avoided; apart from the physical damage this may cause, ties should allow for expansion of the stem. String, even of the tarred and longer lasting types, cannot be expected to last for more than three or four years at the most and some kinds of string may last for only a single season. **Plastic-coated wire** is longer lasting and can be both cheap and quickly fixed in place.

For bulkier stems that need to be kept in place for many years, other methods have to be devised. **Loops of rubber** placed around the stems (pieces of old bicycle tyre, for instance) and fixed by wire to the wall or fence with nails can be both strong and long-lasting. Shreds of strong cloth can serve the same purpose. Whatever means of attaching is used, it must secure the plant without damaging it.

TRAINING CLIMBERS

Once planted, the young climbers will often need some guidance. The support, whatever it is, will already be in place and the developing shoots can easily be trained in the right direction. Initially, a few loose ties with soft string may be needed but thereafter the shoots can be allowed to clamber up for themselves.

With some plants, like the climbing roses, the new shoots will need to be tied in at regular intervals, but this can usually be left until after flowering, when pruning takes place. In order to encourage strong growth from close to the base of the plant, it is often a good idea to pinch back the young shoot or shoots, selecting the strongest to form the future main frame-

(Above) The morning glory *(Ipomoea purpurea* 'Huberi') twines its way up any support, such as trellis.

work of the climber. With many climbers it is best during the first few years to establish a framework of branches which are firmly fixed to their support and which will bear successive generations of shoots over the succeeding years. These shoots will eventually carry the flowers, so it is important that they are well distributed.

It is often difficult to start off self-clingers such as ivy and the climbing hydrangeas and any buffeting winds will prevent the shoots from attaching themselves to the support. For these it is generally wise to peg down any long shoot to the ground, parallel to the base of the wall. The resultant side-shoots will then grow out and fasten onto the support more readily. Once they are fixed, they can grip with a limpet-like hold.

Any self-clinging stem that comes loose from the wall or other support will need to be tied in or removed, for they have a tendency, especially during windy weather, of pulling more of the plant away from its support.

Pruning Climbers

*P*runing is a subject that often alarms and worries gardeners and nowhere is the lack of pruning or overpruning more obvious than with climbers trained to walls fences or pergolas. But pruning need not be daunting – indeed it can be a good deal of fun once the fundamental principles are understood. A well-pruned climber is an attractive sight and one can admire the skill of the pruner. Bad pruning, on the other hand, can make the plant look ugly and is certainly far worse than no pruning at all. Above all, pruning should never allow the plant's natural grace and beauty to be spoilt.

Pruning is not essential for all climbers. Large climbers that have clambered into lofty trees require little pruning – it may be impossible in any case – and the plants are left to nature. In more confined spaces, however, pruning is needed to keep plants within bounds. A honeysuckle or rose would soon obscure and block an archway or pergola if it were not carefully pruned and trained; unruly climbers can cause concern. Some climbers certainly benefit from a regular routine of pruning, which serves both to train the plant and to promote flowering; many climbers, such as wisteria, that flower on lateral spurs from the branches, respond well to such treatment.

Annual climbers or those whose annual stems are produced from a perennial rootstock (herbaceous climbers) need no pruning, although their shoots may need some training to get them to grow in the required direction. This can be achieved simply by tying them in occasionally, if required. At the end of the season the dying growths are simply removed at ground level, or close to the base of the plant.

The pruning of woody climbers is more complex. It is no good wading in as the mood dictates and clipping without regard. All this will do in most instances will be to promote vigorous vegetative growth at the expense of flowering. The severity of pruning depends to some extent on personal

(Left) The pruning of climbing roses is all-important if they are to give of their best and flower profusely, as over this arch.

preference and, perhaps more important, on the space available. Light pruning allows for a looser, more natural and softer look that is generally more pleasing. Having said this, a well-trained and carefully pruned wisteria, with its twisting branches, can look very effective, even during the winter when it is devoid of leaves.

The prime factor governing pruning is the time of year in which the plant flowers. In general, those that bloom in the spring flower on last season's shoots, while those that flower from midsummer onwards and in the autumn do so on the current season's shoots. Pruning should be carried out to

allow as much time as possible between pruning and flowering so that the plant builds up substantial new growth (potential flowering shoots) in between. Pruning too late will reduce the plant's flowering potential, but if you prune too early, you may well rob the plant of its blossom.

CLIMBERS WHICH FLOWER ON LAST SEASON'S GROWTH

The great majority of climbers in fact **flower on growths made the previous season**, so pruning should take place the moment flowering has finished – generally in late spring or early summer. Pruning simply consists of cutting back growths that have flowered to strong replacement shoots (or a strong bud) which will carry the following year's bloom. If there are too many possible replacement shoots, they will need to be thinned, being careful not to damage those that are required. Any weak shoots or branches can be removed at the same time. The end result should be attractive and well-balanced specimens with ample shoots to carry future flowers.

CLIMBERS WHICH FLOWER ON THIS SEASON'S GROWTH

Conversely, **those climbers that flower on the current season's shoots**, often in summer and autumn, are best pruned during the winter or early spring. With these there will be no obvious replacement shoots as the plants will be dormant or only just starting into growth. Shoots that have flowered the previous summer and autumn can be pruned back to a strong bud or buds near the base of the shoot, leaving the framework of the plant intact. These buds will subsequently grow out and will produce the current season's flowers. A word of caution here: if pruning is left too late in the spring then the plants may not be able to produce sufficient growth to flower fully. Clearly where tender subjects are involved some compromise has to be reached: pruning should not be carried out until all danger of severe frosts have gone. As pruning proceeds any weak, diseased or unwanted growth can be readily removed.

OTHER CLIMBERS

Of course there are exceptions to these rules. **Climbers grown for their foliage** rather than their flowers, such as the ivies, can in effect be pruned at almost any time of the year; as a general rule, however, prune deciduous species in the autumn and evergreens in the spring. **Climbers which produce ornamental fruits** should not be pruned after flowering, otherwise the

display of fruits will be removed before they have had a chance to mature; such subjects need to be pruned with caution and, generally speaking, require very little if any pruning. In temperate gardens **tender climbers** need to be pruned carefully, generally leaving the operation until well into the spring for those that flower on the current season's growths, otherwise

severe frost may attack the cut areas, causing severe die-back or even death. Likewise, with **climbers that flower on the previous season's growth** it is critically important to prune very soon after flowering in order to promote strong new shoots which have the longest possible time to mature before winter comes along. If shoots are badly frost-damaged, leave them alone until the new shoots emerge from lower down the stems or from the base of the plant, then prune back accordingly.

THE FRAMEWORK

Once a framework has been established, then a regular system of pruning can commence. Routine pruning for all climbers consists of first removing all weak, diseased or dead growths in the late winter or early spring. Then prune according to flowering season, as discussed above. Never leave any snags (lengths of stem below a cut without buds) for these will die back and may invite disease.

It would be wrong to think that all climbers need regular pruning. In their early years, many climbers require only minimal pruning. Weak growers as well as young plants require very little, removing only sufficient growth to encourage branching and to stimulate growth.

(Above) Careful pruning of roses maximizes their flowering potential while keeping them neatly trained on a wall.

(Left) Vigorous climbers like *Hydrangea petiolaris* can be allowed to clamber up large trees, needing little or no pruning.

As the season progresses, some shoots may well grow out away from their support and these may hamper access, especially if plants are growing close to paths. Such shoots can be tied in or, if the plant is already crowded, they can be removed altogether. As pruning proceeds, any ties can be checked to see if they need to be loosened or replaced.

Some climbers naturally produce numerous **suckers** (*Muehlenbeckia* for instance) and this is quite natural. Most should be left, although some thinning will do no harm. Where climbers have an ample framework of woody branches, then suckers are unwanted and are best removed; they are easy to remove when young, pulling them away from the plant by hand; if cut, they will certainly resprout.

CONSERVATORY CLIMBERS

Many tropical and subtropical climbers have a very extended flowering season, and some can flower throughout much of the year. Pruning time is less critical as the plants will soon put on new growth after pruning, which is best done when flowering is not at its peak. Many tropical evergreen climbers require pruning only to cut back unwanted extension growth and keep them within bounds. Growth in a warm conservatory will be more rapid and extensive than in a cool one and plants may become extremely entangled or they may overpower neighbouring plants, to the detriment of the latter. It is important not to allow things to get out of control – it is easier to prune occasionally and effectively rather than to wait until a huge amount of pruning is required.

RENOVATION PRUNING

There comes a time in the life of many climbers when they become old, displaying a lack of vigour and reduced flowering.

(*Left*) Many tropical climbers, such as *Petraea volubilis,* are rampant and floriferous. They can be pruned at any time, as they will readily put on new growth.

Some climbers reach this stage in just a few years, others may go on for many years without any apparent loss of vigour at all: wisteria can take twenty or more years to fill an allotted space and will then go on for many many years unhindered. Some climbers will respond readily to drastic renovation, by cutting back all the branches to the main trunk or trunks, or even cutting back the entire plant to within 30cm (12in) of the ground. The resultant shoots will be vigorous and may need thinning if there are too many, but they can be trained from the start. Roses, honeysuckles and most clematis, particularly vigorous types such as *C. armandii* and *C. montana* will respond to drastic renovation.

Other climbers will not respond to this treatment and a severe cutting back may well kill them. Wisteria and pea-flowered climbers in the Leguminosae (pea and bean) family are notable examples. For these the best advice is to replace them with young healthy plants. If unsure, it is often wise to do a partial renovation, cutting back part of the plant only and seeing what happens. If new shoots arise from the base of the plant, then the following year the rest can be cut back, training in the new shoots from the previous year at the same time. Partial renovation can be undertaken over two or three years if necessary.

Hard pruning may be the answer to renovating a particular climber once but it should not become the norm, for succes-

(Left) Ipomoea horsfalliae is a vigorous evergreen subtropical climber, in flower most of the time. It can be pruned to keep it in check.

(Right) Wisteria, a rampant climber, can be pruned into a free-standing standard 'tree'.

sive hard prunes will either promote excessive lush non-flowering growth or weaken the plant severely. Many climbers settle down after a few years to produce more flowers and less extensive vegetative growth; at this stage they often require minimal pruning to keep them in check.

SPUR PRUNING

Certain climbers, notably wisterias, flower on short lateral shoots close to the main branches; these are called spurs. Pruning aims mainly at building up a series of spurs, for the more spurs there are the more flowers there will be. Spur pruning can generally be tackled in two stages. In the summer, long lateral shoots are shortened by about half their length. In the winter these same shoots are trimmed back further to about three buds of the shoot base. Only those long young shoots required to extend the framework of the climber are left unpruned. The shoots which arise from pruned stubs are treated the same way in the

following year, and so on. Gradually the spurs are built up along the branches and the resultant buds will eventually be flower buds rather than vegetative ones. By the times of its maturity a large wisteria will have a complicated system of short spurred branches with relatively few long extension growths being produced. Wisterias require patience and it may take up to eight years from planting before one comes into bloom.

Wisterias and bougainvilleas can also be **pruned to form a standard**. Young plants are restricted to a single stem which is secured to a stout pole. Tipping the leading shoot when it reaches the desired height (a standard trunk can be anything from 1–3m (3–10ft)) will encourage the formation of lateral shoots. The lowermost shoots are

removed to keep the trunk clear, so that a tree-shape is produced, but the others are treated as above, by establishing a rigorous system of spur pruning. In the case of standards, once the outline framework has been established, no further extension shoots are allowed and all the shoots are subjected to spur pruning.

As a final word on the subject it is perhaps wise to stress that there are no hard and fast rules to pruning. The principles outlined above apply to the majority of climbers but not to all of them. Not every gardener will agree on the correct method to prune certain subjects or when to prune them.

The specific pruning of clematis and roses is dealt with in the relevant chapters. For pruning codes, *see page 31*.

Care of Climbers Throughout the Year

*I*n temperate regions the less hardy climbers may well require some form of winter protection in the open garden, especially in severe winters. The most vulnerable part of the majority of climbers is the base, close to the soil, for if this is killed then the whole upper part of the plant will also die, even though, in some instances, plants may sprout from below ground when the spring arrives. The base, or indeed the whole plant, can be protected with fern fronds or bracken, hessian, horticultural fleece or even newspaper. Whatever is used it needs to be securely held in place otherwise winter gales will carry it off. Plastic is generally unsuitable, causing a humid environment which attracts moulds and rot as well as pests such as slugs and snails. Modern forms of horticultural fleece are excellent and not too expensive but they should be kept away from prickly plants which will readily ensnare and ruin it.

Many tender or half-hardy climbers can be grown under glass, which will protect them throughout the winter. Conservatories, in particular, are glorious places to grow climbers, providing plenty of light, warmth and the necessary height. Backing walls and pillars offer excellent support for climbers, which can then furnish colour and interest throughout the year, allowing the conservatory to be enjoyed even when the weather is inclement.

(Right) A conservatory used as an additional sitting room is greatly enhanced by housing tender pot plants, shrubs and climbers in it, making it agreeable to sit in all year round. The *Abutilon* provides height and decorative yellow blooms.

MAINTENANCE CALENDAR

Spring

- Finish pruning climbers that flower on the current year's shoots (⟨⟩s code in the main text). Prune those species that have already bloomed, i.e. those that flower on the previous season's wood (⟨⟩ in text).
- Remove any diseased, damaged or unwanted growth.
- Lightly fork around the base of the plant and apply a slow-release fertilizer such as bonemeal, removing any weeds at the same time.
- Check for signs of pests and diseases, especially aphids, caterpillars, slugs and snails; spray accordingly.
- Tender and most evergreen climbers can be planted; for tender ones (in temperate gardens) wait until the worst frosts are over. In tropical gardens plant in the spring or during the coolest time of year and water regularly there after until the plants are established.

Summer

- Continue to prune climbers that have flowered on the previous season's wood; prune as soon after flowering as possible. Leave or only partly prune plants which have interesting autumn fruits otherwise these will be lost. The first stage spur-pruning of climbers such as wisteria can commence.
- Continue to check for signs of pests and disease, especially aphids, caterpillars, red spider mites and weevils; the last two in conservatories especially. Mildew and blackspot may be a problem on roses. Spray accordingly.
- Tie in shoots that block pathways or access or prune them out altogether.
- Water any plant that shows signs of wilt; regularly water newly planted climbers. Help conserve moisture around the plants by applying fresh mulches (well-rotted manure, compost, bark chippings, coir are all suitable).
- Take semi-hardwood and hardwood cuttings of woody climbers, especially if existing climbers are to be replaced the following year.
- Feed plants with a well balanced fertilizer (preferably low in nitrogen but high in trace elements), especially to plants that are not growing strongly or show any obvious signs on the leaves of mineral deficiency such as premature yellowing, mottling, partial necrosis or un-natural purpling or bronzing of the foliage.

Autumn

- Collect seeds of interesting species for sowing during the winter; especially those of annual and herbaceous climbers.
- Clear up fallen leaves from the base of the plants; they may harbour pests and diseases over winter.
- Plant hardy deciduous climbers.
- In cooler regions protect the lower part and roots of the more tender climbers; straw, fern fronds, hessian, horticultural fleece are all effective, even newspaper protected from the wet.

Winter

- Complete spur pruning of climbers that had the first stage in the summer (see page 27).
- Clear excess growth from around gutters and windows lest they cause blockages or spoil paintwork.
- Check wooden supports for signs of rotting, especially those parts in or close to the soil; replace if necessary.
- Check ties to make sure they are not too loose or too tight; replace if necessary.
- Sow seeds of woody climbers; if necessary use a propagator to ensure germination; stratify seed if required.
- Commence pruning climbers that flower on the current season's shoots ; start with the hardiest types.
- Prepare areas of ground where new climbers are to be planted.
- Renovation work on walls, fences etc. is best carried out during the winter.

Climbers for Special Purposes

DECIDUOUS CLIMBERS FOR TEMPERATE GARDENS

FULL SUN OR HALF-SUN

Actinidia deliciosa
Ampelopsis species
Aristolochia macrophylla
Campsis radicans, *C.* × *tagliabuana*
Clematis 'Bill Mackenzie', *C. flammula*, *C. montana*, many large-flowered cvs
Jasminum officinale
Lonicera etrusca, *L. periclymenum*
Parthenocissus species
Schizophragma hydrangeoides
Vitis coignetiae, *V. vinifera* and cvs
Wisteria floribunda, *W. sinensis* and cvs

SHADE

Akebia quinata
Celastrus orbiculatus
Clematis macropetala, *C. montana* and cvs
Hydrangea petiolaris
Lonicera caprifolium, *L. periclymenum* and cvs, *L.* × *tellmaniana*, *L. tragophylla*
Rosa 'Aloha', 'Madame Grégoire Staechelin', 'Gloire de Dijon', 'Madame Alfred Carrière', 'Danse du Feu'
Parthenocissus species
Schisandra chinensis
Schizophragma hydrangeoides

EVERGREEN CLIMBERS FOR TEMPERATE GARDENS

FULL SUN OR HALF-SUN

Berberidopsis corallina
Clematis armandii, *C. cirrhosa*
Hedera species and cvs
Jasminum officinale
Lonicera giraldii, *L. henryi*, *L. japonica*
'Halliana'
Passiflora caerulea
Rosa banksiae, *R. bracteata*
Stauntonia hexaphylla
Trachelospermum asiaticum, *T. jasminoides*

SHADE

Euonymus fortunei var. *radicans* and cvs
Hedera helix and cvs
Holboellia coriacea
Hydrangea serratifolia
Lapageria rosea and cvs
Pileostegia viburnoides

TEMPERATE CLIMBERS GROWN FOR THEIR FOLIAGE

* deciduous
Actinidia kolomikta *
Ampelopsis species *
Euonymus fortunei var. *radicans* and cvs
Hedera canariensis, *H. colchica*, *H. helix* and cvs
Holboellia coriacea
Humulus lupulus 'Aureus'
Jasminum officinale 'Aureum'
Lonicera japonica 'Aureomarginata'
Parthenocissus henryana *, *P. quinquefolia* *, *P. tricuspidata* *
Sinofranchetia chinensis *
Vitis 'Brant', *V. coignetiae* *, *V. vinifera*

CONSERVATORY CLIMBERS GROWN FOR THEIR FOLIAGE

Cissus discolor
Epipremnum aureum and cvs
Ficus pumila and cvs
Monstera deliciosa
Philodendron bipennifolium, *P. scandens*, *P. melanochrysum*, *P. erubescens* and cvs

CLIMBERS WITH BERRIES OR FRUITS

* deciduous; + annual or herbaceous perennial
Actinidia chinensis *, *A. polygama* *
Ampelopsis brevipedunculata *
Billardiera longiflora
Celastrus orbiculatus *, *C. scandens* *
Humulus lupulus +
Kadsura japonica
Lablab purpureus +
Lagenaria siceraria +
Lardizabala biternata
Lonicera etrusca, *L. periclymenum* and cvs, *L. henryana*
Periploca graeca *, *P. laevigata*
Stauntonia hexaphylla
Trichosanthes cucumerina +
Tropaeolum speciosum +
Vitis vinifera and cvs

TEMPERATE SELF-CLINGING CLIMBERS

Asteranthera ovata
Campsis radicans
Decumaria sinensis
Euonymus fortunei var. *radicans*
Hedera canariensis, *H. colchica*, *H. helix* and cvs
Hydrangea petiolaris
Parthenocissus henryana, *P. quinquefolia*, *P. tricuspidata*
Pileostegia viburnoides
Schizophragma hydrangeoides

CLIMBERS TOLERANT OF ACID OR ALKALINE SOILS

Campsis species and cvs
Fallopia baldschuanica
Hedera species and cvs
Jasminum species and cvs
Lonicera species and cvs
Parthenocissus species
Passiflora caerulea
Rosa; most species and cvs
Solanum species and cvs
Wisteria species and cvs

CLIMBERS FOR TEMPERATE COASTAL REGIONS

Clematis; many species and cvs
Hydrangea petiolaris
Passiflora caerulea
Solanum crispum

FLOWERING CLIMBERS FOR CONSERVATORIES

* requires cool shade
Allamanda cathartica
Beaumontia grandiflora
Bomarea caldasii
Bougainvillea cvs
Cobaea scandens
Hardenbergia violacea
Hoya carnosa
Ipomoea species and cvs
Jasminum mesnyi, J. polyanthum
Lapageria rosea and cvs *
Mandevilla species
Mitraria coccinea *
Mutisia decurrens

Pandorea jasminoides and cvs
Passiflora antioquiensis, P. quadrangularis
Plumbago auriculata
Solandra maxima
Solanum jasminoides, S. seaforthianum
Stephanotis floribunda
Tecomaria capensis

HERBACEOUS PERENNIAL CLIMBERS

Aconitum hemsleyanum
Bowiea volubilis
Clematis viticella and cvs, *C.* 'Jackmanii'
Codonopsis convolvulacea, C. forrestii,
  C. nepalensis
Dicentra chrysantha, D. scandens
Humulus lupulus and cvs
Ipomoea purpurea
Lathyrus grandiflorus, L. latifolius
Thladiantha dubia
Tropaeolum speciosum, T. tuberosum
Vincetoxicum ascyrifolium

ANNUAL CLIMBERS

* short-lived perennial climbers in frost-free
gardens, more permanent in warmer climates
Cobaea scandens *
Eccremocarpus scaber *
Gloriosa superba *
Ipomoea purpurea, I. tricolor
Lablab pupureus *
Lathyrus odoratus and cvs
Maurandya barclaiana *
Mina lobata
Rhodochiton volubile *
Thunbergia alata *
Tropaeolum majus, T. peregrina *
Tweedia caerulea *

*I*n order to cut down on repetitive, but important information in the text, the following condensed information appears in symbol form at the end of each entry.

ASPECT:
  ☼ requires full sun
  ◑ requires semi-shade
  ● requires full shade

HARDINESS *(see page 18)*:
 -15°C (5°F) fully hardy
  -5°C (23°F) frost hardy
   0°C (32°F) half-hardy
  10°C (50°F) tender
These categories indicate likely hardiness.

PRUNING *(see page 24)*:
  ⚘ prune immediately after flowering
  ⚘s prune in spring
  ⚘w prune in winter
  ⚘ no regular pruning required

SOIL ACIDITY:
  ▯ requires an acid soil

Example:
  ☼ ◑ -5°C (23°F) ⚘s ▯
This plant requires full sun or semi-shade, acidic soil and a temperature that does not fall below -5°C (23°F); it should be pruned in spring.

One or more of the following symbols may appear before the name of a species or cultivar.

  ✓ indicates a plant especially
     recommended by the authors

  ⊞ indicates plants that are particularly
     well suited to conservatories

  ○ indicates annual and herbaceous
     climbers suitable for subtropical and
     tropical, as well as temperate, gardens.

  ♛ Royal Horticultural Society's Award
     of Garden Merit.

Temperate
Deciduous
Climbers

Introduction

S ome of the very best climbers are decid-uous species and cultivars, indeed many of them are among the most popular grown in our gardens: the climbing hydrangea (*H. petiolaris*) the ever-popular wisterias, per-haps the most glorious of all hardy climbers, and various vines (*Vitis, Ampelopsis* and *Parthenocissus*). Although deciduous climbers include the many species and cultivars of clematis, rose and honeysuckle, these are dealt with separately, as they are large enough subjects to merit their own chapter.

Deciduous climbers are grown for their flowers as well as their foliage, and some produce the most wonderful autumn leaf colours, as splendid as those of trees such as the maples. A high wall clothed in Virginia creeper (*Parthenocissus quinquefolia*), turning from bright green to crimson and scarlet in the autumn is an unforgettable sight. Others, such as *Celastrus*, continue the show long after leaf-fall by producing a rash of colourful fruits. Even in midwinter the leafless branches of some of these climbers have an austere beauty of their own; few can rival a venerable wisteria with its gnarled and twisted trunks which possess a majesty few other plants can rival.

BEST USE OF DECIDUOUS CLIMBERS
Because they lose their 'coat' in the autumn, deciduous climbers are generally not suit-able for covering unsightly walls or fences or for screening purposes. For these situa-tions there is a large range of evergreen climbers to choose from that will provide a more permanent cover (*see page 84*). Deciduous climbers are particularly valu-able when a permanent curtain of green foliage is not required: if walls or fences need regular painting or other maintenance treatment, it is much easier to get behind deciduous rather than evergreen subjects. Where dense shade is required in summer, but lighter shade in the winter, deciduous types are ideal. In most gardens it is the mix-ture of evergreen and deciduous climbers,

together with a careful selection of comple-mentary trees and shrubs, that will produce the most pleasing and lasting effect.

Apart from the tropical species and cultivars, given in a separate chapter (*see page 122*), most deciduous climbers can be planted at almost any time from late autumn until spring, weather permitting.

Container-grown specimens can in fact be planted almost throughout the year; how-ever, those planted in spring and summer will require careful attention in the form of regular watering and heavy mulches to prevent the roots from drying out.

Tender species are best planted out in the spring, and even then should be protected

(*Above*) Luxuriant foliage is provided by many of the deciduous climbers, including *Actinidia kolomikta,* with its pink-splashed leaf tips.

(*Left*) The climbing hydrangea (*H. petiolaris*) clings to the wall around an arched entrance, enlivening the garden with its white inflorescent blooms in summer.

(*Right*) Wisteria is one of the most popular and attractive deciduous climbers. Its sweet-smelling, pendent racemes appear in early summer.

initially, in case the weather should turn cold and windy. Wise gardeners will protect such plants through the winter too, even when they are well established, insuring against loss by taking cuttings during the summer. These can be kept in a frame or greenhouse over winter in case the parent plants succumb to low temperatures.

ACTINIDIA
(Actinidiaceae)

A genus of usually hardy, twining, mostly deciduous climbers grown for their handsome leaves and some for their fruits; the Chinese gooseberry or kiwi fruit is the best-known species.

The leaves are simple and alternate, often heart-shaped, while the small flowers, often white, are borne in small clusters on the lateral shoots, but are occasionally solitary; plants have either male, female or hermaphrodite flowers. The fruits are fleshy, sometimes edible, berries.

Actinidias are easily grown in most average garden soils, though not in dry soils, and are ideal subjects for walls, fences, pergolas or when trained on stout poles. Most prefer cool, partially shaded positions, especially those that avoid sun during the midday hours. *A. kolomikta* however, does best on a sunny south- or west-facing wall.

Young plants are best placed in their permanent positions in early spring. Those species or varieties grown for their fruits should be planted in twos or threes to ensure a good fruit set. Propagation is from midsummer layerings or cuttings placed in a propagating frame.

Some species, especially *A. kolomikta* and *A. polygama*, are greatly attractive to cats which will chew the leaves and the young shoots.

✓ *A. arguta*
Vigorous climber to 15m (50ft). Leaves oval or oblong, 8–13cm (3¼–5¼in) long, dark shiny green above, paler beneath and downy along the veins; leaf stalk long and pinkish. Flowers fragrant, white, rather globular, 1.5–2cm (½–¾in) across, with purple anthers; male and female flowers borne on separate plants; summer. Berries greenish-yellow, oblong, 2.5cm (1in) long, edible but rather tasteless. Fruits are widely eaten in Japan. Japan, Korea, Manchuria
-8°C (18°F) W

'Ananasnaya': vigorous with attractive, fragrant flowers and small fruits in large clusters. **'Issai'**: self-fertile clone. **'Meader Female'**: one of the finest fruiting clones. **'Meader Male'**: good male clone for pollination purposes.

var. ***cordifolia*** has more heart-shaped leaves with purple stalks.

A. callosa
Vigorous climber to 10m (33ft), with hairless young shoots. Leaves oval or oblong, 7.5–12.5cm (3–5in) long, with a straight or rounded base, hairless. Flowers white or cream-coloured, 1.8–2.5cm (¾–1in) across; late spring to early summer. Fruit egg-shaped 1.8–2.5cm (¾–1in) long, green tinged with red and spotted. N India, Himalaya, W China
-5°C (23°F) W

A. coriacea
Vigorous, often semi-evergreen, to 8m (26ft); young shoots hairless, turning dark brown with age and speckled with white. Leaves leathery, lance-shaped or oval, tapered at both ends, 7.5–12.5cm (3–5in) long, dark green above but paler beneath. Flowers deep rather lurid red with yellow anthers, 1.2–1.3cm (½ in) across; early summer. Fruit rounded to egg-shaped, about 1.8cm (¾ in) long, juicy, brown dotted with white. Sometimes found under the name *A. henryi* in nurseries, though that is a distinct but closely allied species. W China (Sichuan)
-5°C (23°F) W

Actinidia deliciosa (hermaphrodite clone)

✓ ▦ *A. deliciosa*
(*A. chinensis*)
CHINESE GOOSEBERRY, KIWI FRUIT
A handsome climber for a large old wall. Vigorous, 9–10m (30–33ft), with reddish hairy shoots. Leaves heart-shaped, pointed, 13–20cm (5¼–8in) long, dark, rather vivid green above, greyish downy beneath; leaves of flowering shoots smaller, rounded and notched at the apex. Flowers white, turning cream, then buff-yellow, 3.8–4cm (1½ in) across, fragrant; late summer and early autumn. Fruit egg-sized, covered in reddish-

brown hairs, gooseberry-flavoured. Introduced from Hubei in 1900 by E. H. Wilson. Both male and female plants should be planted to ensure fruit set, although there is a hermaphrodite clone available. Plants grown for fruit are best kept at a minimum temperature of 7°C (45°F). China

☀ -8°C (18°F) ⅄ℓw

'**Aureovariegata**': leaves marked with yellow and cream. Important commercial clones for fruit production are: '**Bruno**' (large-fruited, female); '**Hayward**' (female); '**Jenny**' (hermaphrodite); '**Matua**' (male); '**Tomuri**' (male).

A. henryi

(*A. callosa* var. *henryi*)
Rather like *A. deliciosa* but distinguished by its slightly ribbed young shoots, clothed in curly reddish bristles. Leaves ovate or oblong, 7.5–12.5cm (3–5in) long, with a heart-shaped or rounded base, green above contrasting with the bluish-green under-surface. Flowers white, 1.2–1.3cm (½in) across; late spring to early summer. Fruit cylindrical, 1.8–2.5cm (¾–1in) long. China (Yunnan)

☀ -5°C (23°F) ⅄ℓw

✓ A. kolomikta ♀

A handsome and striking climber to 2–4m (6½–13ft) with slender stems. Leaves heart-shaped, coarsely toothed, 7.5–16cm (3–6½in) long, remarkable for their coloration, some or all having the terminal half creamy-white flushed with pink. Flowers

small, white, slightly fragrant, 1.2–1.3cm (½in) across, male and female on different plants; early summer. Fruit yellowish, oval in outline, 2.5cm (1in) long, sweet to taste. This species was first introduced to cultivation round about the middle of the nineteenth century; the form usually cultivated is the male plant. Probably the most decorative species, it is worth a place in any garden where a sunny, sheltered wall can be provided. Young plants may take a year or two before the leaf colours are produced.
N China, Japan, Manchuria

☀ -17°C (1°F) ⅄ℓw

'**Arctic**': a very hardy form with purple young leaves; mature leaves zoned with pink, white and green. '**Krupnoplodnaya**': leaves red in the summer. '**Arnold Arboretum**': a form with small, sweet-tasting fruits.

A. melanandra

Vigorous climber to 10m (33ft) or more, with hairless stems. Leaves oblong or oval, abruptly pointed, 7.5–10cm (3–4in) long, green above but bluish-green beneath. Flowers white, 1.8–2.5cm (¾–1in) across, male with purple anthers; early to midsummer. Fruit egg-shaped, 2.5–3cm (1–1¼in) long, reddish-brown with a plum bloom. Central China (Hubei and Sichuan)

☀ -5°C (23°F) ⅄ℓw

✓ A. polygama

SILVER VINE
Slender-branched climber to 4.5–6m (15–20ft). Leaves

Actinidia kolomikta

elliptic or oblong, sometimes heart-shaped, 7.5–12.5cm (3–5in) long, with a bristly-toothed margin, green, sometimes tipped white or cream, tinged with bronze when young. Flowers fragrant, white, 1.8–2.5cm (¾–1in) across, male, female or hermaphrodite; early summer. Fruit egg-shaped, translucent canary-yellow, 2.5–4cm (1–1½in) long, juicy and edible, though poorly flavoured. This species is often confused with the more widely grown *A. kolomikta*; however, the leaves of *A. polygama* are tapered or

rounded at the base, rather than heart-shaped.
Central Japan

☀ -17°C (1°F) ⅄ℓw

A. purpurea

Like *A. arguta* but less vigorous, seldom more than 8m (26ft). Leaves oval or oblong, 7.5–12.5cm (3–5in) long, dull green above, green and downy beneath. Flowers white, 1.2–2cm (½–¾in) across; early summer. Fruits small, egg-shaped, about 2.5cm (1in) long, purple when ripe, edible and sweet. SW China (W Sichuan, Yunnan)

☀ -15°C (5°F) ⅄ℓw

A. venosa

Similar and closely related to *A. callosa*; however, the leaves of this species have prominent netted veins and both the sepals and flower stalks are clothed in rusty down.

AKEBIA
(Lardizabalaceae)

A subtly beautiful genus of twining climbers grown as much for their elegant foliage as for their small reddish or purplish flowers. They are vigorous growers, suitable for covering walls, fences or pergolas, and even old tree stumps. The flowers are borne in drooping racemes with those at the base larger and female. The large, attractive fleshy fruits are unfortunately only rarely produced in cultivation.

Akebias thrive in any good garden soil but they resent disturbance and, once planted, they should ideally not be moved.

✓ A. quinata

Stems to 10m (33ft) or more if unchecked. Leaves vivid green, usually with 5 oblong, untoothed leaflets; only evergreen in mild winters or in the warmer localities. Flowers with a spicy vanilla fragrance; female rich chocolate-purple, 2–3.5cm (¾–1½in) across, male pale purple, only 7–8mm (⅓in); late spring. Fruits, if produced, sausage-shaped, greyish-violet or purple,

Akebia quinata (showing both male and female flowers)

6.5–10cm (2½–4in) long. China, Japan, Korea
☼ ☀ -20°C (-4°F) ✾

A. × pentaphylla

A hybrid between the two species which is found both in the wild and in cultivation; intermediate in habit and appearance between the two parent species.

A. trifoliata

Similar to *A. quinata* but always deciduous. Leaves with 3 leaflets that have an irregular margin and notched apex. Flowers purple, the female 1.8–2cm (¾in) across; spring. Fruits, if produced, sausage-shaped, pale violet, 7.5–12.5cm (3–5in) long. China, Japan
☼ ☀ -20°C (-4°F) ✾

AMPELOPSIS
(Vitaceae)

A handsome genus of deciduous tendrilled climbers grown mainly for their attractive foliage, though a few produce clusters of small, rather interesting fruits. Flowers small, generally greenish. Most of the species are too vigorous for small gardens and require ample space in which to mature satisfactorily. *Ampelopsis* are easy to grow provided they are given a warm, sheltered niche in the garden and a loamy soil.

Plant in autumn or early spring, tying in young stems to their supports as they extend to start them off. The shoots require some support and plants are ideal on a sheltered pergola where the shoots can be tied in and trained. Alternatively, plants can be trained up stout posts, allowing the shoots eventually to hang free, which can give a very pleasing effect.

Like most members of the grape vine family, the species and varieties are easily rooted from short cuttings of firm young growths taken in midsummer.

A. aconitifolia
(*Vitis aconitifolia*)
Slender climber with hairless young shoots. Leaves luxuriant, very variable in shape and size with basically 3 or 5 leaflets, 2.5–7.5cm (2–3in) long, each deeply cut

into 3–5 toothed lobes, glossy green above but paler and duller beneath. Flowers greenish; late summer to early autumn. Berries dull orange, 6mm (¼in) long. China

☼ ● -25°C (-13°F))ℓw

Var. *glabra*: leaves usually 3-parted, lobed and toothed.

A. arborea
(*A. bipinnata, Vitis arborea*)
PEPPER VINE
Handsome climber to 10m (33ft); stems slender, purplish, scarcely hairy. Leaves large, twice or thrice pinnate with numerous oval leaflets each 3.5–5cm (1½–2in) long, dark green above, paler and downy beneath. Flowers small, greenish; summer. Berries dark purple, 8mm (⅓in) across. In the very mildest areas it may behave as a semi-evergreen. Cultivated since about 1700. SE USA, Mexico

☼ ● -15°C (5°F))ℓw

✓ A. brevipedunculata
(*A. glandulosa* var. *brevipedunculata, Cissus brevipedunculata, Vitis heterophylla* var. *cordata* and var. *amurensis*).
A vigorous climber with rough, hairy young stems. Leaves hop-like, 3- or occasionally 5-lobed, with a heart-shaped base, 5–15cm (2–6in) long, long-stalked, deep green above but paler and rough-hairy beneath. Flowers greenish (summer), followed by attractive small, bright amethyst-blue or purple, berries 6–8mm (¼in). Unlike the other species, a

Ampelopsis brevipedunculata (in fruit)

restricted root run is preferable if plants are to grow well and set plenty of fruit. China, Japan, Korea, E Siberia

☼ -5°C (23°F))ℓw

'Citrulloides': leaves deeply 5-lobed. ⊞ **'Elegans'** (*A. heterophylla* var. *variegata*): young shoots pinkish and leaves freckled and splashed with pink and white. A tender cultivar, only at its best on a warm sheltered wall in the mildest regions; often sold as a pot plant.

var. *maximowiczii* (*Vitis heterophylla* var. *maximowiczii*): plants exhibit an extraordinary range of leaf shapes and sizes even on the same plant; berries porcelain-blue. Less hardy than the type and often sold in nurseries as *A.* or *Vitis heterophylla*.

A. chaffanjonii
(*Vitis chaffanjonii*)
Allied to *A. megalophylla* but with smaller leaves, rarely exceeding 30cm (12in) and with 5 or 7 leaflets that are shiny green above and strikingly reddish-purple beneath. Berries red, turning black. Introduced from Hubei in western China by E.H. Wilson at the turn of the present century. W China

☼ -5°C (23°F))ℓw

A. cordata
(*Vitis indivisa*)
A vigorous climber to 10m (33ft) with rather warted bark; shoots with or without tendrils. Leaves rounded or oval, 5–13cm (2 5¼in) long, with a slightly heart-shaped base and sharply toothed margin. Flowers greenish, in branched clusters on slender stalks; mid- to late summer. The berries are small, blue or greenish-blue. The shoots die back part-way during the winter and generally break off at the nodes. S and SE USA

☼ ◑ -25°C (-13°F))ℓw

A. delavayana
A vigorous climber to 8m (26ft) with hairy, pinkish young stems which are noticeably swollen at the nodes. Leaves with 3 or 5 narrowly oval, rather tapered leaflets which are coarsely toothed, 4–10cm (1–4in) long, somewhat downy beneath. Flowers small, greenish; mid- to late summer. Berries attractive, dark blue,

6mm (¼in). Rare in cultivation. W China

☼ ◑ -15°C (5°F) ⅄ℓw

✓ *A. megalophylla*
(*Vitis megalophylla*)

Vigorous, handsome, hairless climber to 10m (33ft) with bluish-green young shoots. Leaves large, pinnate or bipinnate, 45–60cm (18–24in) long, with 7 or 9 oval to oblong leaflets, deep green above but bluish-green beneath. Flowers green, in a loosely branched inflorescence; late summer. Berries dark purple turning black, 6mm (¼in). A strong grower with the largest leaves of any *Ampelopsis* in cultivation. Ideally it requires a stout post to 5m (16ft) tall or an old tree to clamber up. W China

☼ ◑ -15°C (5°F) ⅄ℓw

ARISTOLOCHIA
(Aristolochiaceae)

An extraordinary and quite remarkable group of plants, mostly from the tropics. The climbing species possess twining stems and deciduous heart-shaped leaves. The flowers of *Aristolochia* are curious, more interesting than beautiful: there is no corolla but the calyx is strangely inflated, partly tubular but bent to resemble a siphon; this curious twist gives the genus its common name of Dutchman's pipe.

They require a good loamy soil and respond to liberal summer mulches and plenty of space. Plants can be propagated easily, by dividing existing plants or from cuttings, and are best planted out in spring.

▦ *A. californica*
(*Isotrema californicum*)

A vigorous climber to 4–6m (13–20ft), with downy stems and leaves similar to *A. tomentosa*. Flowers solitary, 5cm (2in) long, on slender stalks, dull purple, the tube double-bent; early to midsummer. SW USA (California)

◑ -5°C (23°F) ⅄ℓ

✓ ▦ *A. chrysops*

Handsome climber to 6m (20ft) with finely downy young shoots and leaves. Leaves oval with a heart-shaped base, dull green, 4–10cm (1½–4in) long. Flowers solitary or paired 48–52mm (2in) long, a typical Dutchman's pipe shape with a downy yellow tube, a bright yellow throat and spreading lobes of deep reddish-purple, sometimes almost black; early summer. Fruit 5–6.5cm (2–2½in) long, 6-ribbed. Introduced in 1904 by E.H. Wilson. W China

◑ -5°C (23°F) ⅄ℓ

✓ *A. durior*
(*A. macrophylla, A. sipho, Isotrema sipho*)

DUTCHMAN'S PIPE

Vigorous, quick-growing climber to 6–10m (20–33ft). Leaves pale green, heart- or kidney-shaped. Flowers clasped by a large oval bract, usually in pairs on separate stalks, each 6.5–8cm (2½–3¼in) long, with a yellowish-green tube and 3 flat, spreading lobes which are yellowish-brown bordered with purplish-brown; early summer. Equally good for walls, pillars or pergolas. E USA

☼ ◑ -10°C (14°F) ⅄ℓ

✓ *A. moupinensis*
(*Isotrema moupinensis*)

Vigorous climber to 6m (20ft), with downy stems. Leaves heart-shaped, 6–12.5cm (2½–5in) long, rather downy beneath. Flowers solitary, pendulous, about 4cm (1½in) long, with an inflated pale green tube and spreading yellow lobes, dotted with reddish-purple, margin green; early summer. Fruits about 7.5cm (3in) long, with 6 prominent ridges. First discovered in the late nineteenth century in the district of Moupin (Sichuan Province) by the French missionary Père David. W China

◑ -15°C (5°F) ⅄ℓ

A. tomentosa
(*Isotrema tomentosum*)

Vigorous climber to 7–10m (23–33ft), densely downy overall. Leaves oval or rounded with a heart-shaped base, 7.5–20cm (3–8in) long, dull pale green. Flowers solitary, greenish-yellow with a brown throat and yellowish lobes, 4cm (1½in) long; summer. Fruits angular, 5cm (2in) long. Rare in cultivation. SE USA

☼ ◑ -10°C (14°F) ⅄ℓ

BERCHEMIA
(Rhamnaceae)

Deciduous twiners with alternate leaves and small greenish flowers carried in terminal clusters, grown primarily for their ornamental sausage-shaped fruits which are rarely set in cooler gardens. They are scarcely worth growing for their flowers, but the plants can be quite ornamental in fruit.

B. scandens
(*B. volubilis*)

SUPPLE JACK, VINE RATTANY

Stems hairless, to 3–5m (10–16ft). Leaves oval, 3–7.5cm (1¼–3in) long, with a fine bristle-like tip, a wavy margin and 9–12 pairs of veins. Flowers small, greenish-white. Fruits dark blue or nearly black, about 1cm (2.5cm) long; mid- to late summer. Rarely sets fruit in cooler climates. SE USA

☼ ◑ -15°C (5°F) ⊗ℓ

B. racemosa

Similar to *B. scandens* but can be very much more vigorous, to 12m (40ft). Leaves oval with a heart-shaped base, pale beneath, turning yellow in the autumn. Flowers in mid- to late summer. Fruits green when young, changing to red and finally black when mature. Japan, Taiwan

☼ ◑ -15°C (5°F) ⊗ℓ

'Variegata': leaves more creamy-white than green, with the variegation more pronounced towards the shoot tips.

CAMPSIS
(Bignoniaceae)

This genus contains two of the most glorious of all deciduous climbing plants whose striking trumpet-shaped flowers in shades of red or orange give them an exotic appearance. They grow best in a sub-tropical or Mediterranean climate; in temperate regions they are hardy when grown on a warm wall. *Campsis* require a good loamy soil and a sunny position if they are to flower well. The roots should not be allowed to dry out during the summer months and mulching around the base of the plant will help to conserve moisture.

Both species and their hybrid are easy to cultivate. They are best planted in spring and for the first year or two left to fill the wall space allotted to them. Thereafter treat as other climbers, pruning shoots to within a few buds of the old wood after the leaves have fallen or in the early spring. Propagate from cuttings of both stems or roots, by the careful removal of suckers, or by layering. Although they are self-clinging, support from nails driven into the wall will aid the heavier stems.

C. grandiflora
(*C. chinensis, Bignonia grandiflora, Tecoma grandiflora*)
CHINESE TRUMPET VINE
Stems 4–10m (13–33ft),

partly twining, with few aerial rootlets. Leaves with 7 or 9 oval, coarsely toothed, hairless leaflets. Flowers in drooping clusters at the ends of shoots, deep orange and red, 5–7.5cm (2–3in) long; late summer and autumn. Pod-like fruits are rarely produced in temperate gardens. China
☼ -10°C (4°F) ⅄ℓs

'Thunbergii' (*Tecoma thunbergii*): a hardier cultivar whose smaller orange flowers have reflexed lobes; tolerant of salt spray.

✓ C. radicans
(*Bignonia radicans, Tecoma radicans*)
TRUMPET VINE
Differs from *C. grandiflora* in having more vigorous stems, to 12m (40ft) with many more clinging roots, leaves with 7–11 leaflets which are downy beneath and slightly larger flowers 6–8cm (2½–3¼in) long at the tips of the current season's shoots; late summer and early autumn. In some parts of the USA, such as around Salt Lake City, this fiery climber has become almost a weed, clambering over trees and electric and telegraph poles. SE USA
☼ -20°C (4°F) ⅄ℓs

'Atropurpurea': flowers scarlet.
'Crimson Trumpet': flowers deep velvety red; leaves deep green.
✓ **'Flava'** (forma *flava*, 'Yellow Trumpet'): flowers yellow; leaves rather pale green. **'Minor'**: less vigorous with smaller orange and scarlet flowers; midsummer.
'Praecox': flowers scarlet; midsummer. **'Speciosa'**: habit

Campsis radicans

more shrubby and less climbing, to 4–5m (13–16ft); flowers deep orange-red.

✓ C. × tagliabuana
(*Tecoma tagliabuana, T. grandiflora* var. *princei*)
A hybrid between *C. radicans* and *C. grandiflora* which is more or less intermediate in character.
☼ -15°C (5°F) ⅄ℓs

'Coccinea': flowers brilliant red.
✓ **'Madame Galen'**: flowers rich apricot set against dark green leaves; very fine; readily available.

CELASTRUS
(Celastraceae)

A genus of vigorous hardy deciduous climbers and shrubs, related to the spindle trees (*Euonymus*), grown for their magnificent displays of brightly coloured autumnal fruits. The climbing species are highly suitable for covering old walls, trellises, pergolas, trees or stout posts stuck into the earth. They succeed in most average garden soils but tend to be gross feeders and relish regular feeds and mulches.

The leaves are alternate and toothed and the flowers small, greenish-yellow or whitish, and of little attraction. Some species possess hermaphrodite flowers, although the two most well known, *C. orbiculatus* and *C. scandens*, bear male and female flowers on separate plants; with these it is essential to ensure that a plant of each sex is planted, otherwise no fruits will be produced.

C. glaucophyllus

Hairless plant to 7m (23ft) tall; shoots green at first but becoming purplish-brown, scarcely twining. Leaves oval and shallowly toothed, 5–10cm (2–4in) long, green above but bluish-green beneath. Flowers small, greenish, rather inconspicuous; early to midsummer. Fruits 10mm (½in) long, yellow when ripe, splitting to reveal bright scarlet seeds. A distinctive plant first introduced by E.H. Wilson in 1904 and only occasionally seen in cultivation today. W China
☀ -15°C (5°F) ✿

C. hookeri

To 7m (23ft); young shoots reddish-downy at first. Leaves oval, pointed, coarsely toothed, 7.5–15cm (3–6in) long, with reddish down on the veins beneath. Flowers inconspicuous, greenish, in small lateral clusters; early

summer. Fruits orange, about 7mm (¼in) long, containing red-coated seeds. Vigorous in cultivation and sets abundant fruit. Himalaya, S China
☀ -15°C (5°F) ✿

C. hypoleucus
(*Erythrospermum hypoleucum*)

Like *C. glaucophyllus* but young shoots covered in a purplish waxy bloom; to 5m (16ft). Leaves larger, 10–15cm (4–6in) long, dark green above and striking blue-white beneath. Flowers small, yellowish, in racemes up to 20cm (8in) long; early to midsummer. Fruits green, the size of a large pea, splitting to reveal a yellow interior and red-coated seeds. China
☀ -15°C (5°F) ✿

✓ C. orbiculatus
(*C. articulatus*)

ORIENTAL BITTERSWEET

Very vigorous, ultimately reaching 14m (46ft); young stems twining and armed with pairs of spines at each bud. Leaves oval or more or less rounded, shallowly toothed, 5–12.5cm (2–5in) long. Flowers green, in small clusters, only 4mm (⅙in); early summer. Fruit green, pea-sized, eventually turning black and splitting to reveal a golden inner surface and shining scarlet seeds of great beauty. Magnificent in the autumn; the fruits generally survive until after Christmas. Hermaphrodite clones exist in cultivation, but plants grown from seed are usually either

Celastrus orbiculatus

male or female. NE Asia
☀ ☀ -15°C (5°F) ✿
'Diana': fine female clone.

C. rosthornianus

Elegant hairless climber to 7m (23ft), with very slender shoots and rather pendulous branches. Leaves oval to lance-shaped, shiny green, finely toothed, 4–7.5cm (1½–3in) long. Flowers greenish, of no great beauty; early to midsummer. Fruit in small groups, pea-sized, orange-yellow, splitting to reveal startling scarlet-coated seeds, borne well into the New Year. W China
☀ ☀ -15°C (5°F) ✿

C. rugosus

Vigorous climber to 7m (23ft) tall, with hairless stems. Leaves oval, coarsely toothed and distinctively rough above, 6.5–15cm (2½–6in) long. Flowers small, greenish, solitary or in small clusters;

early to midsummer. Fruits orange-yellow, about 8mm (⅓in) long, eventually splitting to reveal red-coated seeds inside. W China
☀ -15°C (5°F) ✿

✓ C. scandens

AMERICAN BITTERSWEET, STAFF TREE

Handsome twiner ultimately reaching 10m (33ft). Leaves are oval to elliptic, finely toothed, 5–10cm (2–4in) long. Flowers small, yellowish-white in terminal clusters, male and female on separate plants; early to mid summer. Fruits in heavy masses 5–7.5cm (2–3in) long, each pea-sized and splitting to reveal an orange inside and brilliant scarlet-coated seeds. Introduced into cultivation as long ago as 1736 and one of the most splendid species to grow, though it requires a lot of room. E North America
☀ -40°C (-40°F) ✿
Hermaphrodite Group: Plants with hermaphrodite flowers which set fruit readily. **'Indian Brave'**: male clone. **'Indian Maiden'**: female clone.

CIONURA
(Asclepiadaceae)

There is only one species in this genus. It is grown for its handsome foliage and its clusters of sweetly scented flowers. The species used to be included within the tropical genus *Marsdenia*.

▦ *C. erecta*

(*Marsdenia erecta*)

Vigorous climber with slender twining stems to 3m (10ft). Leaves paired, with a heart-shaped base, 3.5–6cm (1½–2½in) long. Flowers white, sweetly scented, 1cm (½in), 5-lobed, borne in many-flowered lateral clusters 5–10cm (2–4in) long; summer. Fruits narrowly egg-shaped, 7.5cm (3in) long. Great care must be taken when pruning as the cut stems exude a milky sap which is not only poisonous but can blister the skin; wear gloves when handling the plant. SE Europe
☼ -5°C (23°F) ⚘✿

CLEMATOCLETHRA
(Actinidiaceae)

Deciduous climbers closely related to *Actinidia*. They are easily cultivated on most well-drained loamy soils, but in cool regions they require the protection of a sheltered wall or fence; in milder districts they can be trained on stout stakes or over tree trunks. Propagation is from cuttings taken in late summer.

The leaves are alternate and in the cultivated species are margined by fine bristle-like teeth. The flowers are usually 5–petalled and have 10 stamens. The fruit is a small, rounded berry with persistent sepals at the base.

These unusual and luxuriant climbers are well worth trying in milder, frost-free regions.

Cionura erecta

C. actinidioides

Vigorous climber to 12m (40ft), sometimes more, with hairless young shoots. Leaves oval to heart-shaped, 4–7.5cm (1½–3in) long, with slender stalks. Flowers white tinged with rose, about 10mm (½in) across, carried in small lateral clusters; early summer. Berries black or purplish-black, 6mm (¼in).
SW China
☼ ◑ -5°C (23°F) ✿⚘

✓ *C. integrifolia*

Closely related to *C. actinidioides* but a finer plant, reaching only half the height. Leaves oval to oblong, hairless, green above but bluish-green beneath. Flowers white, fragrant, slightly smaller; early summer. First discovered by the Russian traveller Potanin in 1887, while he was travelling in Gansu.
W China
☼ ◑ -5°C (23°F) ✿⚘

C. lasioclada

To 6m (20ft), with downy young shoots. Leaves oval, 5–10cm (2–4in) long with hair-tufts in the vein angles beneath. Flowers white, in small lateral clusters; midsummer. Berry black, 8mm (⅓in). Rare in cultivation.
W China
☼ ◑ -5°C (23°F) ✿⚘

C. scandens

Handsome vigorous climber, to 8m (26ft), with densely bristly young shoots. Leaves oblong to almost lance-shaped, pointed, 5–12.5cm (2–5in) long, green above but bluish-green and downy beneath. Flowers white, 7–8mm (⅓in) across, in small lateral clusters; early summer. Berry red when ripe, 8mm (⅓in). Equally effective grown against a wall as on a tree.
W China
☼ ◑ -10°C (14°F) ✿⚘

COCCULUS
(Menispermaceae)

Deciduous or evergreen climbers and erect shrubs with entire or lobed, alternate leaves. The small flowers are unisexual and 6-parted, borne in lateral clusters. The fruit is spherical, fleshy and one-seeded.

✓ *C. carolinus*

CAROLINA MOONSEED, CORAL BEADS, SNAILSEED

Twining woody stems to 5m (16ft), downy. Leaves oval or heart-shaped, 5–12.5cm (2–5in) long, sometimes with 3 or 5 lobes, whitish-downy beneath. Flowers white, the male ones in lateral clusters, the female in racemes, usually on the same plant; midsummer. Fruits red, about 6mm (¼in) across, in dense clusters. SE USA
☼ -15°C (5°F) ✿⚘

C. orbiculatus

(*C. trilobus*)

To 3.5–4.5m (11½–15ft) with twining, downy stems, becoming woody with age. Leaves heart-shaped or oval, occasionally with 3–5 lobes, 3.5–10cm (1½–4in) long, downy beneath, particularly when young. Flowers cream; late summer. Fruits about 1cm (½in) across, black with a blue bloom. An attractive sight in autumn when covered in fruits, though to fruit well it needs plenty of sunshine. China, Japan, Korea, south to Java
☼ ◑ -10°C (14°F) ✿⚘

DECUMARIA
(Hydrangeaceae)

Decumaria barbara is sometimes deciduous but is treated with the evergreen *D. sinensis* (see page 89).

FALLOPIA
(Polygonaceae)

Fallopia contains the Russian vine, a rampant climber that often receives bad publicity because of its invasive nature. But for large buildings and for tall screens or barriers there are few quicker growing or more effective climbers. In full flower plants have an attractive, cloud-like effect. All the species are vigorous woody twiners with alternate heart-shaped leaves and were formerly in the genus *Polygonum*. The small flowers are borne in lax terminal and lateral panicles and usually have 5 segments, of which the 3 outer are winged or ridged on the back. The fruit is a 3-angled nut, enclosed by the perianth which persists.

They can be grown on a large wall, provided there are supporting wires, or over pergolas, but they are probably best when left to scramble up an old tree. They will succeed in most average soils and are readily propagated from soft cuttings in summer or hardwood cuttings in winter. Plants will sprout readily from the base if they are heavily pruned.

Fallopia aubertii

F. aubertii
(*Polygonum aubertii,*
Bilderdykia aubertii)
RUSSIAN VINE
Similar to *F. baldschuanica*, differing mainly in having narrower, erect, rough panicles carrying smaller, white or greenish flowers (summer and early autumn) which become pinkish when in fruit.

This species has been much confused with *F. baldschuanica* in gardens, with many of the plants sold and grown under the name *F. baldschuanica* being in fact *F. aubertii*, which is generally more common in cultivation.
W China, Tibet
☼ ◑ -15°C (5°F) ⋎ₛ

F. baldschuanica ♔
(*Polygonum baldschuanicum,*
Bilderdykia baldschuanica)
MILE-A-MINUTE VINE,
RUSSIAN VINE
A generally rampant twiner to 12m (40ft), sometimes more, producing very woody stems in time. Leaves 2.5–10cm (1–4in) long, hairless and pale green. Flowers small, white or pale pink, borne in broad drooping panicles 20–40cm (8–16in) long; summer to early autumn. Afghanistan, W Pakistan, southern Central Asia (Turkmenistan to Kazakstan)
☼ ◑ -15°C (5°F) ⋎ₛ

F. multiflora
(*Polygonum multiflorum*)
Less vigorous, with slender red stems twining to 4.5m (15ft); occasionally semi-evergreen. Leaves heart-shaped, 5–12.5cm (2–5in) long, dark shiny green. Flowers white or greenish, in loose downy panicles; early to midsummer. China, Taiwan
☼ -15°C (5°F) ⋎ₛ

HYDRANGEA
(Hydrangeaceae)

The climbing members of this popular genus attach themselves to walls by aerial roots produced from the stems, similar to those of ivy. They have opposite leaves and bear their flowers in flat-topped clusters. *H. petiolaris*, the common climbing hydrangea, is one of the most popular and widely sold wall climbers, which looks particularly effective on old buildings.

They thrive in well-drained soils, especially when enriched by mulches of compost or well-rotted manure. Shoots of young plants may need to be tied to a support before they begin to cling by themselves. Cuttings of well-ripened shoots placed in a propagating frame in the summer root fairly readily.

H. anomala

Very similar to *H. petiolaris* but flower clusters less flat, the creamy fertile flowers (early summer) have fewer stamens (9–15) and the leaves have coarser teeth. Far rarer in cultivation than the ordinary climbing hydrangea, but it can be equally effective in flower. Himalaya to W China
☼ ◑ -10°C (14°F) ⌇ℓₛ

✓ H. petiolaris ♀

(*H. anomala* subsp. *petiolaris*)
CLIMBING HYDRANGEA
To 15m (50ft), though it can be trained to walls only 3–4m (10–13ft); older stems have peeling brown bark. Leaves broadly oval, toothed, 5–11cm (2–4¼in) long. Flower clusters 15–25cm (6–10in) in diameter, with characteristic enlarged white, outer, sterile flowers; early to midsummer. Widely grown and suitable for walls or fences of any aspect; especially

Hydrangea anomala

valuable on a north wall where it will flower well. Although it will reach a great height, this valuable plant is also ideal when trained on lower walls, up to 2m (6½ft). It can also be allowed to climb up trees or indeed it can be very effective when used to cover old tree stumps when it will eventually develop a bush-like habit. Sometimes confused in nurserymen's catalogues; some of the plants offered as *Schizophragma hydrangeoides* turn out to be this plant. Japan, Korea, Taiwan
☼ ◑ ● -20°C (-4°F) ⌇ℓₛ

H. serratifolia

is an evergreen climber
(*see page 94*).

JASMINUM (Oleaceae)

Although described in the chapter on evergreen climbers, these species often behave as deciduous subjects in the colder regions where they can be grown, especially during a severe winter:
J. beesianum, *J. dispermum*, *J. officinale*, the commonly grown sweetly-scented summer jasmine, and *J. × stephanense* (*see pages 94–5*).

MENISPERMUM (Menispermaceae)

A small genus of woody or semi-woody twiners with

deciduous, alternate, long-stalked leaves. The flowers are unisexual, the male and female borne on separate plants. Each fruit contains one crescent-shaped seed; often known as 'moon seeds'. They are attractive in fruit, but plants of both sexes are needed if fruits are to be produced.

✓ M. canadense

CANADA MOONSEED,
YELLOW PARILLA
Vigorous, quick growing climber, to 3–5m (10–16ft), spreading by underground suckers; stems slender, producing a dense tangle. Leaves oval to heart-shaped, usually with 3–7 shallow, angular lobes; dark green

above, paler and strongly veined beneath. Flowers greenish-yellow, rather inconspicuous, in long-stalked lateral racemes; early to midsummer. Fruits blackish when ripe, blackcurrant-like, about 7–9mm (⅓in), in long loose clusters. Although no pruning is actually necessary, the plant may be tidied by removing weak or dead wood, but this is a difficult task with such a tangled mass of stems; it may be preferable to cut the plant nearly to the ground every two or three years in the winter. Fruits ripen in the autumn; both fruits and seeds are poisonous. E North America
☼ -10°C (14°F) ✿

✓ *M. dauricum*

Similar but less often seen in gardens. Leaf-lobes more pointed and racemes of flowers shorter and denser, being produced in pairs above each leaf axil; early to midsummer. Fruits slightly larger. Treat as *M. canadense*. NE Asia from Siberia to China
☼ -15°C (5°F) ✿

MUEHLENBECKIA
(Polygonaceae)

Semi-woody shrubs or climbers from the southern hemisphere. The leaves are alternate and the unisexual flowers are green or whitish, deeply 5-lobed. The fruit is a 3-angled nutlet enclosed in the other persistent flower-parts.

Menispermum dauricum

M. complexa

MAIDENHAR VINE, NECKLACE VINE

To 6m (20ft), producing numerous slender, tangled, dark, interlaced stems. Leaves vary enormously in size and shape from rounded to oblong, heart- or fiddle-shaped, 3–18mm (⅛–¾in) long, dull green and hairless with a rough warty stalk. Flowers greenish-white, about 4mm (⅛in) long, in terminal and lateral spikes about 1.5cm (⅛in) in length; autumn. Not beautiful but a curiosity for those wanting something different. Best used to disguise an old tree stump in a sheltered position. Will generally resprout if killed to the ground by frost.
New Zealand
☼ ◑ 0°C (32°F) ✿
   var. *trilobata* (*M. triloba, M. varians*) has deeply 3-lobed leaves.

M. sagittifolia

Climbing shrub to 4m (13ft). Leaves arrow-shaped to lance-shaped, 4–9cm (1½–3½in) long; upper leaves linear. Flowers greenish-white, in slender racemes, very similar to *M. complexa*. New Zealand
☼ ◑ 0°C (32°F) ✿

PAEDERIA
(Rubiaceae)

A small genus seldom seen in our gardens but well deserving to be tried if plants can be acquired. The one species commonly grown will succeed on most average garden soils, provided they are well-drained.

P. scandens
(P. chinensis, P. wilsonii)
Vigorous climber to 5m (16ft).
Leaves dark green, oval, finely
pointed, 5–15cm (2–6in)
long, downy beneath; young
growth with an unpleasant
foetid odour. Flowers tubular,
white with a purple throat,
8–12mm (⅓–½ in) long, in
branched clusters at the shoot
tips among smaller, narrower,
leaves; midsummer to early
autumn. Fruits pea-sized,
orange when ripe.
China, Japan, Korea
☼ 0°C (32°F) ⋎⌀s

PARTHENOCISSUS
(Vitaceae)

A genus of about 10 species of
rapid-growing ornamental
climbers from North
America, eastern Asia and the
Himalaya, grown primarily for
their handsome foliage which
often turn rich colours in the
autumn (the best colours are
produced on walls of north
and east aspect). The shoots
usually climb by suckered,
branched tendrils; the
suckers, which attach
themselves firmly to wall,
fence, pillar or tree, serve to
distinguish this genus from its
two close allies, *Vitis* and
Ampelopsis. Their culture is
the same. They are mostly
excellent for covering large
and unsightly walls and
building and, once established,
are rapid growers.
 The greenish, rather
insignificant flowers are borne

Parthenocissus quinquefolia

in lateral branched panicles,
the flowers often being
followed by small blue or black
berries, especially during hot
dry summers.

✓ P. henryana ♀
(Vitis henryana)
The finest and most handsome
species; rather vigorous, to
10m (33ft). Leaves with 3–5
oval, coarsely toothed leaflets,
4–12.5cm (1½–5 in) long; leaf
coloration very striking, rich
dark velvety green or bronze
above with the veins picked out

in pink, red or purple, turning
deep red in the autumn.
Flowers small, greenish, in
terminal leafy clusters
15–17.5cm (6–7in) long; mid-
to late summer. Berries small,
dark blue. Central China
☼ ● -5°C (23°F) ⋎⌀s

P. himalayana
(Ampelopsis himalayana)
Vigorous climber with hairless
stems to 10m (33ft). Leaves
with 3 oval, toothed leaflets
5–15cm (2–6in) long, deep
green above but paler bluish-

green beneath, turning rich
crimson in the autumn.
Flowers greenish, in branched
clusters; mid- to late summer.
Berries small, deep blue.
Himalaya
☼ 0°C (32°F) ⋎⌀s
 var. *rubrifolia*: leaves smaller,
 purple when young. W China.

P. inserta
(P. quinquefolia var. *vitacea,*
Vitis or *Ampelopsis inserta)*
Vigorous climber often
confused with *P. quinquefolia*
but lacking the sticky suckers
on the tendrils which instead
coil around suitable supports
or insert themselves into
crevices. Flowers greenish;
mid- to late summer. Leaves
with 5 elliptic leaflets, rather
larger and a brighter green but
also turning brilliant crimson
in the autumn.
E, Central and SW USA
☼ -15°C (5°F) ⋎⌀s
 var. *laciniata* *(P. quinquefolia* var.
 laciniata): leaflets deeply toothed,
 giving the plant a striking
 appearance. SW USA

✓ P. quinquefolia
(Vitis quinquefolia)
VIRGINIA CREEPER
Vigorous and handsome
climber to 15m (50ft) tall,
with slender hairless stems that
are reddish at first. Leaves
composed of 5, sometimes 3,
oval, coarsely toothed leaflets,
2.5–10cm (1–4in) long, dull
green above but paler and
bluish-green beneath; foliage
turning a rich vivid crimson in
the autumn. Flowers small,
greenish; mid- to late summer.

Parthenocissus quinquefolia

Parthenocissus tricuspidata 'Robusta'

Berries in clusters, bluish-black. C and E North America ☼ -25°C (-13°F) ⑂s

Cultivated for many years with records going back as far as 1629. *P. quinquefolia* is the true Virginia Creeper though this common name is often wrongly applied to *P. tricuspidata* whose correct common name should be the Japanese creeper.

var. *engelmannii* (*Vitis* or *Ampelopsis engelmannii*): leaves smaller than the type, pleasantly bluish-green during summer but turning fiery red in autumn. **var.** *hirsuta* (*Ampelopsis graebneri*): shoots, leaves and inflorescences hairy; leaves with very intense autumn coloration. **var.** *murorum* (*P. radicantissima*, *Ampelopsis hederacea* var. *murorum*): tendrils abundant, with more and shorter branches enabling the shoots to cling very tightly to their supports; southern USA. **var.** *saint-paulii* (*P. saint-paulii*): young shoots and under-surface of the leaves finely downy; leaflets more deeply and sharply toothed than the other varieties.

P. thomsonii
(*Cayratia thomsonii*, *Vitis thomsonii*)

Closely related to *P. henryana*. A delightful plant, rather hardier and more graceful than *P. henryana*. Leaves glossy green, with 5 oval leaflets, 2.5–10cm (1–4in) long, sharply toothed in the upper half, turning rich scarlet and crimson in the autumn. Flowers greenish; mid- to late summer. Berries small, black. Assam, China, Himalaya ☼ ☀ -5°C (23°F) ⑂s

✓ P. tricuspidata ♔
(*Ampelopsis tricuspidata*, *Ampelopsis* or *Cissus veitchii*)

JAPANESE CREEPER

Very handsome and vigorous climber to 20m (66ft). Leaves shiny, very variable in size and shape; heart-shaped and scarcely lobed when young, or with 3 leaflets, while in mature plants they are coarser and generally 3-lobed, to 20cm (8in), vivid crimson in the autumn. Flowers yellowish-green, in branched clusters; mid- to late summer. Berries dull dark blue. One of the largest and most spectacular of all climbing plants and one that is commonly planted. It is commonly found under the name *Ampelopsis veitchii* in catalogues or as 'Virginia Creeper', a common name that rightly applies to *P. quinquefolia*. China, Japan

☼ ☀ -15°C (5°F) ⌇s

'Atropurpurea': leaves large, red in spring and autumn, green tinged blue, turning purple in the summer. **'Aurata'**: leaves yellowish, somewhat marbled. **'Beverley Brook'**: leaves small, red in autumn. **'Green Spring'**: young leaves red-tinged, later glossy green. **'Lowii'**: an elegant cultivar with rather small 3–7-lobed leaves which are crinkled and have fine autumn colours. **'Minutifolia'**: Leaves large, glossy green, turning purple and pink. **'Purpurea'**: leaves red tinged with purple. **'Robusta'**: leaves glossy, usually trifoliate, red and orange in autumn. **'Veitchii'** JAPANESE IVY: leaves smaller than the typical plant, oval or 3-lobed, reddish purple, even when young.

PERIPLOCA
(Asclepiadaceae)

Deciduous or evergreen twining climbers or shrubs native to the Old World, with paired, untoothed leaves, grown for their clusters of small hoya-like flowers and handsome silky-seeded fruits which are borne in pairs. The stems exude poisonous milky juice when cut. Easily grown

climbers, especially good on fences, pergolas and arches.

P. graeca
SILK VINE
Stems brown, hairless, twining to 9m (30ft) tall. Leaves oval, 5–12.5cm (2–6in) long, dark green and shiny. Flowers brownish-purple inside and greenish-yellow outside, in clusters 5–7.5cm (2–3in) across; each flower 2.5cm (1in) across, with 5 spreading lobes; mid- to late summer. Fruits cylindrical, 12–13cm (5–5¼in) long. SE Europe, Turkey

☼ -15°C (5°F) ✿

P. laevigata (see page 99).

✓ P. sepium
CHINESE SILK VINE
A smaller and more delicate climber to 3m (10ft) tall. Leaves lance-shaped to narrowly oval, 4–10cm (1½–4in) long, shiny and dark green. Flowers fragrant, dark purple inside and greenish outside, 2cm (¾in) across, in clusters of 2–9, the lobes recurved and woolly on the margins; early to midsummer. Fruits twisted, 10–15cm (4–6in) long. Somewhat hardier than *P. graeca*.
N. China

☼ -15°C (5°F) ✿

SARGENTODOXA
(Sargentodoxaceae)

The family *Sargentodoxaceae* contains but a single species,

S. cuneata, at one time included in the family Lardizabalaceae as a species of *Holboellia*.

✓ S. cuneata
(*Holboellia cuneata*)
Vigorous twining climber to 8m (26ft), or more. Leaves with 3 oval, untoothed, leaflets 5–12.5cm (2–6in) long, rather dark glossy green and borne on long stalks. Male and female flowers greenish-yellow, 18–22mm (¾–⅞in) across, borne on separate plants in loose drooping racemes, 10–15cm (4–6in) long; late spring to early summer. Berries clustered, about 6mm (¼in), purplish-blue when ripe. Rare in cultivation; this plant's hardiness is not fully established. The species was first discovered in 1887 by the Irish plant collector, Augustine Henry. Central China

☼ ☀ -5°C (23°F) ⌇

SCHISANDRA
(Schisandraceae)

Handsome twining climbers grown for their beautiful waxy flowers and, in favoured localities, for their unusual beaded fruits.

There are some 25 species of *Schisandra* which grow in tropical and warm temperate Asia and eastern North America; they are deciduous or evergreen woody climbers with alternate leaves. The flowers have 5–20 similar sepals and petals; male and

female flowers are borne on separate plants; both sexes must be planted if fruit are wanted.

They thrive best in a rich loamy soil with plenty of well-rotted compost or manure in the form of mulches.

Propagation is by means of half-ripened wood in summer, in a propagating frame.

✓ S. chinensis
To 9m (30ft) with red young shoots with wart-like lenticels. Leaves elliptic to oval, sparsely toothed, 5–10cm (2–4in) long. Flowers in clusters of 2 or 3 on slender stalks, fragrant, pale pink, 13–20mm (½–¾in) across, with 6–8 'petals' which soon fall; mid to late spring. Fruits, scarlet when ripe, in a pendulous spike to 7.5cm (3in) long, remaining on the plant during most of the winter. A very handsome climber when fruiting.
China, Japan, Korea and neighbouring NE Siberia

☼ ☀ -17°C (1°F) ⌇s

S. coccinea
BAY STAR VINE, WILD SARSPARILLA
To 5m (16ft), with slender branches. Leaves oval to elliptic, 5–15cm (2–6in) long, rather fleshy. Flowers crimson, 10mm (½in).
SE USA

☼ -7°C (20°F) ⌇s

S. grandiflora
To 6m (20ft) with reddish young shoots. Leaves more or less oval, toothed, 6–12.5cm (2½–5in) long, hairless. Flowers fragrant, solitary,

Schisandra rubriflora

Schisandra rubriflora (in fruit)

pendulous, white to cream or pale rose-pink, about 25mm (1in) across, with 5–7 'petals'; mid- to late spring. Fruit red, in pendent spikes 7.5–15cm (3–6in) long.
W China, NE India
☼ -15°C (5°F) ⊬s

S. henryi
Differs from the other species in having triangular young stems with a wing on each angle. Leaves oval or heart-shaped, 7.5–10cm (3–4in) long, sparsely toothed, shiny above but rather blue-green beneath. Flowers white, about 13mm (½in) across, borne on a stalk to 5cm (2in) long; mid-to late spring. Fruits red, in pendent spikes 5–7.5cm (2–3in) long. China
☼ ◐ ● -7°C (20°F) ⊬s

S. propinqua
To 5m (16ft) with angled young stems. Leaves narrowly oval, 5–12.5cm (2–5in) long, hairless, finely toothed or untoothed. Flowers usually solitary, the outer 'petals' greenish-yellow, the inner orange; mid- to late spring. Berries red, in pendent spikes to 15cm (6in) long. Himalaya
☼ ● -5°C (23°F) ⊬s
> **var. chinensis** (var. *sinensis*): leaves narrower, sometimes marked with white; flowers yellowish in mid- to late summer. Said to be hardier than the type. China

✓ S. rubriflora
Like *S. grandiflora*, but flowers scarlet to dark red.
India, Burma, SW China
☼ -15°C (5°F) ⊬s

S. sphenanthera
To 5m (16ft) with reddish-brown, warty young growth. Leaves oval to almost round, 5–10cm (2–4in) long, with tiny marginal teeth. Flowers solitary, hanging on slender stalks, greenish outside, orange

Schisandra sphenanthera

inside, about 13mm (½in) across; mid- to late spring. Berries scarlet in pendent spike 5–7.5cm (2–3in) long. China ☼ ☀ -7°C (20°F) ⋎🌿ₛ

SCHIZOPHRAGMA (Hydrangeaceae)

Climbing shrubs related to, and often confused with, the climbing *Hydrangea* species, differing mainly in that the sterile flowers possess only 1 sepal (not 3–5). Although perhaps less often seen in gardens, they are quite the rival of *Hydrangea* in full flower and a large established plant can be extremely handsome. Plants climb by numerous short aerial roots produced on the underside of the stems which cling closely to their supports. The leaves are opposite and the flowers are borne in a flat inflorescence, with tiny fertile flowers in the middle and showy sterile flowers round the edge.

Schizophragmas flower best on a sunny wall, but they can be grown quite successfully on a north-facing or shady wall. However, they look most attractive when allowed to ascend a large tree, although they may take some years to reach a large size. Cuttings can be rooted in a propagating frame in summer. Generally rather slow to establish.

✓ S. integrifolium
Very handsome climber attaining 12m (40ft) in time. Leaves oval or heart-shaped, 7.5–17.5cm (3–7in) long. Inflorescences up to 30cm (12in) across, bearing large elliptic, creamy-white, sterile flowers 6–9cm (2½ 3½in) at the margin; midsummer.

Slightly less hardy than the following species, but more commonly grown. It greatly dislikes a hot and sunny situation in the garden. Well grown, it is more spectacular than the climbing hydrangea, *H. petiolaris*. China ☼ ☀ ☼ -5°C (23°F) 🌿

S. hydrangeoides
To 12m (40ft) in time, with reddish young stems. Leaves broadly oval, 10–15cm (4–6in) long, toothed, deep green, paler and silky-haired beneath. Inflorescences 20–25cm (8–10cm) across, the marginal sterile flowers with a pale yellow oval to heart-shaped sepal 2.5–4cm (1–1½in) long; midsummer.
Japan
☼ ☀ ☼ -15°C (5°F) 🌿

Schizophragma hydrangeoides

Sometimes mistaken for *H. anomala* or *H. petiolaris*.
✓ **'Roseum'**: sterile flowers tinged with pink; a pretty form.

SINOFRANCHETIA (Lardizabalaceae)

A genus of one species grown for its handsome foliage closely related to *Holboellia* but quite hardy and with all the leaves being trifoliate. The genus was named in honour of Andrien Franchet who did a great deal of work on the plants of China and who died in 1900. Especially fine for covering large old buildings and for clambering up trees; unsuitable for small gardens.

✓ S. chinensis
Very vigorous climber with twining shoots to 15m (50ft); young shoots and slender leaf stalks covered in purplish

Sinofranchetia chinensis

Sinofranchetia chinensis (in fruit)

SOLANUM
(Solanaceae)

The evergreen solanums, including the very popular *S. crispum* and *S. jasminoides*, are described on page 99 but the following species is deciduous.

✓ *S. valdiviense*
Vigorous, more or less climbing, shrub to 3m (10ft) tall, producing suckers. Leaves alternate, oval-lance-shaped, untoothed, to 6cm (2½in) long. Flowers scented, in small racemes in the leaf-axils, mauve or white, about 13mm (½in) across, with a central 'beak' of yellow anthers; late spring to early summer. Fruit is a dull green berry, about 6mm (¼in). It is especially beautiful when the flowers first appear, before the leaves are fully expanded. Introduced from Argentina in 1927 by Harold Comber. Chile, adjacent Argentina.
☼ 0°C (32°F) ⚘

VITIS
(Vitaceae)

This genus contains among its 50 or so species the common grape vine, *V. vinifera*. The species are confined to the Northern Hemisphere, many to the North American continent; however, it is the Asian species that are the most decorative garden plants. Most are vigorous deciduous plants with handsome, often large and usually palmate, leaves. They climb by means of simple or branched tendrils borne opposite the leaves. The small flowers are greenish and of little beauty; they are usually bisexual though they may be male only. These are succeeded by loose or dense bunches of small succulent berries – grapes, edible in some species.

Grape vines are grown for their sumptuous and highly attractive foliage which in some species takes on glorious autumn colours. In addition, in favoured areas, some produce a fine display of fruit. They are good subjects for tumbling over old walls and fences, or for growing up pergolas, poles or tree stumps. The large-leaved species such as *V. coignetiae* and *V. davidii* are excellent when allowed to scramble into old trees. They prefer a well-drained loamy soil, particularly a slightly chalky one, though they will succeed on a wide variety; the addition of well-rotted manure is highly beneficial on

bloom. Leaves trifoliate, deep green above, bluish-green beneath; leaflets oval or elliptic, 6–15cm (2½–6in) long, pointed and untoothed. Flowers small, dull whitish, of no great beauty, in pendent racemes to 10cm (4in) long; male and female are borne on separate plants; late spring. Fruits grape-sized, pale purple, in summer. Fruit is often produced on the female

plant even in the absence of a male partner, which suggests that the plants may not be wholly female. This is a luxuriant and vigorous climber which can look especially fine in a woodland setting. It is grown more for its foliage than for its flowers or fruit. E.H. Wilson introduced this plant into cultivation in 1907. Central and W China
☀ -15°C (5°F) ⚘

poorer soils. Most species like a warm, sunny aspect if they are to produce the best autumn colouring.

Pruning should be carried out before the end of winter or else the cut surface will bleed badly due to the rise of sap. Most grape vines can be readily propagated from short lengths of young, well-ripened wood, one or two node-lengths long, inserted in a cold frame in the autumn. The majority can also be propagated from 'eyes', short one-bud lengths placed horizontally in a sandy compost during the early spring.

Vitis 'Brant'

V. aestivalis

SUMMER GRAPE

Extremely vigorous climber to 15m (50ft); young stems hairless or slightly downy. Leaves very large, 10–30cm (4–12in) long, with 3 or 5 shallow or deep lobes, dull green above but brown with down beneath. Flowers borne in long panicles to 25cm (10in) long; early to midsummer. Berries black with a blue bloom, about 8mm (⅓in), pleasantly flavoured. Central and E USA
☼ ☽ -30°C (-22°F) ⋎ℓ**w**

✓ V. amurensis

Vigorous vine similar in habit to *V. vinifera*. Young shoots reddish and downy. Leaves 3–5-lobed, 12.5–30cm (5–12in) long, deep green, turning crimson and purple in the autumn. Flowers greenish; early to midsummer. Berries

small and black, 7–8mm (⅓in). N China, Japan, Korea, E Siberia
☼ ☽ -25°C (-13°F) ⋎ℓ**w**

✓ V. argentifolia

(*V. aestivalis* var. *argentifolia*) To 10m (33ft); easily distinguished by its bluish white young shoots. Leaves 3–5-lobed, 10–30cm (4–12in) long deep green above, bluish-white beneath. Flowers greenish; early to midsummer. A handsome and striking vine which well deserves to be more widely known. Central and E USA
☼ ☽ -30°C (-22°F) ⋎ℓ**w**

✓ V. 'Brant' ♀

(*V. vinifera* 'Brandt') A superb vine to 7m (23ft) or more; one of the best ornamental grape vines. Leaves

lobed, bright green, 10–22.5cm (4–9in) long, turning bronzy red in the autumn, except for the veins which remain green. Berries purple when ripe, sweet and delicious. Generally believed to be a hybrid between *V.* 'Clinton' and *V. vinifera* 'Black St Peters'. Cultivated in Britain since 1886, having originated in China
☼ ☽ -15°C (5°F) ⋎ℓ**w**

V. californica

Moderately vigorous, to 10m (33ft); young shoots covered at first in a fine grey down. Leaves heart- or kidney-shaped, sometimes 3-lobed, 5–10cm (2–4in) long, green above but downy-grey beneath, turning deep crimson in the autumn. Flowers greenish; early to midsummer. Berries small,

black with a purple bloom, 7–8mm (⅓in). W North USA
☼ ☽ -15°C (5°F) ⋎ℓ**w**

✓ V. coignetiae ♀

Extremely vigorous vine, generally to 10–15m (33–50ft); young shoots ribbed and covered in grey down. Leaves large, rough, broadly heart-shaped, 10–30cm (4–12in) long, with 3–5 pointed lobes, dark green above, rusty brown with down beneath; glorious in the autumn when the foliage takes on hues of orange, mahogany and scarlet. Flowers borne in early to midsummer. Berries black with a purplish bloom, about 12mm (½in). This handsome vine deserves a place in any garden where space permits. It looks particularly

Vitis coignetiae

fine grown on a patio wall or draped over a large tree stump or simply allowed to ramble into a suitable tree. Named in honour of Mme Coignet, daughter of Jean Sisley the French Rosarian, who collected seed in 1887. Japan ☼ ☽ -15°C (5°F) Ⱳw

V. davidii
(*V. armata*, *Spinovitis davidii*)
Luxuriant climber to 8m (26ft) or more with the young stems covered in short, slightly curved, prickles. Leaves variable but basically heart-shaped, 10–25cm (4–10cm) long, with a slender point, shiny dark green above, but bluish- or greyish-green beneath, turning brilliant red in the autumn. Flowers greenish; early to midsummer.

Berries black when ripe, 15–17mm (½–¾in), edible. Introduced from Shensi in 1872 by Père David. China ☼ ☽ -15°C (5°F) Ⱳw
'Veitchii'(*V. armata* var. *cyanocarpa*): less prickly form with fine bronzy green leaves which take on rich red autumn tints; berries with a bluish bloom.

V. flexuosa
An elegant vine with its slender, hairless, stems to 5m (16ft). Leaves thin, heart-shaped or more or less rounded, pointed, 5–10cm (2–4in) long, glossy green above and downy beneath. Flowering in early summer. Berries pea-sized, black when ripe. China, Japan, Korea ☼ ☽ -20°C (-4°F) Ⱳw
var. *parvifolia* (*V. parvifolia*): a

pretty plant with smaller leaves, green with a bronzy metallic sheen, purple beneath when young. Central and S China, Taiwan, E Himalaya

V. labrusca
NORTHERN FOX GRAPE, SKUNK GRAPE
A luxuriant and vigorous vine, to 10m (33ft), or more, with very woolly young shoots. Leaves thick, heart-shaped to rather rounded, unlobed or 3-lobed, 7.5–20cm (3–8in) long, dark green above but rusty with down beneath. Berries dark purplish-black, 15–17mm (½–¾in), with a musky or foxy aroma. This luxuriant vine is very important in the United States as the source of many varieties of grapes. North America ☼ ☽ -25°C (-13°F) Ⱳw

V. mustangensis
(*V. candicans*)
MUSTANG GRAPE
To 10m (33ft) or more; young shoots covered in dense white wool. Leaves basically heart- or kidney-shaped, unlobed or somewhat 3-lobed, 5–12.5cm (2–5in) long, dull dark green above and woolly at first, but always white-woolly beneath. Flowers greenish; early to midsummer. Berries rounded, purplish, 15–17mm (½–¾in), unpleasantly flavoured. S USA ☼ ☽ -5°C (23°F) Ⱳw

V. piasezkii
(*V. sinensis*, *Parthenocissus sinensis*)
Vigorous, though rather slender, climber to 7m (23ft). Leaves 7.5–15cm (3–6in) long, variable in shape on the same stem, 3- or 5-lobed or composed of 3 or 5 separate leaflets, dark green turning bronze and red in the autumn. Flowers greenish; early to midsummer. Berries black, rounded, 8mm (⅓in). Central and W China ☼ ☽ -20°C (-4°F) Ⱳw
var. *pagnuccii* (*V. pagnucci*): form with practically hairless stems but differs little from the type in other respects.

V. quinquangularis
(*V. pentagona*, *V. filifolia* var. *pentagona*)
Another vigorous climber, to 8m (26ft); young shoots white-felted. Leaves oval or heart-shaped, 7.5–15cm (3–6in) long, usually with 3 or 5 shallow lobes, dark green

above but white-felted beneath, a striking contrast. Flowers appearing in early summer. Berries blue-black, 7–8mm (⅓in). First introduced in 1907 by E.H. Wilson. This species deserves to be more widely grown. Central and W China

☼ ☽ -15°C (5°F) ⋎ℓw

✓ *V. riparia*
(*V. odoratissima*)

FROST GRAPE, RIVER BANK GRAPE

Strong-growing vine to 10m (33ft), or more. Leaves broad, heart-shaped, poorly 3-lobed, and coarsely toothed, 10–22.5cm (4–9in) long, shiny bright green on both surfaces. Flowers, borne in panicles up to 20cm (8in) long, are sweetly scented; early to midsummer. Berries purplish-black with a pronounced bluish bloom, 7–8mm (⅓in). Frequently used as a stock on which many French varieties of grape are grafted, due to its 'phylloxera' resistance. Central and E North America

☼ ☽ -40°C (-40°F) ⋎ℓw

V. romanetii

Close to *V. davidii* but leaves narrow heart-shaped, 3-lobed, 15–25cm long (6–10in), dark green above, grey with down beneath. Flowering at the same time. Berries black, 8–12mm (⅓–½in) long. Young growth and thin wood may be cut back by frost. Père David introduced the species to Europe from China in 1872–3. China

☼ -15°C (5°F) ⋎ℓw

Vitis vinifera 'Purpurea'

V. rotundifolia
(*Muscadinia rotundifolia*)

FOX GRAPE, MUSCADINE GRAPE

A vigorous vine to 10m (33ft); the bark does not shred as in other vines. Leaves broad, rather rounded heart-shaped, seldom lobed, 5–11cm (2–4¼in) long, coarsely toothed, glossy dark green above but glossy yellowish-green beneath. Flowers greenish; early to midsummer. Berries dull purple, 16–25mm (⅔–1in), with a pleasant musky flavour. S USA

☼ ☽ -5°C (23°F) ⋎ℓw

✓ *V. vinifera*

COMMON GRAPE VINE

This species is almost too well known to warrant a description. Stems vigorous, reaching 7m (23ft) or more if left unchecked. Flowers early to midsummer. Leaves 3–5-lobed, coarsely toothed and bright green in the usual form. Cultivated for many centuries and today many fine cultivars exist, grown primarily for their fruit (not included here). Probably W Asia

☼ ☽ -15°C (5°F) ⋎ℓw

'Apiifolia' ('Ciotat', 'Laciniosa') PARSLEY VINE, CIOTAT: leaves handsome, dissected, each of the main lobes deeply cut into long narrow divisions. **'Fragola'**: a decorative cultivar with pleasant strawberry-flavoured berries.

'Incana' DUSTY MILLER GRAPE: bears handsome grey-felted leaves, whitish when young, 3-lobed or unlobed; berries black.

✓ **'Purpurea'** TEINTURIER GRAPE: a very striking plant; young leaves are whitish-downy but soon become claret or plum-purple, changing in the autumn to an intense deep dark purple; grapes purple-black when ripe but unpleasant to taste; one of the very finest ornamental vines.

✓ *V. wilsoniae*

Very vigorous, to 5m (16ft) or more, with woolly young shoots. Leaves oval, slightly heart-shaped at the base, wavy-toothed, 7.5–15cm (3–6in), woolly when young but becoming deep green and hairless above while remaining downy beneath, turning fiery red in the autumn. Flowers greenish; early to midsummer. Berries black with a purple bloom, 10–12mm (½in). E.H. Wilson discovered this plant in China in 1902 and the species was named after his wife. Central China

☼ ☽ -15°C (5°F) ⋎ℓw

WISTERIA
(Leguminosae)

Without question one of the most popular group of flowering climbers grown for their luxuriant twining habit and sumptuous racemes of fragrant pea-flowers. Wisterias are some of the most beautiful climbing plants and can be used on walls, or trained on pergolas or up tall trees. They can be grown in any type of soil providing it is well-drained but prefer a sunny, sheltered position.

The genus contains 10 species native to East Asia and eastern North America, with alternate pinnate leaves. The terminal inflorescences are axillary and usually pendulous. The fruit is a flattened pod, generally with several seeds.

Young plants may take a number of years to reach a flowering state but careful training and pruning from an early stage can advance flowering; over-feeding plants will encourage growth at the expense of flower-bud formation. A system of spur pruning is recommended: once the framework branches have been established lateral growths should be pruned each year to encourage the formation of flower buds *(see spur pruning, page 27)*. It is best to prune in two stages; first, after flowering (usually about midsummer) the long laterals should be cut back to about 15cm (6in); second, in midwinter, these are again shortened, leaving only two or three buds to each lateral shoot.

✓ *Wisteria floribunda*
JAPANESE WISTERIA
Vigorous twiner to 10m (33ft). Leaves 25–35cm (10–14in) long, composed of 11–19 oval leaflets. Flowers in drooping, rather slender racemes 15–25cm (6–10in) long, with fragrant violet-blue flowers; late spring to early summer. Pods 7.5–15cm (3–6in) long, velvety. Japan
☼ ◑ -20°C (-4°F) ⚘ ⚘w

Widely grown in gardens, this species has been cultivated for centuries in Japanese gardens and it was introduced into Europe in the 1830s. Many cultivars have been selected over the years. The following are generally in cultivation. Those with long racemes look their best on a pergola or some overhead structure where the flowers can dangle downwards unhindered:

✓ **'Alba'**: flowers white, sometimes tinged with lilac on the keel; racemes 50–60cm (20–24in) long, strongly scented. ♛ **'Beni Fuji'**: flowers lavender-blue, especially well scented. **'Geisha'**: flowers lavender-blue; rare.

✓ **'Multijuga'** ('Macrobotrys', 'Naga Noda'): Flowers fragrant, lilac suffused with bluish-purple, often yellowish at the base of the standard petal, in racemes 90–120cm (36–48in) long; a magnificent form. ♛ **'Rosea'**: flowers purple with a pink standard petal; racemes about 55cm (22in) long. ♛ **'Russelliana'**: flowers

Wisteria floribunda 'Alba'

deep bluish-violet with a deep mauve standard, all marked with cream; probably no longer available. **'Sekine's Blue'**: short racemes of violet-blue. **'Violacea Plena'**: flowers double, lilac; the only double-flowered cultivar.

✓ *W. × formosa*
Probably a hybrid between *W. sinensis* and *W. floribunda* 'Alba'. To 25m (82ft). Leaves with 9–15 leaflets. Flowers pale violet, in racemes up to 25cm (10in) long; late spring to early summer. Garden origin.
☼ -15°C (5°F) ⚘ ⚘w

'Issai': racemes slightly shorter, 17.5–25cm (7–10in), lilac-blue.

W. frutescens
To 9–12m (30–40ft). Leaves 17.5–30cm (7–12in) long with 9–15 oval or oblong leaflets. Flowers scented, mauve with a yellow spot, in erect to arching racemes 10–15cm (4–6in) long; summer. Pods 5–10cm (2–4in) long, hairless. This species is rather uncommon in gardens and is generally less vigorous than its Asian cousins. SE USA
☼ -20°C (-4°F) ⚘ ⚘w

'Magnifica': flowers lilac with a sulphur-yellow blotch on the standard. **'Nivea'** (forma *nivea*): flowers white with a yellow blotch on the standard.

Wisteria venusta

Wisteria venusta 'Violacea'

W. *japonica*
(*Millettia japonica*)
To 12m (40ft). Leaves
15 22.5cm (6–9in) long, with
9–13 bright green, oval to
rounded leaflets. Flowers
white or very pale yellow in
racemes 15–30cm (6–12in),
that are often branched; mid-
to late summer. Pods hairless,
7.5–10cm (3–4in) long. A
plant for growing up a stout
tree but rare in gardens. Japan
☼ -15°C (5°F) ⚘ ⚘**s**

W. *macrostachya*
To 8m (26ft); closely allied to
W. frutescens. Leaves usually
with 9 oval to narrowly elliptic
leaflets. Flowers lilac-purple in
dense racemes 15–35cm
(6–14in) long; late spring to
early summer. Pods hairless,
7.5–12.5cm (3–5in) long. S
USA
☼ -20°C (-4°F) ⚘ ⚘**w**

✓ W. *sinensis*
(*W. chinensis*)
CHINESE WISTERIA
Very vigorous climber to 30m
(98ft), especially if allowed to
grow unhindered. Leaves
25–30cm (10–12in) long,
usually with 11 leaflets.
Flowers fragrant, in rather
broad drooping racemes,
20–30cm (8–12in) long,
mauve or lilac; late spring,
occasionally later. Pods

12.5–15cm (5–6in) long. The
finest species for the average
garden. China
☼ -15°C (5°F) ⚘ ⚘**w**
   'Alba': flowers white, powerfully
   scented. ♔ **'Caroline'**: flowers
   deep purple-blue, very fragrant.
   'Jako': racemes dense, lilac, 30cm
   (12in) long, fragrant. **'Plena'**:
   flowers lilac, double. ✓ **'Prolific'**
   ('Oosthoek's Variety'): a Dutch
   cultivar with longer racemes than
   the type, produced in great
   abundance. **'Sierra Madre'**:
   flowers lavender-violet with a
   whitish standard, very fragrant.

W. *venusta*
To 9m (30ft). Leaves 20–35cm
(8–14in) long, with 9–13 oval
to oblong leaflets. Flowers
slightly fragrant, white with a
yellow blotch on the standard,
in short, broad, arching
racemes 10–15cm (4–6in)
long, all open at the same time;
late spring to early summer.
It has the largest flowers
(2.5–3.5cm/1–1½in long) of
any cultivated wisteria. Pods
velvety, 15–20cm (6–8in)
long.
Not known in the wild;
derived from Japanese gardens.
☼ -20°C (-4°F) ⚘ ⚘**w**
   'Alba Plena' (forma *plena*, 'Shiro
   Kapitan'): flowers white,
   double. **'Violacea'** ('Murasaki
   Kapitan', var. *violacea*): flowers
   purplish.

Honeysuckles

Introduction

Honeysuckles are among the most loved of all climbing plants and have long been associated with cottage gardens, archways and arbours. They are grown for their pretty, often powerfully fragrant flowers. Many are attractive to bees or night-flying moths and the New World species, with their scarlet, tubular flowers are pollinated by humming-birds in those areas where these birds occur. Honeysuckles are ideal for training up walls, trellis, fences or pergolas or for hiding old tree stumps. They grow best in a loamy soil which does not dry out for long periods and they appreciate being mulched and fed during the summer. In common with clematis, they prefer their roots and lower stems to be in shade and their upper stems and flowers to be in the sun. The shiny berries are attractive to birds seeking a source of food.

Honeysuckles belong to the genus *Lonicera*. With some 180 species scattered around the northern hemisphere they display a range of form, from shrubs to vigorous climbers. Of the 60 or so species in cultivation, about a third are climbers. The remainder are non-climbing shrubs and they therefore not included here.

The climbing honeysuckles have twining stems, opposite, untoothed leaves and flowers produced in pairs or in whorls. The flowers are generally tubular with five lobes at the mouth, and usually the flower is two-lipped with four of the lobes forming the upper lip and the fifth making the lower lip. The five stamens often protrude and the flowers themselves are followed by many-seeded berries.

In general, honeysuckles are plants of temperate latitudes. However, the more tender species (*L. hildebrandtiana*, *L. implexa*, *L. similis* and *L. splendida*) will do well in a conservatory where, perhaps surprisingly, *L. sempervirens* and *L. japonica* can also be grown.

After planting, the plants should be cut back by two-thirds to encourage strong

(Left) Honeysuckles mix well with other climbers. Here, *Lonicera etrusca* forms an attractive medley with *Rosa* 'The Garland' and *Clematis viticella* 'Madame Julia Correvon'.

lateral shoots. The strongest two or three stems should be selected to form the main framework and tied in if necessary until they begin to twine in the desired direction. Mature plants need pruning – primarily to reduce their size. Regular pruning consists of removing any weak, congested or dead growth, cutting back long shoots to a suitable pair of buds. This is best done in late winter before the plant shows signs of spring growth. If grown on a fence or tree, little or no pruning will be necessary. Where space is no problem, honeysuckles can be allowed to roam freely to great effect. When the common species such as

L. periclymenum are grown in restricted positions, such as on a pillar or arch, lateral shoots should be cut back in late winter to two or three bud pairs of a main stem.

The flowers of climbing honeysuckes are borne on the current season's shoots. Thus, pruning and training is aimed at producing a framework of permanent branches which will produce the flowering shoots. These framework branches should be renovated after five or six years by hard pruning which will encourage strong new replacement growth from the base. This can be done in gradual stages over two or three years if you wish.

(Above) Lonicera periclymenum and a clematis intermingle successfully through a decorative wrought-iron fence.

(Left) Sweet-smelling honeysuckle makes an attractive climber to train over an arch.

Climbing honeysuckles tend to become bare at the base in time. Cutting back one or two branches close to the ground will encourage new replacement growth.

Honeysuckles are fairly free of pests and diseases although greenfly (aphids) can be a problem. If aphids are not noticed and get a hold early in the season, the plant's leaves can be distorted and the crop of flowers may be destroyed. An insecticide should be applied as soon as aphids are seen. *L. periclymenum* and its cultivars and *L. tragophylla* are particularly affected by aphids especially when they are grown in a sunny position. Planting in a shadier aspect can often overcome the problem. Mildew and leaf miner can also affect honeysuckles.

Honeysuckles are readily propagated by semi-hardwood cuttings taken in midsummer and placed in a propagating frame: hormone rooting powder will improve the chances of success. The species can also be grown from seed.

The fragrant species of honeysuckle should, if possible, be planted where their perfume can be easily appreciated: by a door or window, or over a garden arch or a gateway. Honeysuckles and roses are one of the classic plant combinations, especially in the traditional cottage garden.

Nevertheless, it is preferable to plant honeysuckles next to their companion plants rather than so close that one grows on or through the other, because the honeysuckle stems tend to overpower and strangle those of their companions. Honeysuckles look charming grown with clematis, but if the plants are allowed to grow into one another, the result can be a great interwoven mass which is extremely difficult to disentangle at pruning time. An exception is *C. viticella* and its cultivars, which mix particularly well as they can be pruned to the ground in late winter and all the old stems which have tangled with those of the honeysuckle are easily pulled out. The combination can still be achieved by planting the chosen species or cultivars next to one another but far enough apart to prevent problems.

There are lots of possible associations for honeysuckles, such as with *Hydrangea petiolaris*, jasmines, mutisias, or the wall shrubs *Buddleja fallowiana* or *Philadelphus mexicanus*. The herbaceous everlasting peas, *Lathyrus latifolius*, *L. rotundifolius* and *L. tuberosus*, can look stunning in association with the summer-flowering honeysuckles. The yellows and pinks of honeysuckles make a superb combination with blue ceanothus. The permutations are endless.

LONICERA
(Caprifoliaceae)

L. alseuosmoides

Closely related to *L. henryi*, but less vigorous and with hairless young shoots. Leaves elliptic, pointed, 3–5cm (1¼–2in) long, downy with a hairy margin. Flowers purple outside, pale yellow inside, tubular (not 2-lipped), about 13mm (½in) long, borne in pairs close together at the shoot tips; midsummer to autumn. Berries purplish-black. It is much less commonly available than *L. henryi* and although the flowers are not spectacular, it is worth growing for the foliage and fruit alone. W China (Sichuan)
☼ ☀ -15°C (5°F) ⚑s

✓ *L. × americana* ⚹

A hybrid between *L. caprifolium* and *L. etrusca*. Moderately vigorous, deciduous, with stems reaching 7m (23ft). Leaves oval, rather pointed, the uppermost united into cups just below the flowers. Flowers fragrant, creamy-yellow flushed with reddish-purple, 2-lipped, 4.5–5cm (1¾–2in) long, borne in the cups formed by the upper leaves and also above them in branched clusters; summer to autumn. Berries red. A lovely hybrid with the general growth of *L. caprifolium* (with which it is sometimes confused) and the branched flower clusters of *L. etrusca*. It is a prolific bloomer with a sweet, powerful scent and is regarded as one of the best honeysuckles. It will tolerate full sun but prefers some shade. Despite its name, *L. × americana* is European in origin: it was named 'americana' by Philip Miller who mistakenly thought it came from North America. It is sometimes found under the name *L. × italica* in catalogues and garden centres but this name applies to a different species. SE Europe
☼ ☀ -15°C (5°F) ⚑s

✓ *L. × brownii*

(*L. etrusca* var. *brownii, L. sempervirens* var. *brownii*)
SCARLET TRUMPET HONEYSUCKLE
A beautiful hybrid which combines the charm of *L. sempervirens* with the hardiness of *L. hirsuta*; the latter parent is only rarely cultivated. Deciduous or semi-evergreen with the general characteristics of *L. sempervirens*, growing to 4m (13ft). Leaves oval, bluish-green. Flowers scarlet with an orange throat, 2-lipped, though not strongly so, downy outside, 3.8–4.2cm (1½–1¾in) long; late spring to early autumn. Garden origin
☀ ☀ -20°C (-4°F) ⚑s

> ✓ **'Dropmore Scarlet'**: a fine scarlet-red cultivar noted for its very long flowering season.
> **'Fuchsioides'**: flowers glowing orange-scarlet, borne early and late in the season.

✓ *L. caprifolium* ⚹
EARLY CREAM HONEYSUCKLE,
ITALIAN WOODBINE
Deciduous with stems twining to 7m (23ft), though generally

Lonicera × brownii 'Dropmore Scarlet'

less. Leaves oval, bluish-green especially beneath, the upper 2 or 3 pairs united below the whorls of flowers to form a series of cups around the stem. Flowers fragrant, yellowish-white tinged with pink, 2-lipped, 3.5–5cm (1½–2in) long; early summer. Berries shiny orange-red. This is a magnificent plant which many people consider to be the finest garden honeysuckle especially noted for its fragrance. It does not like to be grown in a soil which dries out, and grows best in light shade, although it will tolerate both sun and deeper shade. *L. caprifolium* is sometimes confused with *L. periclymenum*; however the leaves are a distinctive bluish-green above and the uppermost are united in pairs around the stem just below the flowers — this never happens in the latter. Europe, W Asia
☼ ☀ ☀ -20°C (-4°F) ⚑s

> **'Anna Fletcher'**: flowers lemon-yellow with no pink tinge.
> **'Pauciflora'**: flowers smaller, tinged rose-pink on the outside.

L. ciliosa
WESTERN TRUMPET
HONEYSUCKLE
Similar to *L. sempervirens* but differing in having the upper pair of leaflets united into a cup with 2 pointed ends and the flowers clearly 2-lipped.
N. USA
☼ -20°C (-4°F) ⚑s

L. etrusca
ETRUSCAN HONEYSUCKLE
A moderately vigorous, deciduous or semi-evergreen climber, reaching 4m (13ft). Leaves oval, green above, bluish-green beneath and softly downy, the upper pairs fused at their bases around the stem. Flowers fragrant, yellowish at first, becoming gradually flushed with red, but eventually turning deep yellow, 2-lipped, 4–5cm (1½–2in) long; summer to autumn. Berries red. This is a vigorous grower and a profuse bloomer with a long flowering season. Its lack of hardiness is a drawback in cooler temperate regions but it makes an attractive conservatory plant where it can grow up a pillar or be trained against a wall.
Mediterranean region
☼ -10°C (14°F) ⚑s

> **'Donald Waterer'**: flowers red and cream, aging to yellow. **'Superba'**: a particularly vigorous, free-flowering cultivar with large clusters of cream flowers which turn orange.

L. giraldii
Evergreen climber with tangled growth reaching 2m

(6½ft), the young shoots covered with yellowish hairs. Leaves narrowly oblong, hairy on both surfaces. Flowers bright red-purple, yellowish and hairy inside, 2-lipped, 2–2.5cm (¾–1in) long, borne in short clusters at the shoot tips; summer to early autumn. Berries purplish-black. S China (Sichuan)

A striking plant related to *L. japonica*. The flowers are small but borne freely. The yellowish hairs of the young growth give the plant a distinctive character.
☼ ☽ -15°C (5°F) ⌇℮ₛ

L. × heckrottii

A handsome hybrid between *L. × americana* and *L. sempervirens* which flowers profusely. A deciduous, weak-stemmed shrub attaining some 3m (10ft). Leaves oblong or oval, green above, bluish-green beneath, hairless and with a very short stalk, the uppermost pairs encircling the stem. Flowers pink with a deep yellow throat, 2-lipped, 3.5–4cm (1½in) long, fragrant, in whorls or long-stalked clusters at the shoot tips; summer to early autumn. Berries red. The plant is more a shrub than a climber; the weak stems usually need to be supported by wires attached to the wall. It grows slowly and dislikes too much direct sunlight. Garden origin
☽ ☀ -15°C (5°F) ⌇℮ₛ

'Gold Flame': plant vigorous with dark green leaves and flowers flushed with deep purple, deep

Lonicera etrusca

Lonicera henryi (in fruit)

yellow inside, borne in dense, rounded clusters. The plant offered under this name by some nurseries is in fact *L. × heckrottii* itself, so plants should be selected when in flower from nurseries and garden centres.

L. henryi

Vigorous evergreen or semi-deciduous climber with stems reaching as much as 10m (33ft), with the young shoots covered in short bristly hairs. Leaves narrowly oblong to oval, deep green above, paler and rather shiny beneath.

Flowers purplish-red, 2-lipped, 1.8–2cm (¾in) long, borne in clusters at the shoot tips; summer to autumn. Berries purplish-black. Suitable for a large wall or fence. Although the flowers are small and not as beautiful as those of many of the other species of honeysuckle, the foliage of this species is handsome and, in autumn, the plant is covered with attractive shiny berries, carried in profusion in some years. W China
☼ ☽ -25°C (-13°F) ⌇℮ₛ

✓ ▦ **L. hildebrandtiana**
GIANT HONEYSUCKLE, GIANT BURMESE HONEYSUCKLE
Very vigorous, evergreen climber, sometimes semi-deciduous, with hairless stems which can reach 20m (66ft) or more. Leaves large, broad oval or rounded, dark green above, paler and glandular beneath. Flowers fragrant, white or cream at first, gradually changing to orange or yellow-brown, 2-lipped, very long and slender, 9–16cm (3½–6½in), borne in axillary pairs or at the shoot tips; summer. This giant honeysuckle produces the largest flowers of any species. It is not hardy in temperate latitudes and only rarely does one see a flowering specimen out of doors on a sunny, sheltered wall. Given greenhouse protection it does well and makes an unusual and attractive subject for the conservatory. Young plants can take several years to establish and are often shy flowerers at first. S China, Burma, Thailand
☼ 5°C (41°F) ⌇℮ₛ

▦ L. implexa
MINORCA HONEYSUCKLE
A compact evergreen climber reaching a height of 2.5m (8ft), sometimes more. Leaves oval or oblong, strikingly bluish-green beneath, greener above, the upper pairs forming cups around the stem and surrounding the stalkless flower clusters. Flowers yellow flushed with pink outside,

downy, white turning to yellow inside, 4–4.5cm (1½–1¾in) long; summer. An attractive species, but slow-growing and too tender for most cool temperate gardens. Mediterranean region
☀ ◑ 0°C (32°F) ⅄S

🔲 *L. japonica*
JAPANESE HONEYSUCKLE
Stems vigorous, reaching as much as 10m (33ft), softly hairy. Leaves evergreen, bright green, usually oval, sometimes lobed, especially on vigorous vegetative shoots. Flowers very fragrant, opening white, sometimes with a purple tinge, but soon turning yellowish, 2-lipped, downy outside, 3–5cm (1¼–2in) long, in stalked pairs in the leaf axils; late spring to autumn. Berries small, black and shiny. A rampant species whose flowers are less attractive than those of most honeysuckles but it has a long flowering season and a wonderful fragrance. A good plant for covering (and concealing) large tree stumps, old fences or garden walls. *L. japonica* was first introduced into gardens in 1806. In the United States, especially in the east, it is naturalized and has become a weed. Plants can be pruned back hard if necessary in the spring and will sprout vigorously as a result. China, Japan, Korea
☀ ◑ -25°C (-13°F) ⅄S
  'Aureoreticulata' ('Variegata'): a less vigorous, small-leaved cultivar with stems reaching only 3m (10ft). Leaves have a bright yellow midrib

and veins; some are distinctly lobed. An attractive, commonly grown cultivar which is less hardy than the type and may suffer damage in a severe winter. To produce lots of flowers, it should be grown against a warm sheltered wall. ✔ **'Halliana'**: the best-known cultivar with very fragrant flowers which have the upper lip divided almost to midway. The main flowering time is summer, though flowers are produced now and then through to the autumn and even sporadically through mild winters. **'Hall's Prolific'**: stems to 6m (20ft) bearing oval leaves, and abundant flowers even on young plants. Var. *repens*: leaves quickly becoming hairless, often stained with brown-purple on the veins beneath and often lobed.

L. periclymenum
COMMON HONEYSUCKLE, WOODBINE
Stems twining and scrambling, reaching as much as 7m (23ft) in the wild, usually less in gardens. Leaves deciduous, oval or oblong, generally pointed, green above, rather bluish-green beneath, the upper unstalked but not united into a cup below the flowers. Flowers deliciously fragrant, usually opening white but gradually turning yellowish, often with a reddish or pink flush, 2-lipped, 3.5–5cm (1½–2in) long with a slender downy tube, borne in a series of dense whorls at the ends of the shoots; summer. Berries shiny red. This is prized as much for its beauty as for its powerful scent which is strongest in the early morning

Lonicera periclymenum, the wild honeysuckle

and late evening. It can be grown on a wall or fence or allowed to clamber over a tree stump or another large shrubs. The wild species is sometimes cultivated but has largely been replaced by some superior cultivars.
Europe, N Africa, W Asia
☀ ◑ ● -25°C (-13°F) ⅄S
  ✔ **'Belgica'**, ♀ EARLY DUTCH HONEYSUCKLE: habit bushier than in the wild species, stems purplish, up to 3m (10ft), flowers purplish-red outside, fading to yellowish-pink, pale yellow inside; late spring

Lonicera periclymenum 'Serotina'

to midsummer. ✔ **'Graham Thomas'** ♀: an extremely vigorous, long-flowering cultivar with white flowers which turn yellow and are copper-tinted. ✔ **'Serotina'** ♀ (*L. periclymenum* var. *semperflorens*, 'Florida') FLEMISH, LATE DUTCH or LATE RED HONEYSUCKLE: leaves rather narrow and flowers dark purple outside, paling with age, pinkish-cream inside; midsummer to autumn. A popular, vigorous cultivar which gives good value as the flowers are often produced spasmodically until the first autumn frosts.

✔ 🔲 *L. sempervirens* ♀
TRUMPET HONEYSUCKLE, CORAL HONEYSUCKLE
A vigorous and generally

Lonicera periclymenum 'Belgica'

evergreen climber growing to 10m (33ft). Leaves oval, deep green above, bluish-green and somewhat downy beneath, the upper 1 or 2 pairs united around the stem to form oblong or rounded cups. Flowers rich orange-scarlet outside, yellow inside, unscented, each tubular, 3.5–5cm (1½–2in) long with 5 more or less equal lobes, borne in 3 or 4 dense whorls at the shoot tips; spring to late summer. Berries red. This beautiful plant is hardier than is generally assumed. It will survive outdoors in all but the coldest districts, providing it has the shelter provided by a wall. *L. sempervirens* is perhaps the finest North American species, but it is not a particularly common garden plant, having largely been replaced by hybrids to which it has contributed – *L. × brownii* and *L. × heckrottii*. Unfortunately *L. sempervirens* is not scented but the beautiful flowers more than compensate for this deficiency. Although usually evergreen, some or all of the leaves may be lost during a cold winter.

S and E USA

☀ ☽ -25°C (-13°F) ⑂ℓs

'**Magnifica**': semi-evergreen, flowers red outside, yellow within. '**Sulphurea**' (forma *sulphurea*): flowers plain yellow. '**Superba**': deciduous with scarlet flowers.

▦ **L. similis**

Closely related to *L. japonica* and represented in gardens by var. **delavayi**. Leaves oval to lance-shaped, green, hairless above but with a thick felt of grey hairs beneath. Flowers pale yellow, sweetly scented, 2-lipped, 5–8cm (2–3¼in) long with a slender tube and protruding stamens, borne in stalked pairs in the leaf axils or in loose heads at the shoot tips; mid- to late summer. Berries black. Not commonly cultivated but worth growing in a protected position.

SW China

☀ 0°C (32°F) ⑂ℓs

▦ **L. splendida**

Stems up to 4.5m (15ft). Leaves evergreen, oval or oblong, bluish-green, stalkless, the uppermost pairs fused together at their bases. Flowers reddish-purple and glandular outside, cream inside, 2-lipped, 2.5–5cm (1–2in) long, borne in a stalkless head consisting of 3–5 whorls, one above the other; mid- to late summer. Closely related to *L. periclymenum* and *L. etrusca*. This beautiful species is not commonly offered in nurseries, possibly because it is difficult to propagate: it deserves to be better known. The flowers are produced profusely if the plant is given a sunny south-facing wall and it really is a splendid sight in bloom, as its name implies. It needs protection in the winter in areas subject to hard frosts. It is fast-growing, often reaching up to 2m (6½ft) in a single season.

Spain.

☀ 0°C (32°F) ⑂ℓs

Lonicera × tellmaniana

✓ **L. × tellmaniana** ♀

REDGOLD

A hybrid between *L. tragophylla* and *L. sempervirens* 'Superba'. Deciduous with vigorous stems to 5m (16ft). Leaves oval, green, the uppermost pairs forming cups around the stem below the flowers. Flowers glowing yellow, unscented, 2-lipped, 4.5–5cm (1¾–2in) long, with protruding stamens, borne in clusters at the shoot tips; late spring to midsummer. A glorious plant and perhaps the best of the hybrid climbing honeysuckles. It is excellent grown on a shady wall where it will produce its large flowers (which open from bronze-flushed buds) in great profusion. In the United States this honeysuckle is often sold under the name 'Redgold'. Garden origin.

☀ ☽ ☀ -20°C (-4°F) ⑂ℓs

✓ **L. tragophylla** ♀

Deciduous, with hairless young shoots up to 6m (20ft). Leaves oval, bluish-green, the uppermost pair united into a diamond-shaped cup below the flowers. Flowers bright yellow, unscented, 2-lipped, 7–8cm (2¾–3¼in) long, downy on the outside, borne in 1- or 2-whorled terminal heads of up to 20 flowers; early summer. Berries red. This is one of the largest-flowered and most spectacular honeysuckles. Its preference is for semi-shade, although it will tolerate both sun and full shade.

W China

☀ ☽ ☀ -15°C (5°F) ⑂ℓs

Lonicera × tragophylla

Clematis

Introduction

Clematis are among the most popular, colourful and useful of all climbing plants. In almost any garden you are virtually certain to see one or two draped over a fence, or clinging to a wall or tree. There is now a huge number of species and cultivars available, many of which have been grown for years, ensuring that clematis today rank among the most important of all the climbers in our gardens.

The informality of clematis make them ideal plants for sprawling over and along a wall or fence. In the spring, few sights can equal an old tree adorned with the flowery tresses of pink or white *Clematis montana* or, in the summer, a pillar or pergola bold with the stately bright blooms of one of the large-flowered cultivars like 'Barbara Dibley' or 'Lasurstern'. But many clematis have smaller flowers which, although less significant on their own, are produced in such quantity and over so many weeks, that they make up in numbers what they lack in size. In addition, when all the flowers are over, many species produce a display of silky or feathery seedheads that vie with other autumn fruits for our attention.

Clematis mix well with other garden plants, especially shrubs and the more vigorous herbaceous perennials as well as with trees, and exciting combinations of form and colour can be devised. In fact a clematis grown alone can look rather forlorn confined to a wall or fence – they really prefer to be grown among other plants. Careful combinations of shrubs and clematis can create a focus of interest in the garden, especially if the clematis flowers before or after the shrub – but do not choose the vigorous, all-invasive types which are likely to swamp the shrubs. For instance the small violet-blue flowers of *C.* 'Etoile Violette' look charming festooning *Euonymus* 'Red Cascade', with its carmine fruits. Roses and clematis have always made a special partnership. Over an arch or pergola, try growing *C.* 'Jackmanii Superba'

(*Above*) Different clematis make exciting companions.

with its rich violet-purple blooms with the pale pink climbing rose 'New Dawn', or 'Madame Julia Correvon' with rich, velvety wine-red blooms with the dainty salmon-cream rambler rose 'The Garland'. Honeysuckles and clematis also make interesting companions. One can even mix several different clematis together: *C. flammula*, which has dainty, scented white flowers, works in perfect harmony with C. 'Ernest Markham' or 'Perle d'Azur' and will flower at the same time. Many other similar combinations can be devised.

The genus *Clematis* is distributed throughout all the major continents of the world and contains over 200 species. Although some species have small, greenish-white flowers of little garden value, there are many beautiful and brightly coloured species which deserve attention, some of them delightfully scented. Besides these, there are numerous large-flowered hybrids and cultivars that have been selectively bred over the years. Some of these may be considered to be big and blowsy, however, they do provide bright splashes of colour in the garden from spring through to the late autumn. One or two of the species even manage to flower during the winter.

Clematis are wonderfully versatile plants. Some are tender and need careful protection if they are to succeed, but many have less exacting requirements and can be grown on a variety of supports; walls, fences, pergolas, pillars and trees are all suitable. Besides this, many can be successfully grown among shrubs or other climbing plants, providing an attractive contrast or combination of colours. Indeed, many of the large-flowered varieties are better

(Above) Few climbing plants are better than clematis for clothing pillars, arches and pergolas.

(Left) *Clematis potaninii* festoons a shrub in the wilds of N.W. Yunnan, in China.

grown in association with other plants than in isolation, for the lower half of the plant is often devoid of flowers and this can detract from the beauty of the flowers at the top; roses, cotoneasters, ceanothus and fruit trees past their best are all suitable partners, though everyone can enjoy working out new combinations of plants and colours for themselves.

Not all clematis are woody climbers – there are a number of attractive herbaceous species as well as a few shrubby ones, though they mostly do not concern us here. The climbing species cling by means of their twining leaf stalks which grip any support at hand and many soon make a tangled mass of shoots and leaves unless the stems are carefully spaced and trained from early on – this requires some care as they can be very brittle at this stage. The leaves of some clematis are evergreen and remain through a part or all of the winter. They may become brown and unsightly unless the plants are grown in a very sheltered position in the garden.

The clematis flower is basically rather simple. There are four or more separate, often brightly coloured, petals (in the botanical sense these are in fact sepals, but that need not concern us here). They may be held close together or indeed partly fused to one another to form a bell- or urn-shaped flower though, in the majority of species, they are quite separate and widely spreading. There are numerous stamens surrounding a group of single-seeded fruits or 'achenes' in the centre of the flower. The tip of each achene – the style – elongates after pollination and in many species is densely hairy, thus giving the fruit heads their fluffy or feathery 'old man's beard' appearance.

CULTURE

Clematis prefer a deep, moist loamy soil. Soils that dry out quickly, such as sandy soils or heavy clays, are not generally suitable unless carefully prepared to improve their composition. Although there is no general agreement among gardeners it would seem that a calcareous soil is good, though not essential, for most species. Species and cultivars, except for the more tender ones, will thrive equally well in a sunny or partially shaded position, some even flowering well in almost total shade. However, they are best planted with their roots in a shady moist place, for they will not tolerate strong sun drying out the soil around them. A sheltered site is also preferable, for constant buffeting by the wind may cause damage, especially to the large-flowered cultivars. Large, vigorous species will need strong

(Left) *Clematis* 'Jackmanii Superba' and *C. flammula* make good companions for late summer.

(Right) Late summer-flowering *Clematis viticella* 'Purpurea Plena Elegans' is easy to please.

supports as they tend to become extremely heavy with age.

Young specimens can be planted out in the autumn or early spring, although today, with the advent of healthy container-grown stock, they can be planted out at virtually any time except midwinter. Evergreen species, however, are best planted out in the spring. Young plants, except those of the *C. montana* group, are best pruned back to a strong pair of buds in late winter; this will help to encourage strong young growth.

Most clematis, especially the large-flowered cultivars, respond to regular feeding and to generous mulches during the growing season.

The only major disease of clematis is clematis wilt, which is caused by a fungus. The large-flowered cultivars are especially vulnerable and are often struck without warning by this annoying disease, causing a shoot or several shoots to die back. Occasionally the entire plant may be affected and is then best removed and destroyed. Infected shoots should be cut out from the base, leaving only healthy growth. A suitable systemic fungicide sprayed regularly can greatly help to hold the fungus in check. Deep planting of container specimens (i.e. burying the lower 10–15cm/ 4–6in of the plant) can greatly alleviate this problem; deep-planted speci-

mens will often put up strong shoots from below ground level.

The flowers of many of the large-flowered forms bleach badly in strong sunlight, especially those with blue or pink flowers. Planting in a semi-shaded position is therefore preferable for these, or at least a position that avoids the direct sun during the midday hours.

Clematis are readily propagated from cuttings of semi-mature shoots. This is usually undertaken in midsummer. They root best from internodal cuttings, with the use of rooting hormones and fungicidal sprays to keep the clematis cuttings healthy until they have rooted.

The species can also be grown from seed, which is readily set, often in abundance. Some cultivars will come true from seed but the majority will not and if you want to be sure of perpetuating a particular cultivar then it is far wiser to propagate it from cuttings. Cultivar seedlings, on the other hand, can be very variable and some may be beautiful: it can be fun making a selection of the best of them but it is advisable to destroy all the others.

(Above) *Clematis montana* produces a mass of spring flowers. Vigorous, hardy and reliable, it has provided our gardens with a host of fine cultivars.

(Left) A medley of clematis festoon the shrubs below a window.

PRUNING

Most people find pruning a complex subject and the pruning of clematis in particular impossible. However, the procedure is really quite simple, provided a few general rules are obeyed, bearing in mind that the object of pruning is to promote strong, healthy growth and a good crop of flowers, while at the same time keeping the plant in check to some extent. Clematis can be placed into three major groups according to their pruning requirements and this grouping has been followed in the following pages.

GROUP A *(see page 72)*

Clematis that flower early in the year on the previous year's growths (*C. alpina*, *C. montana* and *C. chrysocoma* for instance) should be pruned immediately after flowering, although pruning is mainly done to remove old or weak growth or to reduce the size or bulk of the plant. Pruning these later in the year will only remove the following year's flowers. They can in fact be left unpruned all together, if desired. Evergreen species like *C. armandii* should be pruned lightly and with discretion, though some gardeners appear to get away with a more vigorous assault on such plants.

GROUP B *(see pages 75, 76, 79)*

The second group includes all the species and cultivars that flower from midsummer onwards on the current season's growth. This includes two main types: the herbaceous climbers such as *C. viorna* and *C. viticella* and the vigorous late-flowerers such as *C. flammula*, *C. tangutica* and *C. vitalba*. With the former it is only necessary to remove all dead growth in the spring (this often means taking back plants almost to ground level). The latter, however, tend to produce a mass of permanent top growth with bare tangled stems beneath after a year or two. Some of the larger stems can be pruned hard back in the spring to encourage new growth. Alternatively the whole plant can be cut back to about a metre (3ft 3in) or as little as 30cm (12in), leaving a few healthy buds at the top of each stem.

GROUP C *(see page 81)*

The third group consists of most of the large-flowered cultivars and hybrids, with the exception of the *C. viticella* group. Little pruning is required other than to remove dead or old shoots and to train and untangle new growths. Most of these flower from the early summer onwards on short shoots produced from those of the previous season.

If a later display is desired, early flowering can be sacrificed wholly or in part by pruning back growth in the spring, although care should be taken not to leave this too late. Many of these cultivars will, under normal circumstances, produce a later second crop of flowers, though generally far fewer than the midsummer flush.

GROUP A CLEMATIS

These clematis flower early in the year on growth made during the previous year. Pruning (if any) should be undertaken immediately after flowering and should consist mainly of reducing the size or bulk of the plant, or removing old, weak or dead growth.

CLEMATIS ALPINA AND ALLIES

Semi-vigorous deciduous species whose leaves have 9 leaflets and solitary nodding flowers which have 4 petals and numerous narrower petal-like staminodes, transitional between the petals and the stamens. They are among the most beautiful and elegant species, ideal for combining with other wall shrubs.

✓ *C. alpina* ♚

ALPINE CLEMATIS
To 2–3m (6½–10ft); young stems often flushed with red or purple. Flowers pale to deep blue or lilac-blue with a contrasting white centre, open bells, 2.5–3.7cm (1–1½in) long; staminodes spoon-shaped, shorter than petals; mid- to late spring. One of the most delightful species, ideal for the small garden with limited space. Central and N Europe, W Asia

☀ -25°C (-13°C) ♚

'**Columbine**': flowers bell-shaped, pale lavender; petals long-pointed. '**Constance**': flowers semi-double,

deep purplish-pink, 5cm (2in) long. ✓ '**Frances Rivis**' ('Blue Giant'): ♚ large mid-blue flowers, 5–7cm (2–2¾in) long. '**Frankie**': flowers pale to mid-blue, 6cm (2½in) long; staminodes white tipped pale blue. '**Helsingborg**': ♚ flowers deep purple-blue with finely pointed petals, 4–5cm (1½–2in) long. '**Inshriach**': flowers rather small, dark lilac to pale mauve; staminodes greenish, tipped mauve. '**Jacqueline du Pré**': flowers large, pink with a silvery edge to the petals. ✓ '**Pamela Jackman**': flowers deep blue, 4cm (1½in) long. '**Pink Flamingo**': semi-double pale pink flowers, 4–6cm (1½–2½in) long. '**Ruby**': flowers reddish-purple with a white centre. '**Willy**': flowers pale pink, deeper at the base of the petals, 4–6cm (1½–2½in) long.

Subsp. *sibirica*: similar in general characteristics to the species but leaves paler green and flowers creamy-white. Sweden to N China, Siberia. '**Gravetye**': flowers large, creamy; early flowering. ✓ '**White Moth**': lovely white-flowered cultivar.

✓ *C. macropetala*

Semi-vigorous to 4m (13ft); stems slender, slightly angled. Flowers blue or violet-blue, 6–9cm (2½–3½in) across, with spreading petals and with numerous similar, though smaller staminodes; late spring to early summer. A very beautiful and free-flowering species which has been cultivated in Europe for more than two hundred years.

Clematis macropetala

Excellent for a wall or fence, or for tumbling down a bank or retaining wall. W and N China, Siberia

☀ -25°C (-13°C) ♚

'**Ballet Blanc**': flowers small, 5–6.5cm (2–2½in) but fully double, white. '**Blue Bird**': semi-nodding mauve-blue flowers, 7.5–10cm (3–4in). '**Jan Lindmark**' (*C. alpina* 'Jan Lindmark'): flowers mauve. ✓ '**Maidwell Hall**' ('Blue Lagoon'): ♚ flowers pure blue. ✓ '**Markham's Pink**' ('Markhamii'): ♚ flowers rosy-mauve flushed with pink at petal bases, with a white centre. '**Rosy O'Grady**': flowers semi-double, bright deep pink. '**Snowbird**': flowers white; late-flowering. '**White Swan**': flowers white, 7.5–10cm (3–4in), freely produced.

✓ *C. verticillaris*

Very similar to *C. alpina*, with thin hairless stems. Leaves untoothed or with a few coarse teeth. Flowers purple or bluish-purple with a whitish centre, 5–7.5cm (2–3in) long, open bells; late spring to early

summer. A less good garden plant than *C. alpina*, being more difficult to cultivate and certainly not as handsome. E North America

☀ -25°C (-13°C) ♚

CLEMATIS ARMANDII AND ALLIES

Vigorous or semi-vigorous evergreen species usually with 3-parted, untoothed leaves, occasionally pinnate. Flowers borne in large lateral clusters, each with 4–7 petals spreading widely apart. They require sheltered positions in the garden.

C. armandii

Vigorous plant to 6–10m (20–33ft) eventually. Leaves leathery, deep glossy green; leaflets large, oblong or lance-shaped, 7.5–15cm (3–6in) long, 3-veined. Flowers in rather dense clusters, white or cream, sometimes flushed with pale rose-pink, 5–6cm (2–2½in) across; mid- to late

Clematis armandii 'Snowdrift'

spring. The finest of all the evergreen clematis; plants make a heavy tangled mass after a few years unless the shoots are trained carefully each season. Introduced to cultivation by E.H. Wilson in 1900.
W and Central China
☼ ☀ -15°C (5°F) ♀∅

✓ **'Apple Blossom'**: young leaves bronzy-green; flowers pink in bud, later white, sometimes flushed soft pink. **'Snowdrift'**: good-sized flowers of pure white, very fragrant.

✓ *C. finetiana*
(*C. pavoliniana*)
Rather like a small-flowered version of *C. armandii*, growing to 5m (16ft). Leaves leathery, dark green; leaflets usually 3, oval, hairless, 5–10cm (2–4in) long, 3-veined. Flowers fragrant, pure white suffused with green on the outside, 3.5–4cm (1½in) across, with 4 petals; early summer-flowering.
W and Central China
☼ -10°C (14°F) ♀∅

✓ *C. × jeuneana*
A beautiful plant likened to a small-flowered *C. armandii*, said to be a garden hybrid between *C. armandii* and *C. finetiana*. To 5m (16ft). Leaves rather like *C. armandii*. Flowers silvery-white flushed with pink on the outside, 2–2.5cm (¼–1in), with 5 or 6 spreading petals; late spring to early summer.
☼ ☀ -10°C (14°F) ♀∅

⊞ *C. meyeriana*
Vigorous plant to 7m (23ft); stems wiry, purplish-brown, hairless. Leaves leathery, deep green. Flowers white, 2.2–2.6cm (1in) across, with 4 petals notched at the tips; late winter to early spring. S and SE China, S Japan, Philippines
☼ ☀ -10°C (14°F) ♀∅

✓ *C. quinquefoliata*
To 4–5mm (13–16ft); stems ribbed, downy. Leaves pinnate; leaflets 5–10cm (2–4in) long, hairless except along midrib above. Flowers white 3.8–5cm (1½–2in) across, with 4–6 narrow petals; late summer to early autumn. Fruits very handsome, with yellowish-brown silky plumes. Closely related to *C. meyeriana* and equally scarce in cultivation.
Central and W China
☼ -10°C (14°F) ♀∅

CLEMATIS MONTANA AND ALLIES

Amongst the hardiest, most floriferous and vigorous

Clematis montana var. *wilsonii*

deciduous species. Leaves 3–parted. Flowers 4–petalled, solitary or in small groups at the leaf axils. The more vigorous types make excellent specimens for clambering up trees. Deservedly popular.

C. montana
Stems 5–12m (16–40ft), rather wiry, becoming thick, woody and entangled with age. Leaves deep green, sometimes tinged red. Flowers white, 5–6.5cm (2–2½in) across, on slender stalks, borne in small clusters, usually vanilla-scented. One of the most popular garden clematis, easily grown on most garden soils in almost any aspect, being equally at home on a wall, fence, pergola or sprawled over a tree or tree stump. Most cultivars grow to 5–7m (16–23ft) in height. Late-spring to early summer, occasionally with a few flowers later. Himalaya, W China
☼ ☀ ● -20°C (-4°F) ♀∅

'Alba': leaves pale green, flowers whitish. **'Alexander'**: leaves pale

Clematis montana 'Tetrarose'

green; flowers creamy-white, sweetly scented, 7–9cm (2¼–3½in) across. ✓**'Elizabeth'**: ♈ leaves purple-green; flowers large, pale pink, vanilla-scented, 5–6.5cm (2–2½in) across. **'Freda'**: ♈ leaves bronzed; flowers cherry-red, the petals edged crimson. **'Lilacina'**: flowers pale mauve. **'Marjorie'**: vigorous; flowers semi-double, cream with pink and orange overtones. **'Mayleen'**: leaves bronze-flushed; flowers large, pink. **'Odorata'**: sweetly scented pale pink flowers. **'Percy Picton'**: less vigorous plant than the others, with deep pink flowers. **'Peveril'**:

flowers to 8cm (3¼in) across, pure white. **'Pink Perfection'**: leaves purple-green; flowers pink 5–7.5cm (2–3in) across. **'Superba'**: flowers large, white; vigorous grower. ✓**'Tetrarose'**: ♈ leaves purplish-green; flowers rather fleshy, purplish-pink, 7.5–9cm (3–3½in) across. **'Undulata'**: flowers numerous, white flushed with mauve; strong grower. **'Vera'**: dark green leaves and fragrant pink flowers. ✓forma *grandiflora* ('Grandiflora'): ♈ leaves dark green; flowers white, 7.5–10cm (3–4in) across; particularly good on a north wall or fence. ✓**var. rubens**: young stems and leaf stalks reddish-purple, and foliage purplish; flowers rose-red, 5–6.5cm (2–2½in) across. W China **var.** *wilsonii*: flowers glistening white (greenish at first), rather small, on downy stalks, strongly scented, from early to midsummer. Central China

✓ *C. chrysocoma* var. *sericea*

(*C. montana* var. *sericea*, *C. spooneri*)
To 6m (20ft), often less; young stems and leaves covered in dense brownish-yellow down. Flowers white or soft pink, 5–7cm (2–2¾in) across; borne in profusion from late spring to early summer, then intermittently until autumn. (*C. chrysocoma* itself is smaller and semi-shrubby, scarcely if ever climbing.) SW China ☀ ☼ -15°C (5°F) ⚘

'Rosea': flowers soft pink with yellow stamens.

Clematis chrysocoma var. sericea

C. gracilifolia

To 4m (13ft); stems greenish, ribbed. Leaves 3-parted to pinnate with up to 7 leaflets. Flowers white, 3.8–5cm (1½–2in) across; late spring to early summer. A graceful plant, like a smaller version of *C. montana*. W China
☀ ☼ -15°C (5°F) ⚘

C. × vedrariensis

A vigorous hybrid between *C. chrysocoma* var. *sericea* and *C. montana* var. *rubens*. To 7m (23ft); stems ribbed and hairy. Leaves dull purplish-green, coarsely toothed, densely hairy beneath, particularly when young. Flowers pale rose-pink, 5–6.5cm (2–2½in) across, solitary on long slender stems, with 4–6 petals; late spring to early summer. Similar in habit and general features to *C. montana* var. *rubens* but with the hairiness of *C. chrysocoma*.
☀ ☼ -20°C (-4°F) ⚘

'Hidcote': flowers smaller, deep pink. **'Highdown'**: flowers mid-pink, average size. ✓**'Rosea'**

(*C. spooneri* var. *rosea*): flowers rose-pink, large, 7.5–10cm (3–4in) across.

CLEMATIS CIRRHOSA AND ALLIES

Two evergreen species bearing small lateral clusters of dainty bell-shaped, 4-petalled flowers, each with a small cup-shaped pair of fused bracts situated midway along the flower stalks. For warm, sheltered situations.

✓ *C. cirrhosa*

VIRGIN'S BOWER
To 3m (10ft), with slender stems. Leaves deep green, glossy beneath, oval or heart-shaped, occasionally 3-lobed, 2–2.5cm (¾–1in) long, turning bronze and purplish in the autumn. Flowers delicate, drooping bells, dull white or creamish, often spotted with reddish-purple inside, 4–7cm (1½–2¾in) long, faintly scented; winter to early spring. Fruits silky white. Mediterranean Europe, Turkey, Cyprus
☀ ☼ -15°C (5°F) ⚘

✓ ▦ var. *balearica* ♈

(*C. balearica*, *C. calycina*)
FERN-LEAVED CLEMATIS
Taller, to 5m (16ft) with more finely divided, rather ferny-looking leaves, green in summer but strikingly bronzy-purple during the autumn and winter. More free-flowering. Balearic Islands, Corsica

✓**'Freckles'**: ♈ flowers cream

Clematis cirrhosa

flushed with pink, heavily spotted maroon-red inside, 6.5cm (2½in) long. **'Wisley Cream'**: leaves undivided, pale green; flowers cream.

✓ ▦ *C. napaulensis*

(*C. forrestii*)
Vigorous, to 10m (33ft), with greyish young shoots. Leaves with 3 or 5, 3-lobed leaflets, each 4–9cm (1½–3½in) long. Flowers creamy-yellow with purple stamens, narrow, drooping, silky bells, 1.2–2.4cm (½–1in) long; late autumn to late winter. Himalaya, SW China
☀ -10°C (14°F) ⚘

The following species is unrelated but is best considered here.

▦ *C. afoliata*

(*C. aphylla*)
An extraordinary species with clambering rush-like stems to 1.5m (5ft), sometimes more. Leaves absent but represented by green stalk-like tendrils

2.5–10cm (1–4in) long.
Flowers greenish-white,
fragrant, 2–2.5cm (¾–1in)
long, in small clusters, the
male and female flowers quite
distinct and borne on separate
plants; petals 4–6, spreading;
late winter to early spring.
Plants are rather sprawling and
should be tied into the wall or
allowed to clamber over a
neighbouring shrub.
New Zealand
☼ -10°C (14°F) ⚘

GROUP B (1) CLEMATIS

Herbaceous climbing species
and cultivars that flower from
midsummer on, on the
current season's growth and
whose stems die back partly or
wholly to a woody base during
autumn and winter. Pruning
should consist of cutting out
all dead or weak growth in the
early spring. The larger-
flowered, more vigorous
cultivars of *C. viticella* can be
treated as under Group B (II),
pruning all stems hard back to
within 30cm (12in) of the
ground in early spring.

CLEMATIS TEXENSIS
AND ALLIES

Small-flowered herbaceous or
deciduous, semi-herbaceous
species with pinnate leaves.
The attractive pendulous, bell-
shaped flowers are borne on
slender stems, which are often
thick and fleshy; each flower
has 4 petals.

C. crispa

BLUE JASMINE, MARSH CLEMATIS
Semi-woody climber to 2m
(6½ft), sometimes more.
Leaves with 3–7 leaflets. Bell-
shaped flowers are pale bluish-
purple, 3–5cm (1¼–2in) long,
solitary, nodding; petals are
strongly recurved near the tip
and have a whitish, wavy edge
to them; summer.
SE USA
☼ -25°C (-13°F) ⚘s
   'Distorta': petals slightly twisted.

C. fusca

Semi-herbaceous climber to
3m (10ft) high, often less;
stems angled, downy when
young. Leaves with 5 or 7 oval
or heart-shaped leaflets.
Flowers bell-shaped, solitary,
reddish-brown, violet inside,
1.8–2.4cm (¾–1in) long; early
to midsummer.
NE Asia
☼ -25°C (-13°F) ⚘s
   var. *violacea*: flowers violet;
   Korea

C. pitcheri

(*C. cordata*)
Partly herbaceous climber to
4m (13ft). Leaves with 3–7
leaflets, the terminal leaflet
sometimes replaced by a
tendril. Flowers bell-shaped,
solitary, purplish-blue,
greenish-yellow inside, 2–3cm
(¾–1¼in) long; late spring to
early autumn. Unlike its allies,
C. pitcheri only dies back a little
during the winter and, as a
result, requires rather lighter
pruning.
Central USA
☼ ☼ -30°C (-22°F) ⚘s

Clematis texensis 'Gravetye Beauty'

C. texensis

(*C. coccinea*)
Partly herbaceous climber to
2–3m (6½–10ft). Leaves
bluish-green with 4–8 leaflets,
often terminating in a sort of
tendril. Flowers red, scarlet or
purple, 2.5cm (1in) long,
solitary, petals slightly
recurved at the tip;
midsummer to early autumn.
In cold areas some winter
protection is generally
advisable. It is tolerant of
rather drier soils than most
clematis. The deep red-
flowered forms are the finest
(a unique colour among
clematis). S USA (Texas)
☼ -25°C (-13°F) ⚘s

The following are hybrids with
C. patens and various large-
flowered hybrids: they should
be treated as for Group B (I),
pruning them hard back early
in the year to promote fresh
flowering shoots:
   'Countess of Onslow': to 3m
   (10ft); flowers pink with a deeper
   bar of colour down the centre of

each petal. Rare in cultivation.
   ✓**'Duchess of Albany'**: ♛ to
   3–4m (10–13ft); bell-shaped
   flowers erect, deep pink, pale lilac-
   pink on the petal margins; plants
   generally die back to ground level
   each winter. **'Etoile Rex'**: flowers
   to 5cm (2in) long, cerise to mauve
   with a silvery margin to the petals.
   ✓**'Etoile Rose'**: flowers cherry-
   purple, the petals edged with
   silvery-pink; plants die back to
   ground level each winter.
   'Gravetye Beauty': flowers
   crimson, narrowly bell-shaped at
   first but the petals gradually spread
   outwards. **'Ladybird Johnson'**:
   flowers dusky red, petals edged
   with purple. **'Major'**: flowers to
   3cm (1¼in) long, scarlet outside,
   pale yellow or white inside.
   'Passiflora': flowers 2cm (¾in)
   long, scarlet. **'Princess of Wales'**:
   flowers deep pink with contrasting
   yellow stamens. ✓**'Sir Trevor
   Lawrence'**: flowers cherry-red;
   delightful.

C. viorna

LEATHER FLOWER, VASE VINE
To 2–3m (6½–10ft). Leaves

pinnate, with 5 variously shaped leaflets, 2.5–5cm (1–2in) long. Flowers dull reddish purple, greenish-yellow or whitish inside, 2.5–3cm (1–1¼in) long, solitary nodding bells; early to midsummer. Plants die right down to a resistant woody base during the winter. E USA
☼ ◑ -30°C (-22°F) ⌇✐s

CLEMATIS VITICELLA AND ALLIES

An important group of mostly small-flowered species and cultivars widely grown in gardens and among the most reliable and easy of clematis. They are deciduous and semi-woody, dying back partly or wholly during the winter; they are all best pruned hard back in the spring, to at least 30cm (12in) of the ground, to encourage strong flowering shoots.

✓ *C. campaniflora*
Closely related to *C. viticella* but often more vigorous, reaching 6m (20ft). Small nodding flowers borne in profusion, 2–3cm (¾–1¼in), whitish tinted with blue and rather cupped; midsummer to early autumn.
Portugal, S Spain
◑ -20°C (-4°F) ⌇✐s

✓ *C. viticella*
Variable, to 2–4m (6½–13ft), with slender stems. Leaves 3-parted; leaflets oval to lance-shaped, 2.5–7.5cm (1–3in)

Clematis viticella 'Purpurea Plena Elegans'

long, often 2- or 3-lobed but untoothed. Flowers blue, purple or rose-pink, fragrant, 3.5–5cm (1½–2in) across, nodding on long slender stalks; petals 4, spoon-shaped; midsummer to early autumn. One of the finest and most floriferous species. Many good cultivars have been produced, ranging from small- to large-flowered ones; many are of hybrid origin between this and various other species. S Europe
☼ ◑ -20°C (-4°F) ⌇✐s ▯

✓ **'Abundance'**: to 5m (16ft); flowers open bell-shaped, delicate lilac-purple, flushed wine-red with deeper veins, 5–7.5cm (2–3in) across. **'Alba Luxurians'**: ♈ flowers white suffused with pale mauve, often green-tipped, 5–7.5cm (2–3in) across; anthers dark. **'Ascotiensis'**: ♈ very floriferous, with azure-blue flowers, 9–12.5cm (3½–5in) across. **'Betty Corning'**: flowers bell-shaped, pale lilac flowers, 5cm (2in) across, slightly scented; petal tips recurved. **'Caerulea Luxurians'**: flowers violet. **'Duchess of Sutherland'**: flowers small, wine-red with a pale

Clematis viticella 'Madame Julia Correvon'

band down the centre of the petals.
✓**'Ernest Markham'**: ♈ to 2.5m (8ft), with velvety petunia-red flowers, 9–10cm (3½–4in) across.
✓**'Etoile Violette'**: ♈ to 5m (16ft) tall; flowers freely produced, deep violet-purple, 7.5cm (3in) across; anthers cream ☼.
'Kermesina': to 5m (16ft) tall; flowers wine-crimson, prolific; probably the same as *C. viticella* 'Rubra'. **'Lady Betty Balfour'**: to 5m (16ft) tall; flowers rich velvety violet-purple, fading purple-blue, 12.5–15cm (5–6in) across; anthers yellow ☼. **'Little Nell'**: flowers small, pale mauve. ✓**'Madame

Julia Correvon': ♈ flowers wine-red, open bell-shaped, 7.5–9 (3–3½cm) across; anthers yellow. **'Margot Koster'**: flowers 10cm (4in) across, lilac-pink. **'Marmorata'**: flowers bluish-grey, with 4 petals. **'Mary Rose'**: flowers rather small, double, amethyst-blue. **'Minuet'**: ♈ flowers erect, white banded with pale purple, 5cm (2in) across. **'Mrs Spencer Castle'**: small double flowers, heliotrope-pink. **'Plena'**: has double flowers larger than the type, 5–7cm (2–2¾in) across, rosy-purple. ✓**'Polish Spirit'**: ♈ flowers rich purple-blue, 5-8cm (2–3¼in) across, anthers red. **'Purpurea'**: flowers plum-red. ✓**'Purpurea Plena Elegans'**: ♈ abundance of fully double deep bluish mauve flowers, paler on the reverse, 5–8cm (2–3¼in) across. ✓**'Royal Velours'**: flowers deep velvety purple, 5–7.5cm (2–3in) across. **'Rubra Grandiflora'**: flowers large, carmine, with 6 petals. **'Venosa Violacea'**: ♈ flowers white veined purple, 8cm (3¼in) across. ✓**'Ville de Lyon'**: to 3m (10ft); flowers bright carmine-red, 10–12.5cm (4–5in) across, deeper at the margins; anthers yellow. **'Voluceau'**: flowers petunia-red.

GROUP B (II) CLEMATIS

Perennial climbers of moderate or vigorous habit flowering on the current season's growth. Plants should be pruned hard back in early spring to about 1m (3ft). Alternatively, lighter pruning will promote earlier flowering; however it is wise to prune one or two shoots hard back each year to promote some young growth from the base of the plant.

Clematis orientalis and allies

Moderately vigorous deciduous climbers with slender stems and pinnate or occasionally 3-parted leaves. Flowers solitary or in lateral clusters, sometimes terminal, yellow or greenish-yellow, each with 4, often rather fleshy, petals. Fruits showy, often borne in quantity. They are strong growers with smallish flowers produced during the summer and autumn, often in large quantities. They are all easily raised from seed and young plants quickly flower; named forms will not necessarily come true from seed.

C. akebioides

(*C. glauca* var. *akebioides*, *C. orientalis* var. *akebioides*)
To 5m (16ft). Leaves bluish-green, pinnate; leaflets 5 or 7, oval to oblong with shallow, rounded teeth. Flowers pendent bells, yellow or greenish-yellow, tinged on the outside with green, bronze or purple, 1.5–2.5cm (½–1in) long; petals fleshy, hairless except on margins; late summer to mid-autumn. An attractive species similar in appearance to *C. tangutica* but with smoother, more fleshy flowers and bluish-green

Clematis akebioides

foliage. SW China (Sichuan, N Kansu, N Yunnan)
☼ ◐ -25°C (-13°F)

C. graveolens

(*C. parvifolia*, *C. orientalis* subsp. *graveolens*)
To 3m (10ft). Leaves bluish-green, bipinnate and rather ferny in appearance, with a few to numerous elliptic or lance-shaped leaflets. Flowers yellow with purplish filaments, 2–3.5cm (¾–1½in) across; petals oval, notched at the apex, widely spreading, densely downy inside; late summer to early autumn. Allied to *C. orientalis* and often sold under that name, but with finer foliage and larger flowers with broader petals.
W Pakistan, W Himalaya
☼ ◐ -15°C (5°F)

C. intricata

(including *C. glauca*)
To 3m (10ft) with slender greenish stems. Leaves bluish-green, pinnate. Flowers yellowish or greenish-yellow, 2.5–4cm (1–1½in) across; petals widely spreading, rather narrow and thin in texture, downy inside; late summer to mid-autumn.
E Siberia, NW China
☼ ◐ ● -30°C (-22°F)

C. orientalis

Moderately vigorous climber to 5–6m (16–20ft); young stems slender greyish- or whitish-green, sometimes tinged with purplish-red. Leaves bluish- or greyish-green, thick and fleshy; leaflets unlobed or with a few blunt uneven lobes. Flowers small, in large clusters, yellowish-green, often tinged or spotted with purplish-red on the outside; petals 10–22mm (½–1in) long, downy on both surfaces, recurved in full flower; midsummer to mid-autumn. Rare in cultivation although many plants appear under the name; *C. orientalis* of catalogues (and also regretfully of some botanic gardens) usually proves to be *C. intricata* or *C. graveolens*, while *C. orientalis* 'Orange Peel' is the Himalayan *C. tibetana* subsp. *vernayi*. To confuse matters, many of the species have been crossed and recrossed to produce a complex selection of fine hybrid cultivars, though only a few have been given names: see list at end of this group. W Asia, southern central Asia, Iran, Afghanistan, Pakistan
☼ -20°C (-4°F)

C. serratifolia

Moderately vigorous climber to 4m (13ft). Leaves bright green, with 3 or 5 sharply toothed leaflets. Flowers pale yellow, lemon-scented, 4–5cm (1½–2in) across; petals wide-spreading, giving the flowers a starry appearance; late summer to early autumn. A free-flowering species that produces a succession of blooms well into the autumn, followed by attractive fruits.
NE China, Korea
☼ ◐ -20°C (-4°F)

✓ *C. tangutica*

(*C. orientalis* var. *tangutica*)
Vigorous quick-growing climber to 4–5m (13–16ft), though often less. Leaves green, pinnate; leaflets sharply toothed except in the upper part. Flowers lemon-yellow, pendent bells or lanterns, 2.5–4.5cm (1–1¾in) long; petals long-pointed, scarcely spreading, shiny and hairless inside but slightly downy outside generally; late summer to mid-autumn. Fruits large and silky, often produced in masses. The best of all the

Clematis tangutica

Clematis 'Bill Mackenzie'

yellow-flowered species; some forms in cultivation are much finer than others and are well worth seeking out. Tibet, W China, Gansu, S Mongolia) ☼ ◑ ● -25°C (-13°F) ⅄ₛ

✓**'Drake's Form'**: flowers exceptionally long and lantern-like, with finely pointed petals.
Subsp. *obtusiuscula* (*C. tangutica* var. *obtusiuscula*): flowers deeper yellow, tinged on the outside with purplish-brown; petals spreading and less pointed. SW China (W Sichuan)

C. tibetana subsp. vernayi

To 3–4m (10–13ft); young stems pale greenish-white, sometimes flushed with purple. Leaves bluish-green, rather fleshy, pinnate or more or less bipinnate. Flowers yellow or greenish-yellow, flushed or spotted with bronze or sometimes purple, nodding open bells 1.5–3.5cm (½–1½in) across; petals usually half spreading,

thick and fleshy, velvety-downy inside but quite hairless outside; late summer to mid-autumn. The thick, fleshy petals have been likened to orange or lemon peel. (*C. tibetana* subsp. *tibetana* itself, occasionally offered by nurseries, has long-pointed leaflets and rather smaller and inferior flowers when compared with the best forms of subsp. *vernayi*). N Nepal, Tibet ☼ ◑ -25°C (-13°F) ⅄ₛ

✓**'Orange Peel'**: the finest cultivar with good-sized, open lantern flowers of great substance with their characteristic thick, waxy petals. *Clematis* L & S 13342 ('Sherriffii') is the same or similar and well worth acquiring; the original collection was made in Tibet by Ludlow & Sherriff; subsp. *vernayi* being particularly common in the mountains around Lhasa. 'Orange Peel' has been crossed with *C. tangutica*, purposefully or inadvertently and the resultant hybrids are the very finest of all the

yellow-flowered clematis of the *C. orientalis* persuasion: ✓**'Bill Mackenzie'**: ♛ like a yellower 'Orange Peel' but with rather larger flowers and greener leaves; free-flowering from midsummer onwards. **'Corry'**: flowers large, 3.5–6cm (1½–2½in) across, clear yellow with thick, widely spreading petals. ✓**'Helios'**: flowers almost as large as 'Corry' but a paler yellow and more star-like, in profusion. **'Lambton Park'**: flowers large, 7cm (2¾in), yellow, nodding.

CLEMATIS VITALBA AND ALLIES

Vigorous deciduous species with rather coarse 3-parted or pinnate leaves and large clusters of generally rather small white, cream or greenish-white flowers with narrow spreading petals. Plants benefit from a hard annual prune in early spring and will become bulky and hard to handle if left unpruned.

C. chinensis

To 8m (26ft); stems ribbed. Leaves pinnate with 5 untoothed leaflets. Flowers small, white, fragrant, 1.2–2cm (½–¾in), in dense lateral clusters; petals 4; autumn. Probably best in milder regions as the late flowers can be easily ruined by frost. W and Central China ◑ -20°C (-4°F) ⅄ₛ

✓ C. flammula
FRAGRANT CLEMATIS
Vigorous climber 4–5m (13–16ft), forming a bushy tangle, bare and woody below if unpruned. Leaves bright dark green, pinnate; leaflets very variable, usually untoothed, though often 2- or 3-lobed. Flowers pure white, beautifully fragrant, 1.8–2.5cm (¾–1in) across, in abundance in large clusters; midsummer to mid-autumn. Especially good for covering low walls and fences, although succeeding best in a sheltered,

Clematis flammula

Clematis vitalba (in fruit)

warm site. S Europe, W Asia
☼ ☀ -20°C (-6°F) ⥾s

✓ C. grata var. grandidentata

To 10m (33ft). Leaves greyish, hairy, with 3 or 5 coarsely toothed leaflets. Flowers white, 2–2.5cm (¾–1in) across, in lax terminal clusters; petals 4 or 5; late spring to early summer. A hardy species little seen in gardens and rather similar to *C. vitalba*; the typical form of the species (var. *grata*), from the Himalaya, is rare in cultivation. W China
☼ -25°C (-13°F) ⥾s

✓ C. terniflora

(*C. dioscoreifolia*, *C. flammula* var. *robusta*, *C. maximowicziana*, *C. paniculata* – not of New Zealand)
Even more robust than *C. flammula*, reaching 10m (33ft), forming a thick entanglement. Leaves dark green, 3-parted or pinnate, untoothed. Flowers white,

hawthorn-scented, 2.2–2.8cm (1in) across; petals 4; autumn. A magnificent climber for a large sunny south wall; a species widely planted in the USA. N China, Japan, Korea
☼ -20°C (-4°F) ⥾s

C. virginiana

Similar to *C. vitalba* but seldom seen outside botanic gardens. E USA

C. vitalba

OLD MAN'S BEARD, TRAVELLER'S JOY
Very vigorous deciduous climber to 15m (50ft), forming a coarse entanglement, the stems becoming thick and bare below if left unpruned. Leaves pinnate, leaflets 5 or 7, usually toothed. Flowers greenish-white, slightly scented of almonds, 1.8–2.5cm (¾–1in) across, in large clusters; petals 4, downy on both sides; midsummer to autumn. Too coarse for all but large gardens and estates where it can look

very effective, especially in fruit, once the leaves have fallen. Most of Europe, except the north, and W Turkey
☼ ☀ -30°C (-22°F) ⥾s

MISCELLANEOUS GROUP B SPECIES

The remaining species in this group represent a miscellany which, although not particularly closely related, all require hard pruning early in the year in order to promote strong flowering shoots.

C. aethusifolia

Graceful deciduous climber to 2m (6½ft); young stems slender, downy. Leaves ferny, rather pale green, pinnate with 3–7 leaflets, each deeply lobed and toothed. Flowers pale whitish-yellow, narrow bells 1.3–2cm (½–¾in) long, in leafy clusters; late summer to early autumn. Although the flowers are not spectacular

they are borne in such a profusion that they make an extremely attractive show. N China, Manchuria
☼ ☀ -25°C (-13°F) ⥾s

C. connata

Vigorous deciduous climber to 7m (23ft); stems slightly ribbed. Leaves bright green, with 3–5 coarsely toothed and sometimes lobed leaflets; leaf stalks flattened at base and surrounding stem as a flattish disk. Flowers bell-shaped, soft yellow, slightly fragrant, 1.8–2.5cm (¾–1in) long, in large lateral clusters; petals 4, slightly ribbed, recurved at the tip; autumn. Himalaya, SW China
☼ ☀ -20°C (-4°F) ⥾s

✓ C. × durandii ♀

A hybrid between *C. integrifolia* × *C.* 'Jackmanii'. Semi-climber to 3m (10ft) tall. Leaves simple, oval, shiny green. Flowers large, dark violet-blue, 7.5–12.5cm (3–5in) across; petals 4, widely spreading. The plant is not a climber in the true sense and the stems need to be tied in carefully to maintain some order to the growths. Summer to early autumn.

☼ ◐ -25°C (-13°F) ⅄ℓ**s**

'Pallida': flowers paler, violet-pink; rather rare.

C. indivisa
(*C. paniculata*)

Vigorous evergreen shrub or climber to 10m (33ft). Leaves glossy green, 3-parted; leaflets oval or slightly heart-shaped, 3.5–7.5cm (1½–3in) long, untoothed, though sometimes lobed. Flowers white with yellow anthers, unisexual, 3.5–7cm (1½–2¾in) across, smaller on female plants, borne in long lose clusters; petals 6–8; late spring to early summer. *C. paniculata* of gardens is generally the hardy Japanese *C. terniflora (see page 79)*. New Zealand

☼ -25°C (-13°F) ⅄ℓ**s**

'Lobata': leaves more deeply lobed and more readily available than the type.

✓ C. 'Jackmanii' ♀
(*C. × jackmanii*)

To 3m (10ft), sometimes more. Leaves rather pale green, usually with 1–5 leaflets. Flowers large, rich velvety violet-purple, 10–12.5cm (4–5in) across, borne mostly in threes, each with 4 or 5 rather flat petals; summer to early autumn. A glorious and much-loved plant widely grown and, with

Clematis 'Jackmanii Superba'

C. montana, probably the most commonly cultivated clematis. This hybrid was raised in 1860 by the famous nursery firm of Messrs Jackman of Woking and led the way to a vast race of large-flowered hybrid cultivars, many with dark, rich colours. Some of the best 'Jackmanii' types are listed below. Although the main flowering season is in midsummer, further flowers are often produced right through until the autumn.

☼ ◐ ● -25°C (-13°F) ⅄ℓ**s**

'Jackmanii Alba': flowers palest grey-white, double but later flowers single. **'Comtesse de Bouchaud'**: ♀ to 3.5m (11½ft); flowers soft rose-pink or cyclamen-pink with yellow stamens, borne freely, each 10–14cm (4–5½in) across; petals 5–7. **'Gipsy Queen'**: ♀ vigorous; flowers rich velvety violet-purple, 12.5–15cm (5–6in) across; petals broad, rounded. ✓**'Hagley Hybrid'**: to 2.5m (8ft); flowers in profusion, shell pink, 12.5–15cm (5–6in) across; petals 5 or 6, pointed and anthers purplish. ✓**'Jackmanii Superba'** ('Madame Grangé'): especially vigorous, to 5–6m (16–20ft); flowers large deep rich violet-purple, each with 5 or 6 broad petals. ☼ ◐ **'Madame Edouard André'**: ♀ to 2.5m (8ft), often less; flowers rich

crimson with yellow stamens, 10–12.5cm (4–5in) across; petals 6. Often starts to flower in late spring. ✓**'Perle d'Azur'**: ♀ to 4m (13ft); flowers pale blue, 12.5–15cm (5–6in) across; petals 4–6. **'Jackmanii Rubra'**: flowers plum-red, double, but late flowers single.

✓ C. × jouiniana

Vigorous hybrid between *C. heracleifolia* var. *davidiana* and *C. vitalba*; stems to 3.5m (11½ft) eventually, semi-climbing only. Leaves with 3 or 5 leaflets. Flowers yellowish-white at first, later white flushed with lilac on the outside, 2.5–3cm (1–1¼in) across, produced in profusion in flat-topped clusters; petals 4; late summer to mid-autumn. The base of the plant is woody to about 1m (3ft 3in) and from this arise annual stems which need to be tied in against walls or fences. Though not scented, the flowers are attractive to butterflies.

☼ ◐ -25°C (-13°F) ⅄ℓ**s**

✓**'Côte d'Azur'**: flowers azure-blue. **'Mrs Robert Brydon'**: flowers pale lavender. **'Oiseau Bleu'**: leaves small; flowers mauve or pinkish. **'Praecox'**: ♀ flowers soft lavender-blue, first appearing in midsummer.

✓ C. lasiandra

Deciduous climber to 5m (16ft); stems slender, rather sticky when young. Leaves dark green, pale beneath, with 3–9 leaflets. Flowers usually dull purple, sometimes white, bell-shaped, 1.1–1.3cm (½in) long; petals with recurved

tips; autumn. China, Japan
☼ ☼ -20°C (-4°F) ⅋ℓₛ

C. petriei
Vigorous evergreen to 4m
(13ft); stems slender. Leaves
bright shiny green, somewhat
glossy, with numerous small
oval or lobed leaflets. Flowers
fragrant, unisexual, yellow
green, nodding open bells,
2cm (¾in) across, borne in
clusters; late spring to
midsummer. New Zealand;
crosses readily with other New
Zealand species.
☼ ☼ -10°C (14°F) ⅋ℓₛ
 ✓'**Limelight**': male selection with
 lime-green flowers and purple-
 flushed foliage. '**Princess**': female
 selection with rather small lime-
 green flowers.

C. phlebantha
Scrambling shrub with ribbed
stems to 2m (6½ft); young
stems white with wool. Leaves
are pinnate, 5–10cm (2–4in)
long, with 5–9, generally 3-
lobed, leaflets, deep green and
silky above, white-woolly
beneath. Flowers usually
solitary, white, 2.5–5cm
(1–2in) across; petals 5–7,
with reddish veins; early to
midsummer. Discovered only
in 1952 by the Polunin, Sykes
and Williams expedition to
Nepal. The stems have to be
tied to supports for they will
not climb unaided. Rare.
Central W Nepal
☼ -15°C (5°F) ❧

C. potaninii
(including *C. fargesii*)
Vigorous deciduous climber to

Clematis petriei

7m (23ft) tall; shoots ribbed,
purplish and downy when
young. Leaves dull green,
bipinnate with 5 basic
divisions; leaflets coarsely
toothed and sometimes 3-
lobed. Flowers satiny white
tinged with yellow on the
outside, 5–6cm (2–2½in)
across; petals usually 6; early
summer to early autumn.
Attractive flowers are
produced over a long season,
though never in great
profusion. The form in which
it is most generally available is
var. *fargesii*.
W China
☼ ☼ -15°C (5°F) ⅋ℓₛ

✓ C. rehderiana
(*C. nutans* var. *thyrsoidea*)
Vigorous deciduous climber to
8m (26ft). Leaves hairy,
pinnate, rather bright green;
leaflets usually 7 or 9, broadly
heart-shaped, coarsely
toothed. Flowers pale
primrose-yellow, cowslip-
scented, nodding bells

1.2–1.8cm (½–¾in) long,
borne in profusion in large
erect clusters; petals 4 or 5;
late summer to mid-autumn.
Himalaya to W China
☼ ☼ -20°C (-4°F) ⅋ℓₛ

C. uncinata
Evergreen or semi-evergreen
to 5m (16ft); stems slender,
hairless. Leaves with 9 or more
leaflets, green above but
bluish-green beneath. Flowers
creamy-white, fragrant,
2.5–3.5cm (1–1½in), borne in
large clusters; petals 4, rather
narrow; summer. First
introduced into cultivation in
1901 by E.H. Wilson but
rarely seen in gardens today.
China, including Hong
Kong
☼ ☼ -20°C (-4°F) ⅋ℓₛ

C. veitchiana ♀
Similar to *C. rehderiana* but
with bipinnate leaves, each
with 20 or more smaller
leaflets; flowers also smaller,
yellowish-white; late summer

to early autumn. It is not as
good a plant as *C. rehderiana* in
gardens, but it may also be
found erroneously under the
name *C. nutans*.
W China
☼ ☼ -20°C (-4°F) ⅋ℓₛ

GROUP C CLEMATIS

This group consists of most of
the large-flowered species and
cultivars, with the exception
of those belonging to *C. ×
jackmanii (see page 80)* and
C. viticella (see page 76). They
mostly belong to, or are
derived from, only two
species, *C. lanuginosa* and
C. patens.
 Usually no pruning is
required, except to remove
dead or unwanted or weak
growth in the late winter or
early spring. However, many
gardeners trim back shoots
slightly to the first strong pair
of buds in the spring, or
alternatively the moment
flowering ceases. Summer
growths need to be spaced out
and trained carefully as they
elongate so as to gain the best
effect when flowering
commences, and to prevent
nasty entanglements. Most of
the cultivars in this group
flower from midsummer
onwards and they often have a
secondary, smaller flush of
blooms in late summer or
early autumn. If desired, they
may be pruned as in Group B
(II), effectively sacrificing the
first flush of flowers for a
larger later display.

✓ *C. florida*

Deciduous or semi-evergreen, to 3–4m (10–13ft); stems wiry, glossy. Leaves dark green with 5–9 elliptic leaflets. Flowers white or cream, 6–9cm (2½–3½in) across, with a greenish band down the back of each petal and a large 'eye' of purple-black stamens; petals 4–6, pointed; early to midsummer. China (Hubei) ☼ ◑ -15°C (5°F) ⚘

Cultivars of this lovely species have been grown in Japanese gardens for several centuries and some were introduced to Europe in the latter half of the eighteenth century. Some of the cultivars often placed under this species are of complex origin, probably involving both *C. lanuginosa* and *C. patens* in past hybridizations; many are not vigorous growers and require more care than most clematis. In the double-flowered forms some, or all, of the stamens are transformed into short, narrow petals, giving the centre of the flower the appearance of an 'anemone' or 'rosette'.

'Alba Plena' ('Plena'): flowers greenish-white, fully double; very similar to 'Duchess of Edinburgh'. ✓**'Duchess of Edinburgh'**: to 3m (10ft) tall; flowers double, pure white with green shading, somewhat scented; late spring to early summer. ✓**'Haku-ôkan'**: flowers semi-double, deep violet with white stamens. **'Proteus'**: flowers double, mauve-pink, 15cm (6in) across, anthers cream; later flowers single and paler.

Clematis florida 'Sieboldii'

✓**'Sieboldii'** (*C. florida* var. *bicolor*): less vigorous, to 2.5m (8ft) at the most; flowers very beautiful, long-lasting, white with a purple anemone-centre, 8cm (3¼in) across ☼.

C. lanuginosa
(*C. standishii*)

Deciduous climber to 3m (10ft). Leaves simple or 3–parted; leaflets heart-shaped. Flowers white to pale lilac, 10–15cm (4–6in) across, borne at shoot tips; petals 6–8, spreading and overlapping; summer to early autumn. Rare in cultivation but this species is a parent of many of the large-flowered garden hybrids. However, as with the other species involved – mainly *C. florida*, *C. patens* and *C. viticella* – the origins of many of these cultivars are complex and grouping them is mainly a convenient way of being able to prescribe the correct cultural treatment. China ☼ ◑ -20°C (-4°F) ⚘ ⚘s

C. patens
(*C. caerulea*)

Deciduous climber to 3–4m (10–13ft); stems slender. Leaves 3-parted or pinnate, with 3–7 leaflets. Flowers creamy-white to whitish-violet or violet-purple, 10–15cm (4–6in) across, produced on short shoots from the previous year's wood; petals 6–8, spreading, not overlapping; summer to early autumn. The form generally in cultivation has creamy-white flowers. China, Japan ☼ ◑ -20°C (-4°F) ⚘

LARGE-FLOWERED CULTIVARS

These are derived primarily from *C. lanuginosa* and *C. patens*, with *C. florida* playing a minor role. Most flower in the period from late spring to midsummer, but often again in the late summer or early autumn. Unless otherwise stated, the flowers are single.

Most thrive in a sunny or half-sunny position, although those whose flowers tend to fade badly are best placed in rather more shade. Cultivars of this association can be left unpruned as for *C. florida* and *C. patens* or, alternatively, may be treated like *C.* 'Jackmanii' and *C. viticella* (pages 80, 76). Double-flowered cultivars often produce paler, single flowers later in the season. ☼ or ◑ unless otherwise stated.

'Aasao': to 2m (6ft), rather compact with creamy-pink flowers, 10–12.5cm (4–5in) across, petals margined deep pink. ✓**'Barbara Dibley'**: to 3.5m (11½ft); petals violet-blue with purple-magenta bars, 12.5–15cm (5–6in) across, petals usually 8; bleaches in strong sunlight; later flowers are paler. ✓**'Barbara Jackman'**: to 3.5m (11½ft); flowers reddish-mauve or purplish with a plum-red bar down each of the 8 petals, 10–12.5cm (4–5in) across; bleaches in strong sunlight. ✓**'Beauty of Worcester'**: to 2.5m (8ft); flowers double, deep violet-blue, 12–16cm (5–6½in) across, anthers creamy-white; later flowers are generally single. ✓**'Bees Jubilee'**: ♔ profuse flowerer, deep pink, with darker banding, 10–12.5cm (4–5in) across. **'Belle of Woking'**: to 3m (10ft); flowers double, mauvish-white, 7.5–12.5cm (3–5in) across; late spring to early summer, often with some green on the outer petals, 8–12.5cm (3¼–5in) across, anthers cream. **'Carnaby'**: flowers deep pink with deeper banding, 7.5–10cm (3–4in) across. **'Corona'**: flowers pale purplish-pink, 10–12.5cm (4–5in) across, anthers red. ✓**'Countess of Lovelace'**: flowers double, bluish-lilac, 10–12.5cm (4–5in) across, anthers cream. **'C.W. Dowman'**: to 3.5m (11½ft); flowers pale pink with darker banding, 10–12.5cm (4–5in) across, anthers cream; petals usually 8; ☼ ●. **'Daniel Deronda'**: ♀ flowers double or single, violet-blue, 12.5–15cm (5–6in) across, anthers cream. **'Doctor Ruppel'**: ♀ free-flowering, deep rose pink with deeper banding, 10–15cm (4–6in) across, anthers chocolate. **'Edith'**: ♀ flowers white, 10cm (4in) across, anthers deep red. **'Edomurasaki'**: flowers dark violet-blue, 12.5–15cm (5–6in) across, anthers red. **'Elsa Späth'** ('Xerxes'): ♀ flowers rich mauve-blue, 12.5–16cm (5–6½in) across, anthers red. **'Fairy Queen'**: flowers flesh-pink banded with deeper pink, 15–17.5cm (6–7in) across. **'Fireworks'**: ♀ flowers blue with petunia-red banding, 15–17.5cm (6–7in) across, anthers deep red. ✓**'Général Sikorski'**: flowers blue, 10–15cm (4–6in) across, anthers cream. **'Gillian Blades'**: ♀ flowers white, 12.5–16cm (5–6½in) across, with wavy petals, anthers cream. **'Guernsey Cream'**: flowers creamy-yellow, 12.5cm (5in) across, anthers cream. **'Henryi'** ('Bangholme Belle'): ♀ to 5m (16ft) tall; flowers creamy-white, 15–17.5cm (6–7in) across, with 6–8 pointed petals; the young foliage has an attractive bronzy hue. **'H.F. Young'**: ♀ flowers pale blue tinged with violet, 10cm (4in) across, anthers cream. **'Horn of Plenty'**: ♀ flowers very rounded, rosy-mauve fading to blue-mauve, 12.5cm (5in) across, anthers dark red. **'John Warren'**: flowers greyish veined carmine-red, 15–17.5cm (6–7in) across, anthers red. **'Kakio'** ('Pink Champagne'): flowers numerous, purple-pink, 10–15cm (4–6in) across,

anthers yellow. **'Kathleen Dunford'**: flowers single or semi-double, rose-purple, 12.5cm (5in) across. ✓**'Kardynal Wyszyński'** ('Cardinal Wyszynski'): flowers late, crimson, 7.5–10cm (3–4in) across, anthers reddish-black. **'King George V'**: rather like 'Fairy Queen' but a deeper flesh pink. ✓**'Lady Londesborough'**: free-flowering, pale mauve turning to silvery-grey with age, 12.5–15cm (5–6in) across; stamens purplish. **'Lady Northcliffe'**: flowers deep lavender blue; anthers white; flowers bleach in strong sunlight; ☼ ●. ✓**'Lasurstern'**: ♀ to 3.5m (11½ft) tall; flowers large, rich purplish-blue, fading to lavender-blue, 15–17.5cm (6–7in) across, anthers creamy-yellow; petals 6–9; flowers fade in strong sunlight; ☼ ●. **'Lincoln Star'**: flowers raspberry-pink, 10–12.5cm (4–5in) across, anthers red; later flowers paler. ✓**'Lord Nevill'**: ♀ to 3.5m (11½ft), flowers rich purple-blue with darker banding, 12.5–16cm (5–6½in) across, anthers purple. **'Marcele Moser'**: rose-mauve petals banded with carmine, 17.5–20cm (7–8in) across, anthers reddish-purple. ✓**'Marie Boisselot'**: ('Mme. Le Coultre'): ♀ to 4.5m (15ft) tall; flowers pinkish in bud but opening pure white, 15–17.5cm (6–7in) across, anthers cream; petals 7–10. **'Miss Bateman'**: ♀ free-flowering, white with red anthers, 7.5–10cm (3–4in) across. ✓**'Mrs Cholmondeley'**: ♀ to 4.5m (15ft); flowers wisteria-blue, 15–17.5cm (6–7in) across, anthers chocolate; flowers fade in strong sunlight; ☼ ●. **'Mrs George Jackman'**: ♀ flowers semi-double, creamy-white, 10cm (4in) across, anthers brown. **'Mrs N. Thompson'**: flowers deep violet with scarlet banding, 10cm (4in)

across, anthers red. ✓**'Nelly Moser'**: to 3.5m (11½ft); flowers pale mauve-pink with carmine-pink banding, 16–17.5cm (6½–7in) across, anthers purplish; flowers fade badly in strong sunlight ☼ ●. ✓**'Niobe'**: ♀ flowers deep velvety red, 10–15cm (4–6in) across, anthers yellow. **'Ramona'**: flowers pale blue, 10–15cm (4–6in) across, anthers dark red; ☼. **'Richard Pennell'**: ♀ flowers deep purple-red, 10–12.5cm (4–5in) across, anthers golden. **'Royal Velvet'**: flowers velvety purple with darker banding, 10–15cm (4–6in) across, anthers red. **'Royalty'**: ♀ flowers semi-double, purple-mauve, 10cm (4in) across, anthers yellow; later flowers smaller, single. **'Silver Moon'**: ♀ flowers silvery-mauve, 10–15cm (4–6in) across, anthers cream. **'Snow Queen'**: flowers white tinted bluish-pink, 15–17.5cm (6–7in) across, anthers red. **'Sylvia Denny'**: flowers semi-double, white, 10cm (4in) across; anthers cream. ✓**'The President'**: ♀ to 3.5m (11½ft) tall; flowers rich deep violet purple with a paler banding and a silvery reverse, 10–15cm (4–6in) across, anthers red. **'Veronica's Choice'**: flowers semi-double, pale lavender flushed mauve, 10–15cm (4–6in) across, anthers cream. **'Vino'**: flowers purple-red, 15cm (6in) across, anthers yellow. ✓**'Vyvyan Pennell'**: ♀ flowers double, lilac, 10–12.5cm (4–5in) across, outer petals often with some green, anthers golden; later flowers blue-mauve. **'Wada's Primrose'**: flowers cream, 10–12.5cm (4–5in) across, anthers yellow; ●. **'W.E. Gladstone'**: free-flowering, to 4m (13ft); flowers pale lavender blue, 16–20cm (6½–8in) across, anthers purple. **'William Kennett'**: to 4m (13ft) tall; flowers lavender blue with a deeper centre, 10–12.5cm (4–5in).

'Marie Boisselot'

'Niobe'

'Nelly Moser'

Temperate
Evergreen
Climbers

Introduction

(Above) The Chilean bellflower *(Lapageria rosea)* luxuriates in the dappled shade of a cool conservatory.

(Left) Tender *Solanum jasminoides* 'Album' is ideal for covering arches and trellis in a warm spot.

(Right) The passion flower *(Passsiflora caerulea)* is a popular evergreen climber.

*E*vergreen climbers have an undeserved reputation for being dull, yet this group contains some of the most beautiful species and cultivars in the world of climbing plants. The extraordinary flowers of the common passion flower (*Passiflora caerulea*), the coral plant (*Berberidopsis corallina*), Chilean bellflower (*Lapageria rosea*) or the species of mutisia are extremely showy and eye-catching and the heady perfume of the jasmines is renowned. The common jasmine is a great favourite for growing by a house door or window, or over an archway where its fragrance can be appreciated readily. In warmer places it can be grown in more open situations and is a good plant to drape over an old wall or tree stump or train on a pergola.

The value of some evergreen climbers, such as the ivies (*Hedera*), lies in their foliage rather than their flowers and, because they carry their leaves throughout the year, these climbers are excellent for covering unsightly walls or fences or planting wherever a permanent green curtain is wanted. Ivy is also invaluable for disguising old tree stumps or unsightly buildings. Contrary to popular belief, it will not harm a wall or building provided they are in a good state of repair: indeed, the beautiful overlapping pattern made by their leaves can be most ornamental. However, the clinging roots may spoil the paintwork of window frames and the vigorous shoots can get under the eaves and lift the roof tiles unless regularly checked.

SITING AND PLANTING

It is important to site evergreen climbers carefully. Many are not hardy and, even if they are, the leaves can easily be damaged by fierce winter winds and frost. On the whole, therefore, the best sites are those that are sheltered: the ideal aspect and the amount of sun required will depend on which plant is being grown.

Planting time is also important. Because evergreen leaves lose moisture even during the winter – and this can severely weaken or even kill a young plant, especially during spells of cold, dry, windy weather, late winter or early spring are a much better time to plant than late autumn or early winter, although early autumn is acceptable in very mild areas. If you have to plant in the autumn, protect plants with a screen of straw or hessian until the spring, and even then do not remove the protection until temperatures have risen sufficiently. Even mature evergreen climbers (especially the tender and half-hardy ones) will benefit from some form of winter protection. It is important to water plants copiously and frequently after planting until they become established.

Most evergreen climbers should be pruned in the early spring or as soon as they have finished flowering – if, indeed, they require any pruning at all. It is not advisable to prune in autumn, since these climbers should be overwintered carrying as much mature growth as possible. None of this advice should discourage the gardener from growing evergreen climbers. They include some of the most attractive species and are well worth a try.

Evergreen species of clematis, roses and honeysuckles can be found in their own specific chapters.

(Right) Sweet-smelling evergreen summer jasmine (*Jasminum officinale*) mixes with *Parthenocissus tricuspidata* and annual nasturtiums.

ARAUJIA
(Asclepiadaceae)

'Araujia' is the Brazilian vernacular name for a small genus of evergreen South American twiners with opposite leaves, grown for their white or pink scented flowers. The corolla has a tube which is inflated at the base and has five lobes at the top. The fruit is a pod containing many seeds, each bearing a tuft of silky hairs. Propagation is by seed or cuttings taken in late summer.

A. sericofera
(*A. albens, Physianthus albens*)
CRUEL PLANT
Stems twining up to 10m (33ft), exuding milky juice when cut. Leaves oval-oblong, 5–10cm (2–4 in) long, dark green above, whitish-felted beneath. Flowers borne in groups of 3–8 in racemes about 5cm (2in) long; strongly scented. Corolla white, often streaked inside with maroon, waxy, strongly scented, the tube about 1.2cm (½in) long with 5 spreading lobes at the mouth, whose diameter is 2.5–3.5cm (1–1½in); late summer. Grooved pods 10–13cm (4–5in) long, yellowish-green. A curious plant which in temperate latitudes can be grown outdoors only in the mildest areas. The common name refers to the fact that visiting night flying moths looking for nectar insert their tongues into the slits in the anthers. As the moths struggle, their tongues become firmly jammed in these slits which are very narrow at the base, and they become trapped. S America
0°C (32°F)

ASTERANTHERA
(Gesneriaceae)

There is only one species in this genus, introduced into cultivation from Chile by the plant collector Harold Comber in 1926. It is a lovely plant which should be grown more often for its sumptuous display of 2-lipped red flowers borne over a long season. Propagation is best by tip cuttings in summer or stem cuttings in late summer to early autumn.

✓ *A. ovata*
Slender stems, covered in white hairs, growing to 4m (13ft) by means of clinging aerial roots produced at the stem nodes. Leaves opposite, roundish, toothed, 1–3cm (½–1¼in) long, clothed with stiff hairs. Flowers produced in the leaf axils, usually 1, occasionally 2 to a flower stalk. Calyx with 5 toothed lobes. Tubular corolla red, 5.5–6cm (2¼–2½in) long, 2-lipped, expanding at the mouth into 5 lobes, the lower lip often striped with yellow; throat whitish inside; summer. Fruit greenish-purple, fleshy. It is not easy to provide the conditions under which this species will flourish: it likes dampish shade but not excessive shading and a slightly acid or neutral, leafy soil suits it best. Too dry a position will produce stunted growth. It may be allowed to creep over the ground as an unusual ground cover, but also looks beautiful if it can be persuaded to climb a mossy tree trunk or mix with other climbers. Chile, W Argentina
-5°C (23°F)

BERBERIDOPSIS
(Flacourtiaceae)

The single species in this genus is considered to be one of the most spectacular of climbing shrubs, with its drooping clusters of waxy, red flowers. The plants like a moist loamy or sandy soil and succeed best on lime-free soils although they will tolerate a slightly alkaline soil, provided some peat is added. Newly planted specimens (the best planting time is spring) benefit from a peat mulch; this helps the roots to establish. They require little pruning other than to remove dead or unwanted growth. Propagation is by cuttings or layering in summer. Fruits produced in cooler latitudes rarely contain viable seeds. Plants should be protected from both drying winds and strong sunshine and in cooler areas it is advisable to protect the base of the plant during the winter. In milder areas the coral plant can be trained up a pillar or even a tree, and can look lovely grown on a pergola or arch where its beautiful flowers can be more easily appreciated.

✓ *B. corallina*
CORAL PLANT
Stems grow to 4.5m (15ft). Leathery leaves alternate, oval or heart-shaped, edged with spiny teeth. Flowers globular, deep red, 1.2cm (½in) across and made up of 9–15 overlapping petal-like segments, forming small drooping clusters borne in the axils of the uppermost leaves and at the shoot tips; summer to early autumn. This species, first brought back from Chile by Richard Pearce in 1826, is now thought to be extinct in the wild. Although hardy, it can be badly damaged by buffeting winds, so wall-protection from the prevailing wind is desirable. Chile
-5°C (23°F)

Berberidopsis corallina

PRUNING GUIDE: *prune immediately after flowering* — S *prune in spring* — W *prune in winter* — *no regular pruning required*

BIGNONIA
(Bignoniaceae)

A genus containing a single species which is called 'cross vine' because when the woody stems are cut transversely a cross-shaped mark can be seen. Its vivid clusters of large flowers make this a spectacular climber when in bloom. It is closely related to *Campsis* but distinguished by the leaf tendrils by which the plant climbs. For culture see *Campsis* (*page 41*).

B. capreolata
(*Doxantha capreolata*)
CROSS VINE, TRUMPET FLOWER
A vigorous climber reaching 20m (66ft) tall in the wild but generally about half that height in cultivation. Stems slender, almost hairless. Leaves opposite, each with 2 oblong to lance-shaped leaflets and a terminal branched tendril with each branch ending in a hook. Funnel-shaped flowers orange-red, 4–5cm (1½–2in) long, spreading at the mouth into 5 rounded lobes, borne in clusters in the leaf axils; summer. Fruits slender, up to 15cm (6in) long, flat and bean-like. This climber is usually evergreen but may become partly deciduous during unseasonally cold weather. It grows fast and is a useful plant for screening an ugly feature.
SE USA
☼ -15°C (5°F) ⌇ℓs
    'Atrosanguinea': leaflets longer and narrower and the flowers brownish-purple.

BILLARDIERA
(Pittosporaceae)

There are nine species in this Australian genus but only one is generally cultivated. They are rather delicate climbers with twining stems and alternate leaves. The 'demure' flowers are followed by a splendid display of colourful blue fruits. Propagation is from seed sown in the spring or cuttings taken in summer or autumn.

B. longiflora ♀
APPLEBERRY
Slender stems, hairless, climbing to 2m (6½ft). Leaves narrowly lance-shaped, untoothed, 2.5–4cm (1–1½in) long. Solitary flowers narrowly trumpet-shaped, scented, greenish-yellow, often becoming tinged with purple, 1.5–3.5cm (½–1½in) long, with 5 petals which are free from one another, although they appear to be united; they are produced in the leaf axils and hang on slender stalks; summer to early autumn. Fruit a cylindrical to globular berry, 2–2.5cm (¾–1in) long, bright blue to violet-blue. This species can be trained on a wall, trellis or even up a tree trunk, or left to clamber among other shrubs or climbers. Plants need to be sheltered from cold winds and strong sunshine, but not completely shaded. Tasmania
☼◐ 0°C (32°F) ⌇ℓs
    'Fructu-Albo' ('Alba'): fruit white. 'Fructu-Coccineo': fruit

red. Both are only rarely seen in cultivation but are well worth seeking out.

CISSUS
(Vitaceae)

A large genus of tropical and subtropical plants which mostly climb by tendrils. They are grown mainly for their attractive foliage and are related to *Ampelopsis*, *Parthenocissus* and *Vitis*. Of the species suitable for indoor culture or tropical conditions, *Cissus discolor* (*page 150*) is perhaps the most splendid. However, the best-known species is undoubtedly the kangaroo vine (*Cissus antarctica*, *page 150*), a tropical species commonly grown as a house plant. Only the species described below is suitable for outdoor culture in temperate latitudes.

▦ *C. striata*
(*Vitis striata*)
MINIATURE GRAPE IVY
A vigorous evergreen climber with angled, hairy stems reaching 5m (16ft). Tendrils slender. Leaves digitate, rather leathery, glossy green, with 3 or 5 obovate, coarsely toothed leaflets. Flowers inconspicuous, greenish; summer to early autumn. Small berries currant-like, dark reddish-purple. Propagation is by semi-ripe cuttings taken in summer.
S Brazil, Chile
☼ 0°C (32°F) ⌇ℓs

DECUMARIA
(Hydrangeaceae)

The two species of *Decumaria* are both cultivated for their handsome foliage and hydrangea-like clusters of flowers. They are woody plants that climb by aerial roots which attach tightly to suitable supports and the leaves are opposite. The small flowers are produced in a terminal inflorescence. The fruit is a ribbed, top-shaped capsule which splits open between the ribs to release many tiny seeds. Decumarias grow best in a moist but well-drained, loamy soil. They are related to the climbing species of *Hydrangea* (*page 45*) and to *Schizophragma* (*page 51*) but distinguished by the absence of sterile flowers, and by their flowers having a larger number (7–10) of sepals and petals. Propagation is by cuttings in late summer to early autumn.

D. barbara
A semi-evergreen, or sometimes deciduous, climber which will reach 9m (30ft). Leaves oval, 7.5–13cm (3–5in) long, untoothed or with shallow teeth towards the tip. Flowers fragrant, white, 6mm (¼in) across, carried in a round-topped inflorescence 5–8cm (2–3¼in) long and wide; summer. Fruit 8cm (3¼in) long, striped white in the lower part. Best grown on a sheltered wall but can look very effective when allowed to climb a tree, especially in

Decumaria barbara

milder sheltered gardens.
SE USA
☼ -15°C (5°F) ♀⊘

D. sinensis

Grows less tall than *D. barbara* with smaller leaves. The cream flowers smell of honey and are borne in a pyramidal inflorescence in late spring to early summer. Central China
◑ 0°C (32°F) ♀⊘

DREGEA
(Asclepiadaceae)

Similar to *Cionura* (*page 42*) but the flowers have oval corolla-lobes; grown for its unusual appearance. Propagation is by seed or cuttings.

D. sinensis

(*Wattakaka sinensis*)
Stems twining, reaching 3m (10ft), the young shoots downy. Oval leaves opposite, heart-shaped at the base, long-pointed at the tip, 3–10cm (1¼–4in) long, densely grey-downy beneath. Fragrant flowers star-shaped, white or cream, dotted and streaked with red, 1.3–1.5cm (½in) across, in a lateral hanging umbel of 10–25 blossoms; summer. Pods borne in pairs, 5–7cm (2–2¾in) long, downy. A botanically interesting plant with dainty flowers. It is available from nurseries, but not often grown in gardens. China
● 0°C (32°F) ♀⊘

EUONYMUS
(Celastraceae)

A large genus of evergreen or deciduous shrubs or sometimes small trees grown for their showy fruits and attractive foliage rather than for their rather inconspicuous flowers. Only the species described below is suitable for training against walls, and it is generally represented in cultivation by var. *radicans*. It produces a dense green curtain of leaves which can be controlled by clipping.

E. fortunei var. radicans

A creeping or climbing evergreen shrub reaching 7m (23ft) high against a wall, the long slender stems self-clinging by means of short roots produced at intervals. Oval leaves dark green, short-stalked, 1.5–3.5cm (½–1½in) long, with shallow teeth. Flowers very small, greenish; mid- to late summer. Fruit capsules small, rounded, pink when ripe, about 6mm (¼in) across, splitting to reveal small bright orange seeds. The normal form of var. *radicans* is the immature phase and, like ivies (*Hedera* species), the growth changes at maturity. Plants will flower and fruit only when the adult phase is reached, and pruning and clipping will prevent some plants from reaching maturity. Mature growth is more bushy and has larger leaves, similar to those of *E. japonicus*. The typical form of *E. fortunei* (var. *fortunei*), which comes from China, is rare in cultivation. China, Japan, Korea
☼ ◑ l -25°C (-13°F) ⊘⊘

Euonymus fortunei var. *radicans* is extremely hardy, indeed in those areas of the eastern USA where ivy is not hardy, this plant is grown on walls as a substitute. Plants are easily rooted from small cuttings taken from older plants. The only pruning needed is to remove untidy or excess growth in the spring to keep the plants tidy, or to train the plant to a required shape.

'Coloratus': reaches 8m (26ft) if given some support and has reddish-purple leaves throughout winter, especially if plants are grown in poor soils; in spring the leaves revert to green. 'Silver Queen': ♈ vigorous, grows to 3m (10ft) tall against a wall or on large tree trunks, soon producing bushy mature growth; leaves creamy-yellow when young, green with white variegations when mature, with the largest reaching 6.5cm (2½in) long. 'Variegatus' ('Argenteo-marginata', 'Gracilis', 'Silver Gem'): similar to var. *radicans* but the greyish leaves have a broad white marginal band, sometimes flushed with red. A pretty cultivar, although plants are not always stable and the leaves may revert to plain green; these reversions should be cut out. 'Vegetus' (var. *vegetus*): generally seen in its adult bushy form, suitable for training against a low wall or fence; mature leaves are broadly oval or roundish, dull green. This cultivar, which comes from the north island of Japan, often produces fruit freely. Growths need to be tied into their supports to train plants into the desired shape.

Ficus pumila (*see page 151*)

HARDENBERGIA
(Leguminosae)

An Australian genus of three species, similar to *Kennedia* but having many smaller flowers in which the blunt keel is shorter than the wings. They are grown for their wonderful airy display of brightly coloured pea-flowers. They are really plants for warm temperate or even subtropical regions: the two species included here will survive outside against a wall in mild districts, but will be killed in a severe winter; they are readily increased by seeds or cuttings and young plants can be overwintered as replacements. They tolerate poor soil, but prefer it to be lime-free.

H. comptoniana ♀
BLUE CORAL PEA

Differs from *H. violacea* in having leaves with 3 or 5 leaflets and blue-purple flowers in which the standard has a white, green-spotted basal blotch; summer.
W Australia
☼ ☽ -5°C (23°F) ♈✿
'Alba'. flowers white.

H. violacea ♀
(*H. monophylla, Kennedia monophylla*)
PURPLE CORAL PEA, FALSE SARSPARILLA

Stems twining up to 3m (10ft). Leathery leaves alternate, oval to linear, 3.5–12.5cm (1½–5in) long, net-veined. Pea-flowers usually violet, sometimes pink or white, the standard with a yellow basal blotch and a notched apex, borne in racemes 5–12cm (2–5in) long; spring. Pods 3–4cm (1¼–1½in) long. E Australia, Tasmania
☼ ☽ -5°C (23°F) ♈✿
'White Crystal' ('Alba'): flowers pure white, produced in late winter.

HEDERA
(Araliaceae)

This small genus of evergreen climbers is a difficult group to classify and botanists are still unable to agree on how many species there are. For many years ivies were labelled 'Victorian' and considered to be dreary and cobweb-ridden, but there has been a considerable revival of interest in them; the many different cultivars offer a wide range of leaf shape and colour and most are readily available. Ivies are commonly grown as pot plants. Outdoors they grow well in a dull, shady corner but they will also grow in full sun and in climates as warm as that of the Mediterranean.

Ivies go through two stages in their growth—a juvenile stage which often lasts a long time, and an adult flowering and fruiting stage. In the juvenile stage the stems produce aerial roots, enabling the plant to cling to a support, and the leaves usually have 3 or 5 lobes. The adult leaves are generally unlobed and arranged in a spiral on the woody non-climbing stem. At both stages, the young shoots have a covering of star-shaped or scale-like hairs; the flowers are greenish and borne in globose clusters and the ripe fruits or berries are black or yellowish.

All the species described below can be grown in any aspect (their tolerance of shade is one of their great

assets) and they are not fussy about soil. The only pruning necessary is to keep the plant to the required size, to remove any long stems which might be caught by the wind or to prevent the adult stage being reached if this is not wanted. Pruning is best done in late spring.

Young plants may take a while to start clinging; they can be helped by being tied close to the wall or other support. Alternatively, long shoots can be laid along the ground against the wall: this will encourage side shoots to grow out straight onto the wall and cling unaided. Propagation is by short young shoots taken in midsummer and placed in a propagating frame. Plants can be layered at any time.

H. azorica
Stems green. Both stems and leaves are thickly covered with a whitish felt when young. Leaves with 5 or 7 lobes, 9–11cm (3½–4¼in) long, bright green. Azores
☼ ☽ l -5°C (23°F) ♈✿

H. canariensis
(*H. algeriensis, H. maderensis*)
CANARY ISLAND IVY, AFRICAN IVY
Stems and leaf stalks smooth, dark red; young shoots have scale-like hairs. Leaves unlobed, 10–15cm (4–6in) long, oval with a heart-shaped base, green in summer, turning bronze in winter. Fruit black. Less hardy than *H. helix* but will succeed in most temperate areas. Canary Islands, N Africa

Hedera hibernica (page 93)

☼ ☽ ☀ -5°C (23°F) ♈✿
✓ 'Gloire de Marengo' ('Variegata'): a decorative fast-growing cultivar, leaves 9–11cm (3½–4¼in) long, green with patchy areas of silver-grey between the veins and an irregular cream margin. which in cooler areas; thrives best on a sheltered wall.
✓ 'Marginomaculata': ♀ a mutation from 'Gloire de Marengo'. Leaves light green with creamy-yellow mottling and often with patches of cream.
'Ravensholst': ♀ leaves large, dark green, some 3-lobed. 'Striata' ('Gold Leaf', 'Golden Leaf'): leaves unlobed, 8–14cm (3¼–5½in) long, dark green with a light green or yellow centre.

H. colchica ♀
PERSIAN IVY
Stems green. Dark green leaves generally unlobed, oval, usually 6–15cm (2½–6in) long but sometimes up to 25cm (10in), thick and leathery, with a heart-shaped base. Fruit black when ripe. N Turkey, Caucasus, N Iran
☼ ☽ l -15°C (5°F) ♈✿

Hedera colchica 'Sulphur Heart'

Hedera colchica 'Dentata Variegata'

Hedera helix in young flower

'Dentata': ♛ a vigorous plant with purplish-brown stems. Leaves unlobed, ovate, 15–20cm (6–8in) long, light green with tiny, widely spaced marginal teeth.

'Dentata Variegata': ♛ leaves unlobed, untoothed or with a few scattered teeth, often with the margins curling under, light green with irregular patches of grey-green and an irregular deep cream margin.

✓ **'Sulphur Heart'** ♛ ('Paddy's Pride', 'Gold Leaf'): stems green, aging to brown. Leaves unlobed with a few marginal teeth, 10–13cm (4–5¼in) long, light green with irregular paler splashes towards the centre, or with yellow veins.

H. helix

COMMON IVY, ENGLISH IVY

The hardiest species of ivy with stems up to 10m (33ft) if allowed. Leaves with 3 or 5 lobes, 4–8cm (1½–3¼in) long, with a strong smell when crushed. Flowers greenish; autumn. Fruit dull black when ripe. Europe, W Asia
☀ ◑ 1 -20°C (-4°F) ⱱ**s**

An enormous number of cultivars, mainly differing in shape, size and colour of leaves, have been produced over the last two or three centuries, and their naming is still somewhat confused, although recent attempts to sort out the

muddle have been reasonably successful. A selection is given below:

'Adam': stems greenish-purple. Leaves 3-lobed, 3–4cm (1¼–1½in) long, pale green, greying with age and with an irregular creamy-white margin, the central lobe directed somewhat to one side. They develop pinkish edges in cold weather. 0°C (32°F)

✓ **'Buttercup'**: ♛ stems and leaves pale green in shade, rich yellow-green in sun. Leaves 5-lobed, 5–7cm (2–2¾in) long, with the central lobe longer than the others. A bright attractive cultivar. -5°C (23°F). **'Cavendishii'**: ♛

stems light green. Leaves 3-lobed, 5–6cm (2–2½in) long, mid-green in the centre with an irregular pale yellow margin which often develops a pink flush in winter. This is one of the quickest cultivars to reach the adult (fruiting) stage. **'Digitata'**: One of the earliest cultivars and extremely hardy; stems greenish-purple. Large leaves deeply 5-lobed, 7–9cm (2¾–3½in) long, dark green with lighter veins, central lobe long and basal lobes reduced. ✓ **'Glacier'**: ♛ stems purplish-green. Leaves with 3 or 5 lobes, 3–6cm (1¼–2½in) long, grey-green with patches of a lighter silvery-grey and a narrow cream margin, basal lobes reduced. A lovely ivy which makes strong growth and provides a cool accompaniment for colourful neighbours. -5°C (23°F). **'Glymii'**: stems and leaves green in summer, turning purple in winter. Leaves very shallowly 3-lobed, 4–5cm (1½–2in) long. **'Goldchild'**: ♥ leaves with 3 or 5 lobes, mid-green with a yellow margin.

✓ **'Goldheart'**: stems deep pink, turning brown with age. Leaves 3-lobed, 4–6cm (1½–2½in) long, dark green with an irregular splash of bright yellow in the middle, central lobe longer. This ivy can be slow to establish but its attractively coloured leaves make it one of the most popular cultivars. It appears in some catalogues as 'Oro di Bogliasco'. **'Gracilis'**: stems purplish-red. Leaves with 3 or 5 lobes, 2–4cm (¾–1½in) long, dark green with lighter veins, turning purplish-red in autumn, central lobe only slightly longer than the others. **'Green Ripple'**: stems greenish-purple. Leaves 5-lobed, 5–9cm (2–3½in) long, heart-shaped at the base, bright green, turning coppery in the autumn, all lobes pointing forward, the sinuses between them twisted. A vigorous ivy with elegant leaves. -5°C (23°F). ✓ **'Heron'**: stems grey-green. Leaves with purplish stalks, 5-lobed, 3–5cm (1¼–2in) long, deep grey-green with whitish veins, basal lobes pointing backwards. ✓ **'Ivalace'**: ♥ stems purplish-green. Leaves with 5 shallow, wavy-margined lobes, 4–6cm (1½–2½in) long, dark shiny green with paler veins, turning coppery in winter; happy on a north-facing wall. -5°C (23°F). **'Kolibri'**: ♥ leaves with 3 or 5

Hedera helix 'Midas Touch'

lobes, light green flecked with grey-green and cream. **'Midas Touch'**: ♥ leaves heart-shaped, yellowish-green variegated with creamy yellow. The stems are red. **'Minor Marmorata'**: stems dull purplish, the young shoots pink-tinged. Leaves 3-lobed, 3–5cm (1½–2in) long, dark green with spots and splashes of whitish-cream, some of which fade with age. Does well on a north-facing wall. ✓ **'Parsley Crested'** ('Cristata'): stems greenish-purple. Leaves unlobed or slightly 3-lobed, the margins strongly waved and crimped, oval to roundish, 4–6cm (1½–2½in) long, bright green with paler veins, turning reddish in winter. -5°C (23°F). **'Pedata'** ♥ ('Caernwoodiana'): stems green. Leaves 5-lobed, 4–5cm (1½–2in) long, dark green with whitish veins, central lobe long and narrow, basal lobes pointing backwards. **'Sagittifolia'**: stems greenish-purple. Leaves spear-shaped, 3–5cm (1¼–2in) long, dark green, with horizontal or backward-pointing basal lobes which are sometimes overlapping. -5°C (23°F)

var. *poetarum* (*H. helix* var. *poetica*): stems pinkish, leaves 5-lobed, 5–7cm (2–2¾in) long, bright green, basal lobes very small. Fruits pale yellowish-orange. Rather a stiff habit. This ivy is commonly known as Italian ivy or poet's ivy. N. Africa, Turkey, Greece

H. hibernica ♥
(*H. helix* 'Hibernica')
IRISH IVY

Stems green. Leaves 5-lobed, 5–9cm (2–3½in) long, dull green with grey-green veins, central lobe large, base heart-shaped. Common in cultivation and very vigorous. Coastal W Europe
☼ ◑ -15°C (5°F) ⧸⌇s
'Variegata': leaves with irregular yellow markings.

H. nepalensis
(*H. himalaica, H. helix* var. *chrysocarpa*)
HIMALAYAN IVY

Stems green, red-brown when young and clothed in yellowish-brown, scale-like hairs. Leaves oval to lance-shaped, 5–10cm (2–4in) long, occasionally with very shallow lobes or teeth, shiny green. Flowers produced in winter. Fruits yellow or orange. Afghanistan, Himalaya to W China and N Burma
☼ ◑ 0°C (32°F) ⧸⌇s

H. pastuchovii
Stems greenish-brown. Leaves leathery, narrowly oval, 4–6cm (1½–2½in) long and sometimes with marginal teeth, dark glossy green. Fruits

black when ripe. Similar to *H. colchica* but with smaller, less leathery leaves. Roy Lancaster introduced this unusual species into cultivation in 1972 but it is not yet widely grown.
W Caucasus
☼ ◑ -15°C (5°F) ⧸⌇s

H. rhombea
JAPANESE IVY

Stems purplish-green, the young shoots with scale-like hairs. Leaves oval or triangular, usually unlobed, 2–4cm (¾–1½in) long, dark green with the veins on the upper surface slightly recessed. Flowers produced in winter. Japan, Korea
☼ ◑ -10°C (14°F) ⧸⌇s
'Variegata': leaves with a regular, narrow cream margin.

HOLBOELLIA
(Lardizabalaceae)

A genus of evergreen twining shrubs with digitately-lobed leaves and separate male and female flowers produced on the same plant. There are five species, all natives of Asia, but only two are generally cultivated, being grown for their lustrous leaves and (in warmer gardens) their spectacular fruit. The small, egg-shaped flowers have fleshy sepals but lack true petals. The male flowers have 6 separate stamens and the females have 3 carpels which develop into fleshy 'pod-like' structures. The genus is related to *Stauntonia* which differs in its thin sepals and joined stamens.

Holboellias thrive in most garden soils and grow in both sunny or shaded positions. Hand-pollination may encourage fruit to form.

H. coriacea

A vigorous climber with stems reaching 7m (23ft), sometimes more, young shoots twining, reddish-purple, hairless. Leaves glossy dark green, rather leathery with 3 large leaflets. Male flowers purplish-white, 1.1–1.3cm (½in) long, borne at the shoot tips or in the leaf axils in small, stalked clusters; female flowers rather larger, greenish-white flushed with purple, in clusters of 3 or 4, usually in the lower axils of young shoots; spring to summer. Fleshy fruits purple, sausage-shaped, rarely produced in cultivation, 4.5–6cm (1¾–2½in) long, containing rows of black seeds. A plant which will readily reach the top of a tall wall but will also happily grow up an old tree; produces flowers, and occasionally fruits, most freely when grown against a sunny wall. But it is for the handsome leaves that it is usually grown. Central China (Hubei)
☼ ◑ 1-5°C (23°F) ⚘

H. latifolia

(*Stauntonia latifolia*)
Similar to *H. coriacea* but the leaves have 3–7 leaflets. Very fragrant flowers, the males greenish-white and the females purplish; spring. Differs very little from *H. coriacea* (some

botanists believe they are variations of the same species) though it is slightly more tender and flowers earlier. Himalaya
☼ ◑ 10°C (32°F) ⚘

HYDRANGEA
(Hydrangeaceae)

The genus is described under Temperate Deciduous Climbers (*page 44*), where the common, more widely grown climbing hydrangea (*H. petiolaris*) is described.

H. serratifolia

(*H. integerrima, Cornidia serratifolia*)
Stems reaching 4m (13ft) or more and, like the other climbing hydrangeas, attaching itself to supports by aerial roots. Leaves leathery, elliptic or obovate, 5–15cm (2–6in) long, sometimes with distantly spaced teeth. Flowers produced in small clusters, several of which make up a panicle 7.5–15cm (3–6in) long; each cluster, at the bud stage, enclosed in 4 papery bracts which fall as the flowers expand. Flowers white, usually all fertile, with 4 petals and 8 stamens; stamens about 6mm (¼in) long, much more conspicuous than the petals; late summer. Sterile flowers are only occasionally produced. Because it lacks the conspicuous sterile flowers of the other species, this hydrangea is not as decorative as its climbing cousins, but it

has the advantage of being evergreen. Chile, Argentina
☼ ◑ 1-5°C (23°F) ⚘s

JASMINUM
(Oleaceae)

A popular genus containing the cheerful winter-flowering wall shrub, winter jasmine (*J. nudiflorum*) and the wonderfully fragrant summer-flowering *J. officinale*. The Latin name *Jasminum* comes from 'Yasmin' which is the Arabic name of the plant.

There are some 450 species of jasmine, native to the Old World tropics and subtropics. They are woody shrubs or climbers, evergreen or deciduous. The leaves can be opposite or alternate, simple, ternate or pinnate. The flowers are solitary or produced in terminal or lateral clusters–they have a 5-lobed calyx and the corolla has 4–9 spreading lobes joined below to form a narrow tube. There are only 2 stamens, usually hidden inside the corolla-tube. The fruit is a small berry, which turns black when ripe.

Jasmines are grown for their wonderful scent: many species provide some of the best fragrant plants for gardens. Most of the cultivated species grown outdoors in temperate regions are evergreen scramblers or twiners. Jasmines prefer a sunny position; although most can tolerate shade, they will not flower well in a shady position.

They can be grown in any well-drained soil, but do not like conditions that are too dry. Propagation is by layering at any time or cuttings taken in late summer and placed in a propagating frame. An essential oil is extracted from the flowers of several white species and used in the perfumery industry.

J. angulare (*see page 151*)

J. azoricum ♀

Stems twining. Leaves opposite, with 3 oval leaflets. Flowers white, flushed with purple in bud, sweetly scented, 2–3cm (¾–1¼in) across, in clusters of 5–25 at the shoot tips; midsummer to early autumn. A pretty species, suitable only for the mildest parts of temperate latitudes; in mild seasons this species will continue to flower into early winter. Madeira
☼ 0°C (32°F) ⚘s

J. beesianum

Stems to 3–5m (10–16ft), often deciduous in colder districts. Leaves opposite, simple, lance-shaped, 2.5–5cm (1–2in) long, often downy when young. Flowers fragrant, pink to rose-red, 8–10mm (¼–½in) across and usually with 6 lobes, borne at the ends of side shoots in groups of 1–3; late spring to early summer. (There are only two pink-flowered cultivated jasmines: the other is *J. × stephanense*.) This is one of the few species to produce fruits regularly, and the glossy black berries remain on the plant in hanging clusters well into winter. W China

☼ -10°C (14°F) 🌿

✓ **J. floridum**

An evergreen or semi-evergreen, scrambling or semi-climbing shrub with angled shoots, reaching 2.5m (8ft) high. Leaves alternate with 3, sometimes 5, oval or broadly oval leaflets. Flowers yellow, 1.2–2cm (½–¾in) long , with 5 lobes, borne in great profusion in terminal clusters on long arching stems; summer to early autumn. A good plant for a warm, sheltered spot in full sun, though now grown less than it used to be. Young plants can be rather shy to flower. W China

☼ 0°C (32°F) 🌿

J. grandiflorum (*see page 151*)

▦ **J. mesnyi** ♆
(*J. primulinum*)
PRIMROSE JASMINE

A strong-growing, rambling evergreen or semi-evergreen shrub which will climb to 3m (10ft) high. Leaves opposite, each with 3 deep green, oval leaflets. Flowers soft yellow, solitary, semi-double, 3–4cm (1¼–1½in) across, with 6–10 lobes; late spring to early summer. A lovely species, most often seen as a conservatory plant in temperate latitudes although it will succeed outdoors in mild areas if given the protection of

a warm, sheltered wall. In tropical regions it usually flowers in winter and spring. It is closely related to winter jasmine (*J. nudiflorum*) and has flowers which are similar, but larger and semi-double. It is perhaps the finest yellow jasmine in cultivation and it is sad that it is not hardier! Older plants become bulky and need careful pruning to keep them under control. W China

☼ 0°C (32°F) 🌿

✓ ▦ **J. officinale** ♆
COMMON JASMINE, JESSAMINE, POET'S JASMINE

Deciduous, or semi-evergreen in milder districts, with angled, twining stems which can reach 12m (40ft) if allowed. Leaves opposite, usually with 7 or 9 elliptic leaflets, each 1.2–6cm (½–2½in) long. Flowers fragrant, about 2cm (¾in) across, with 4 or 5 spreading lobes, white, opening from buds which are usually tinged with pink, carried in terminal clusters of 5–12; summer to autumn. In cooler areas it is best against a sheltered wall or fence where it will often grow up to 2m (6½ft) in a season. Young plants are shy-flowering and too drastic pruning may reduce flowers on established plants. Best left unpruned and allowed to romp, only removing old or dead growth when necessary. It will produce more flowers in warmer areas where the wood ripens better. It should be fertilized cautiously as too

Jasminum officinale

much feeding produces over-lush and over-vigorous growth. *J. officinale* is naturalized in southern Europe and western Asia. Himalaya, S China

☼ ◐ -10°C (14°F) 🌿

Affine' (forma *affine*, 'Grandiflorum'): flowers larger, suffused with pink on the outside. **'Argentovariegatum'** ('Variegatum'): leaves variegated with white. **'Aureum'** ('Aureovariegatum'): leaves with yellow blotches. Though a handsome plant, said to be less hardy than the typical form.

J. polyanthum (*see page 151*)

✓ **J. ×stephanense**

A hybrid between *J. beesianum* and *J. officinale*. A vigorous climber, evergreen in mild districts, stems angled, reaching 7m (23ft). Leaves varying from simple to pinnate with up to 5 leaflets. Fragrant flowers pink, about 1.5cm (½in) across, in terminal clusters of 3–10; summer. The plants of this beautiful cultivated hybrid are the

descendants of a cross made in a garden in Nancy, France, though the hybrid also occurs in the wild; it is the only hybrid in the genus. S China

☼ -15°C (5°F) 🌿

'Variegatum': leaves of young shoots variegated with white or pale yellow.

KADSURA
(Schisandraceae)

Very similar to *Schisandra* (*page 49*), but with its fruit in a globose head instead of in a long spike. It is grown for its attractive red fruits and its leaves which turn rich red and purple in the autumn.

K. japonica

Stems slender, twining, reaching about 4m (13ft). Leaves alternate, dark green, oval or lance-shaped, 5–10cm (2–4in) long. Flowers unisexual, cream with 6–9 petals, fragrant, about 2cm (¾in) in diameter, solitary in the leaf axils of the current year's shoots; summer to early autumn. Berries scarlet, up to 6mm (¼in) long, in a pendulous globose cluster 2.5–3cm (1–1¼in) wide. This rarely grown species needs the shelter of a warm wall to grow well. If fruits are required (and, being attractive, they generally are), both male and female plants must be grown. China, Taiwan, Japan

◐ -10°C (14°F) 🌿

'Variegata': leaves with an irregular cream border.

LAPAGERIA
(Philesiaceae)

This genus is named in honour of the Empress Josephine, Napoleon's first wife, whose maiden name was 'de la Pagerie'. There is only one species, and it is one of the most glorious of all climbing plants, noted for its spectacular waxy bells.

✓ ▦ *L. rosea* ♀

CHILEAN BELLFLOWER, COPIHUE
Stems twining, hairless, reaching 5m (16ft) or more in favoured gardens. Leaves evergreen, leathery, alternate, heart-shaped or oval with 3 or 5 veins, 5–10cm (2–4in) long, dull green above, paler beneath. Flowers pendulous, waxy, pink to rich crimson, sometimes white, often flecked with rose, narrowly bell-shaped, 7–9cm (2¾–3½in) long, borne singly or 2 or 3 together in the upper leaf axils; summer to early autumn. Perianth-segments 6, fleshy. Fruit an oblong 3-sided berry, which is sometimes produced in cultivation.

The Chilean bellflower is the national flower of Chile and has been regarded as one of the finest greenhouse climbers since the middle of the last century when it was introduced to Kew Gardens in England. In mild temperate districts it will succeed on a shady wall and is probably hardier than is generally supposed. The soil must be a deep moist loam which does

Lapageria rosea

not dry out. Hot, dry summers and biting winter winds are the chief dangers, so some winter protection is necessary, together with mulches around the base of the plant during the spring and summer. Frosted plants will usually sprout again from the base. The plant has a rather rambling habit and sends up shoots randomly from the root system.

Propagation is by seed or from layers or cuttings taken in the summer. Seeds sown as soon as the fruit is ripe will germinate readily and plants should flower 4–5 years later. Old or dead wood should be removed each year. Various colour forms and cultivars are available, and you should select the form carefully before

spending any money as the plants are often expensive. Chile, Argentina

☼ 0°C (32°F) ⚘

Var. *albiflora*: flowers glistening white. **'Flesh Pink'**: ♀ flowers pale pink. **'Nash Court'**: ♀ flowers soft pink with a faint marbling. **'Penheale'**: flowers deep red.

LARDIZABALA
(Lardizabalaceae)

A small South American genus of climbing evergreens with two species, only one of which is cultivated. They are grown for their handsome foliage and for their unusual fruits. The flowers are either male or female, and both occur on the same plant. Both have 6 rather fleshy sepals and the female flowers have 3–6 carpels, one of which develops into a sausage-shaped fleshy fruit.

▦ *L. biternata*

Stems twining, reaching 4m (13ft) tall. Leaves ternate to triternate with 3–9 leathery, dark green leaflets. Flowers unisexual, with green and dark chocolate-brown petaloid sepals and small whitish petals, the male ones 8–12mm (¼–½in) long, borne in long drooping spikes; female flowers 15–18mm (½–¾in) long, borne singly in the leaf axils on slender stalks; winter. Fruits fleshy, purple, oblong in outline, 5–7.5cm (2–3in) long. In northern latitudes this plant only succeeds on a warm sheltered wall. Grows well in Mediterranean regions, where flowers and fruits are freely produced, but elsewhere it is a fine plant for a conservatory wall or trellis and deserves to be more widely known. The sweet fruits are edible but not produced reliably in cooler areas. Chile

☼ -5°C (23°F) ✀

Mandevilla laxa (*see page 152*)

MITRARIA
(Gesneriaceae)

Mitraria contains only one species, a beautiful, rather neat plant grown for its show of brilliant orange-red flowers, produced in profusion on mature plants. It was introduced by plant collector William Lobb in 1846.

✓ ▦ *M. coccinea*

Evergreen with slender stems up to 2m (6½ft). Leaves opposite, somewhat leathery, oval, up to 2.5cm (1in) long, toothed, with short hairs on both sides. Flowers orange-scarlet, downy outside, 2.5–3.5cm (1–1½in) long, tubular, slightly inflated, with 4 exserted stamens, produced singly in the leaf axils, each on a drooping, slender stalk 2.5–3.5cm (1–1½in) long; late spring to early autumn. Capsule egg-shaped, about 1cm (½in) long. A lovely plant which does best on a partially shady wall or tree trunk,

Mitraria coccinea

although it will also succeed on a north-facing wall. It will not grow in hot sun or dry conditions; a moist loamy soil with added peat or peat-substitute suits it best. In northern latitudes it makes a fine conservatory plant and flowers mainly in spring and early summer. Chile, adjacent Argentina

☼ -5°C (23°F) ✀

MUTISIA
(Compositae)

A spectacular and distinctive South American genus of about 60 species, only five of which are generally cultivated. They climb by tendrils produced at the ends of the alternate leaves, which can be simple or pinnate. The flowers are in typical 'daisy' heads which are solitary, usually borne on long stalks, and have attractive, petal-like, marginal ray-florets. At the base of the flower-heads are a number of overlapping ovate, pointed bracts with hairy margins.

These magnificent climbers grow best in a well-drained soil with their roots and main stems in the shade, and their heads in the sun. They dislike disturbance but will tolerate light pruning in the spring to keep them tidy. A plant in full flower makes a magnificent display and the colourful flower-heads are long-lasting. Mutisias are thought to be tender, but this is not generally true and they should be tried much more often. They also have a reputation for being short-lived and the plants can sometimes die suddenly, with no obvious cause. However, in some gardens they have been known to live for many years.

They are suitable for a wall or fence but look best when allowed to climb up other wall shrubs, especially old or unwanted ones. Propagation is easiest from seed if it can be obtained.

✓ *M. clematis*

Stems up to 9m (30ft) or more. Leaves pinnate with 6–10 oblong to oval leaflets which are 1.5–3.5cm (½–1½in) long, white-woolly on both surfaces when young, becoming hairless above when older. Tendril 2–3-branched. Flower-heads hanging downwards, 5–6cm (2–2½in) across, with 9 or 10, bright scarlet-orange ray-florets which spread horizontally or are somewhat recurved; late spring to autumn. A vigorous species which may require light pruning to keep it within bounds. *M. clematis* is the easiest species to cultivate. Andes of Colombia and Ecuador

☼ 0°C (32°F) ✀s

✓ ▦ *M. decurrens*

Stems slender, hairless, up to 3m (10ft). Leaves narrowly oblong, stalkless, 7.5–13cm (3–5¼in) long, the base of the blade running down each side of the stem to form a couple of narrow wings. Tendril forked.

Flowerheads 10–13cm (4–5¼in) across, with 10–15 orange or scarlet ray-florets and a yellow disk; summer. This species can be difficult to establish, and is therefore not often seen in gardens, but it is worth the trouble as it is a most glorious sight when in full bloom. It flowers best on a south- or west-facing wall but one which is slightly shaded. Chile, Argentina
☼ -5°C (23°F) ✾

⊞ *M. ilicifolia*

Stems slender, climbing to 4.5m (15ft); young shoots with toothed wings. Leaves stalkless, 2.5–6cm (1–2½in) long, oval-oblong with strong, holly-like spiny teeth on the margin, dark green above and with woolly hairs beneath. Tendrils unbranched. Flower-heads with 8–12, pale mauvish or pink ray-florets and a yellow disk; the whole head is 5–7.5cm (2–3in) in diameter and is borne on a shorter stalk than the other species, 1.2cm (½in) or less; summer and intermittently throughout the year. A lovely plant for a low wall or trellis or for growing through a shrub and the hardiest of the five species described here. It will tolerate harder pruning than the other species. It sets seed well and can also be propagated from layers or cuttings. Chile
☼ -5°C (23°F) ✾

✓ ⊞ *M. oligodon*

Stems up to 1.5m (5ft), the young shoots ribbed and clothed in pale woolly hairs. Leaves stalkless, 2.5–3.5cm (1–1½in) long, oblong with toothed margins, dark green above but with pale woolly hairs beneath. Tendrils unbranched. Flower-heads 4–7 cm (1½–2¾in) across with 6–12, strong, shiny pink ray-florets 3cm (1¼in) long, and a central yellow disk; summer and sporadically until autumn. Chile, Argentina
☼ -10°C(14°F) ✾

M. spinosa

(*M. retusa*)

Stems up to 6m (20ft), with spiny wings when young. Leaves 2.5–6cm (1–2½in) long, stalkless and elliptic to oblong, toothed, sometimes untoothed, hairless, dark green above, either hairless or woolly beneath. Tendrils unbranched. Flower-heads 4–6cm (1½–2½in) across, with 8–10 pink ray-florets 3cm (1¼in) long, and a yellow disk; summer. Chile, Argentina
☼ 0°C (32°F) ✾

Pandorea jasminoides

(*see page 153*)

PASSIFLORA
(Passifloraceae)

For general notes on the *Passiflora* genus, see page 153. In addition to the species described below, the following may be grown in temperate gardens provided that they are given protection from frost: *P. × allardii*, *P. antioquiensis* and

Passiflora × caeruleoracemosa

P. edulis. For descriptions of these species, see the chapter on Conservatory Climbers (*pages 153–4*). For the herbaceous species *P. amethystina* and *P. incarnata*, see page 138.

✓ ⊞ *P. caerulea* ♈

BLUE PASSION FLOWER

Stems vigorous, grooved, hairless, forming a tangled growth up to 5m (16ft) tall or 10m (33ft) in warmer areas. Leaves more or less evergreen, although they may be deciduous in cool temperate regions, usually with 5 or 7 lobes, hairless, the stalks with 2, 4 or rarely 6 glands. Flowers slightly fragrant, solitary, 7–10cm (2¾–4in) across; summer to early autumn, all year round in the tropics. Sepals and petals greenish outside, white or pinkish inside. Corona banded with purple, white and blue; filaments up to 2cm (¾in) long, the inner ones very short, in 4 rows. Fruits egg-shaped, tough-skinned,

orange, 4–6cm (1½–2½in) long. *P. caerulea* is also sold as a pot plant and is a fine subject for a conservatory. It is the parent of more hybrids than any other species of passion flower. Though it is the most commonly grown species in temperate latitudes, it is only really hardy in the mildest areas. Severe winters cut it back to ground level, but the stems will generally grow the following summer. It needs a well-drained soil. The flowers open in sun and remain closed on cloudy days. Propagation is from seed or cuttings struck in midsummer from semi-mature growth. The fruits are edible but lack flavour.
S Brazil, Argentina
☼ -5°C (23°F) ✣

'Constance Elliott': ♔ flowers ivory-white, slightly less free-flowering than the species.

'Grandiflora': flowers 12.5–20cm (5–8in) across.

▦ *P.* × *caeruleoracemosa*

A hybrid of garden origin, bearing spectacular rose-pink flowers all summer; needs a warm, sheltered wall.
☼ -5°C (23°F) ✣

PERIPLOCA
(Asclepiadaceae)

The genus is described with deciduous climbers (*page 49*).

P. laevigata

Stems up to 3m (10ft), twining at the ends. Leaves evergreen or semi-evergreen, hairless, elliptic or lance-shaped, 2.5–5cm (1–2in) long. Flowers greenish outside, purplish-brown and white inside, about 1.2cm (½in) across, in almost stalkless terminal and lateral clusters of up to 15 blossoms; late spring to autumn. Fruit pods spreading, 5–10cm (2–4in) long. N Africa, Canary Islands
☼ -5°C (23°F) ✣

PILEOSTEGIA
(Hydrangeaceae)

A small genus related to *Schizophragma* (*page 51*) and, like that genus, climbing by means of aerial roots. It is grown for its viburnum-like flowers and large, handsome leaves which form a dense covering. The flowers (all fertile) are carried in terminal clusters; there are 4 or 5 sepals and petals and 8–10 stamens.

✓ *P. viburnoides* ♔

(*Schizophragma viburnoides*)
A slow-growing climber reaching 6m (20ft) or more, with scaly young shoots and leaves. Leathery leaves opposite, oblong or obovate, 6–15cm (2½–6in) long, untoothed, dull green. Flowers white or cream, 8–9mm (⅓in) across, with long stamens, borne in dense pyramidal clusters 10–15cm (4–6in) long; late summer to autumn. An excellent, adaptable plant which will grow in any soil and any aspect but most useful for a north-facing wall. In addition

Pileostegia viburnoides

to spring pruning, unwanted growths can be removed as they are produced, during the summer. India, China, Taiwan
☼ ◑ l -5°C (23°F) ✣s

SOLANUM
(Solanaceae)

A large genus of some 1700 worldwide tropical and temperate species, which has given us the potato (*S. tuberosum*) and the aubergine (*S. melongena*). The leaves are alternate and both calyx and corolla are 5-lobed. The five stamens have short filaments and the long anthers lean towards one another to form a kind of 'cone'. The fruit is a berry containing many seeds.

The two species described below are grown for their clusters of pretty flowers borne over a long season. They climb by scrambling: the stems need to be tied to the support, at least initially. Both will thrive on most average garden soils and at midsummer can be propagated from firm young shoots in a propagating frame. They mix beautifully with small-flowered clematis and honeysuckles. The deciduous *S. valdiviense* is described on page 52.

▦ *S. crispum*

A quick-growing, scrambling semi-evergreen, growing up to 5m (16ft). Leaves oval, 6–13cm (2½–5¼in) long. Flowers slightly fragrant, 2.5–3cm (1–1¼in) in diameter, bluish-purple with a yellow cone of anthers, produced in clusters 7.5–15cm (3–6in) across; summer to early autumn. Berries globose, 4–6mm (⅙–¼in) across, cream-coloured when ripe. A lovely plant which needs full sun and prefers a south- or west-facing wall. It does well on chalky soils. In addition to wall culture, it can be used on a fence or trellis, or to cover unsightly structures. Care should be taken when pruning, as not only are the stems rather brittle, but handling or brushing against the leaves gives some people a rash.
Chile, Peru
☼ -5°C (23°F) ⅄ₛ

✓ **'Glasnevin'** ('Autumnale'): ♀ a cultivar with a longer flowering period: in a mild winter a few flowers will often appear. One of the best wall plants; the flowers are deep bluish-purple. Named after Glasnevin Botanic Garden, Dublin, where it originated. Hardier than the type, being able to withstand temperatures of -10°C (14°F).

Solanum crispum 'Glasnevin'

▦ *S. jasminoides*
POTATO VINE
A usually semi-evergreen scrambler reaching 5m (16ft). Leaves oval to lance-shaped, 2.5–5cm (1–2in) long, with a slightly wavy margin, sometimes lobed at the base, or even with separate leaflets. Flowers pale blue with a greyish tinge, 2–2.5cm (¾–1in) across, and with a yellow cone of anthers; summer to autumn. Less hardy than *S. crispum* and needing the protection of a south- or west-facing wall. In bad winters, or colder regions it can be cut to ground level by frost. It does not produce fruit in cooler areas; in the wild, the flowers are followed by purple berries about 1.3cm (½in) in diameter.
S Brazil, Paraguay
☼ ◐ 0°C (32°F) ⅄ₛ

✓ **'Album'**: ♀ flowers white, long-lasting. More commonly grown than *S. jasminoides* itself and considered by many to be more beautiful. **'Album Variegatum'**: leaves variegated with white. Some people consider that the variegation diminishes the impact of the lovely white flowers.

Solanum jasminoides 'Album'

STAUNTONIA
(Lardizabalaceae)

Another genus allied to the better known *Holboellia*. The stamens of *Stauntonia* are joined together while those of *Holboellia* are separate. The genus contains about 15 species from cast and south-east Asia, although only *S. hexaphylla* is in general cultivation.

⊞ **S. hexaphylla**
(Rajania hexaphylla)
A twiner reaching 10m (33ft) tall or more and forming a dense tangled growth. Leaves long-stalked, with 3–7 oval, sharply pointed leaflets, 5–13cm (2–5¼in) long. Flowers fragrant, white-flushed violet, about 1.8cm (¾in) across, with 6 fleshy sepals but no petals. Male and female flowers are produced on separate plants and borne in few-flowered racemes; spring to summer. Fruits fleshy, plum-shaped, purple and juicy when ripe, 2.5–5cm (1–2in) long.

This is a handsome climber suitable for a warm sheltered spot in milder districts and happy on most garden soils. It grows well in Mediterranean regions and in cooler regions makes a good cool greenhouse or conservatory subject. The edible fruits are sweet and succulent when ripe but they are seldom produced in quantity in cultivation, except during a hot summer. As in *Sinofranchetia*, *Stauntonia* will occasionally produce a few fruit even in the absence of a male plant. Plants will sometimes be found under the name *Holboellia hexaphylla* in books and catalogues. S Korea, Japan, Ryukyu Islands
☼ ◐ -5°C (23°F) ❦

Tecomaria capensis
(see page 157)

TRACHELOSPERMUM
(Apocynaceae)

Twining shrubs whose cut stems produce milky sap. The leaves are opposite, leathery and untoothed. The jasmine-like flowers have a 5-lobed calyx and a 5-lobed corolla whose lobes all overlap one another to the right. The fruit is a pair of cylindrical pods, which contain seeds each of which bears a tuft of hairs.

The two cultivated species are grown for their neat leaves and sweetly scented flowers. They will grow in all but the coldest temperate latitudes, provided they are given wall protection. They will tolerate partial shade but grow best in a sunny position. They make fine patio plants grown in a large tub with trellis support. They can be easily trained on a south- or west-facing wall, producing their scented flowers on the old wood. Prune to remove dead wood or weak growth, or to control any unwanted extension growth. Cuttings can be taken in late summer and started in a propagating frame.

Trachelospermum jasminoides

⊞ ***T. asiaticum*** ♀
(T. majus, T. japonicum)
Stems much-branched, reaching 6m (20ft). Leaves dark, glossy, oval, 2–5cm (¾–2in) long. Scented flowers cream, deeper in the throat, and changing to yellow with age, about 2cm (¾in) across, and with erect calyx lobes, in terminal clusters; summer. Pods 12–22cm (5–9in) long. Slightly hardier than *T. jasminoides* but with flowers less powerfully scented. Japan, Korea
☼ ◐ -5°C (23°F) ❦s

✓ ⊞ ***T. jasminoides*** ♀
STAR JASMINE, CONFEDERATE JASMINE
Stems climbing to 9m (30ft) if permitted. Leaves dark, shiny, elliptic, oblong or oblanceolate, up to 10cm (4in) long. Flowers very fragrant, white, about 2.5cm (1in) across and with recurved calyx lobes, borne in terminal and lateral clusters; summer. Pods up to 15cm (6in) in length. This species is often grown in subtropical gardens where it usually blooms in the spring (in the northern hemisphere). China
☼ ◐ -5°C (23°F) ❦s
  'Variegatum': ♀ leaves oval to narrowly lance-shaped, margined and splashed with white, flushed crimson in winter. More widely available than the type and also possibly hardier. **'Wilsonii'**: leaves bronze with pale green veins, usually turning deep red in winter.

Climbing
Roses

Introduction

The rose is the most popular and widely grown of all garden plants and has been cultivated for as long as any of them. Through the processes of selection and hybridization carried out by breeders and nurserymen, a huge variety of cultivars has been produced which offers an enormous range of colour (although a blue rose still remains an unattained dream), flower size and plant habit, from miniatures to shrubs or rampant climbers. Anyone who wishes to specialize in roses should consult appropriate specialist rose books and keep a keen eye on current rose nursery catalogues to see which new cultivars are being offered.

The genus *Rosa* is native throughout the northern temperate region, but by far the largest number of the cultivated species come from eastern Asia, especially China. When forms of the Chinese *R. × odorata* were introduced into Europe at the end of the eighteenth and the beginning of the nineteenth centuries, the repeat-flowering character they possessed was bred into their subsequent hybrids: this is why most modern roses flower throughout the summer. By choosing different species and cultivars with care, it is now possible to have roses in bloom from spring until the first frosts.

Roses work well with other climbers too, especially honeysuckle, clematis and jasmine. A combination of these is invaluable in creating a cottage garden style. Roses also look lovely in association with some of the shrubs which are often grown on walls, such as ceanothus, *Fremontodendron* or myrtle. Roses sometimes develop bare stems at the base and these can be hidden by planting perennials like penstemons, catmint (*Nepeta × faassenii*), peonies, lupins, or spurges like *Euphorbia griffithii* or *E. sikkimensis*, remembering to consider colour combinations and to choose perennials whose flowers complement the colour of the particular rose.

Although they are not in fact true climbers, with tendrils or twining stems,

roses climb by using their thorns to attach themselves to supports and are best regarded as scramblers, rather like brambles. In windy conditions the stems will be blown down unless they are tied carefully. The only scrambling roses which do not need tying are those grown into trees, whose branches and twigs usually give enough support to prevent the rose from falling.

Roses generally like a sunny position, although a few will tolerate semi-shade. Very few roses will bloom in permanent shade. However, they can be planted with their roots in the shade provided that their

(Left) Luxuriant climbers like 'New Dawn' are ideal for covering large pergolas.

(Below left) Climbing roses provide a fragrant walkway below an arch.

(Right) Roses and clematis make a classic companion planting. When chosen to flower at the same time, they are one of the most charming summer sights.

stems can grow into the sun. When planted against a wall they should be placed at least 30cm (12in) away from it; if planted too close, the roots will become very dry as the wall tends to keep the rain off. Many roses look wonderful grown on fences, pergolas and pillars and can also be attractive trained into a tree: plant on the side towards the prevailing wind so that the stems will be blown towards the tree rather than away from it.

Air circulation is important, especially for those roses which are prone to mildew. A plant grown in a hot, sheltered corner, bounded by walls, can transpire excessively through its leaves and become dehydrated. On the other hand, roses do not like to grow in draughty places such as the exposed wind tunnels between buildings – they may survive but will not produce many flowers.

Good drainage is essential as roses dislike waterlogged soils. The type of soil is not of prime importance, although roses grow best in a rich, well-balanced soil. They can be grown on sandy or clay soils too, as long as the latter are not really wet. It is untrue that roses will grow well only on clay soils – any average soil that has been well prepared with the addition of composts and mulches will suit them and only very extreme acidity and alkalinity is a problem.

There is no doubt that roses grow most happily in temperate latitudes. But man's love of the rose is very strong and one often sees attempts to grow roses in a subtropical climate. While it is not easy, it is possible, provided that suitable cultivars are chosen and a strict regime of spraying and fertilizing is adhered to. Generally, cultivars grafted onto a *R.* × *fortuniana* rootstock are the most successful (such as 'Sombreuil', 'Don Juan', 'Blossomtime', 'Royal Sunset' and 'Rosarium Ueteresen'). Those living in the subtropics should join their local rose society or consult books which give advice on the best methods of cultivation.

The directory of climbing roses on the following pages is divided into two main sections. In the first, some seventeen 'climbing' species are described, while the second part deals with a selection of hybrids and cultivars suitable for growing on walls, fences and a variety of garden structures.

PRUNING AND PROBLEMS

The pruning of roses depends primarily on the type of rose and its timing is a subject of much debate. Some gardeners insist that autumn is the time to prune, whereas others will not touch a bush before Christmas. The climbing groups covered here, however, need rather differing treatments. The species, the shrubs and the climbing miniatures need only as much pruning as is necessary to keep them within required limits, or else to remove dead, weak or diseased growth. This is best done after flowering (unless the plants produce ornamental hips which are wanted): in this case pruning can be postponed until late winter. Species

which are trained into trees are rarely pruned because of the difficulty of reaching the branches.

Rambler roses, with the exception of the few repeat-flowering cultivars, are also best pruned after flowering. Old or dead stems can be cut to ground level. The other groups – bourbon, noisette, climbing teas, kordesii and the large-flowered – should be pruned in late winter, to control their growth as well as to remove old or dead wood. A useful tip when removing long rose stems, is to cut them back little by little. If they are cut back to the required length all in one go, the young growths can be damaged as the old thorny stems are dragged out of the plant.

(Above) Roses over arches and pergolas make an interesting feature, but they need careful pruning and training to look good.

PESTS AND DISEASES

Roses are susceptible to a number of common pests and diseases including aphids, caterpillars, red spider mites, capsid bugs, scale insects, grey mould, powdery mildew and honey fungus; plants affected by any one of these ailments should be treated with a suitable proprietary remedy. In addition, the following conditions are specifically associated with roses.

Black spot is probably the most common fungal disease of roses and appears on the leaves as blackish-brown spots surrounded by yellowing tissue. Badly affected leaves fall early, and in a really bad attack the rose can lose all its leaves. The fungus overwinters on fallen leaves, so they must be collected and burnt. To control black spot, plants should be sprayed with a suitable fungicide every two weeks through the growing season. Black spot tends to be less prevalent in industrial areas; in rural districts it is best to choose roses which have resistance.

Rust is another fungus disease which manifests itself as orange patches on the stems and leaf stalks in spring and yellow spots on the upper sides of the leaves in summer, accompanied by orange spore-masses beneath the leaves. Badly affected plants must be burnt, and any fallen leaves should also be destroyed. A fungicide will help to control rust – consult a book or your local garden centre for advice on which fungicide is the best.

(Above) The soft pink rose 'Constance Spry' is one of a new generation of climbing shrub roses. It should be pruned in mid-winter.

Leaf-rolling sawfly is most likely to attack roses growing in sheltered positions. The sawfly is a small black insect which lays its eggs on rose leaves in early summer. The leaves then roll up tightly and the eggs hatch into green caterpillars which eat the rolled leaves. The attack can be controlled by removing and destroying the rolled leaves before the caterpillars hatch out, but if the infestation is more extensive than this, the plants should be sprayed with a suitable proprietary insecticide.

Rose leafhoppers are yellow or greyish insects about 3mm ($\frac{1}{6}$in) long which suck the sap of the rose, resulting in colourless spots and mottled areas. If the adults are disturbed they will leap off the leaves – hence their name. Climbing roses grown on sheltered walls are particularly prone to attack, and badly infested plants can lose all their leaves. Affected rose plants should always be treated with a proprietary systemic insecticide.

(Above) The double yellow-flowered species rose, *Rosa banksiae* 'Lutea', is slightly tender and requires a warm, sheltered corner if it is to flower in profusion. It is a magnificent sight in full flower.

SPECIES ROSES

Most rose species have thorny stems and the thorns or prickles may be large or small, straight or curved and they are sometimes mixed with bristles and hairs, especially on young growth. The leaves are alternate and pinnate, with toothed leaflets. The flowers are either borne singly or in branched clusters. They consist of 5 green sepals, 5 broad prominent petals, a large number of stamens and a cluster of short styles fused together. The flowers are often fragrant, although not always so. The fruit is the familiar rosehip which varies greatly in shape and size. They are usually either globose, pumpkin-shaped or urn-shaped and the colour varies from green to brown, red or black: in some roses they can be as ornamental as the flowers. Most cultivars have semi-double or double flowers in which the stamens are replaced by a profusion of petals.

R. arvensis

FIELD ROSE

A somewhat trailing or rambling shrub reaching 1–2m (3ft 3in–6½ft), or more against a wall. Leaflets 5–7, oval, often bluish-green beneath. Flowers white or sometimes pale pink, single, 2.5–5cm (1–2in) across, fragrant or not, solitary or several in small clusters; summer. Hips rounded to egg-shaped, dark red when ripe, 10–20mm (½–¾in) long. This species is valuable because it is completely shade-tolerant and therefore good for scrambling into trees or up a north-facing wall or fence.
Europe, Turkey
☼ ☽ ● -20°C (-5°F) ✃

R. banksiae

BANKSIAN ROSE, LADY BANKS' ROSE

A vigorous semi-evergreen attaining 12m (40ft). Stems slender, thornless or sparsely thorny. Leaflets 3–7, bright shiny green. Flowers white or yellow, single or double, 2.5–3cm (1–1¼in) across, fragrant, borne in dense clusters; late spring to early summer. This pretty rose exists in white- and yellow-flowered forms, single or double (the double yellow 'Lutea' is the most commonly grown). R. banksiae is rather tender and grows best on a sunny sheltered wall, requiring plenty of sun to ripen the wood. It grows especially well in areas with a Mediterranean climate. Even in the most favoured places Banksian roses take some time to settle down and do not flower freely during the first few years but it is an enchanting sight in full flower. Plants should be pruned carefully because they flower mostly on growths which are two or three years old. Annual pruning should be avoided, but every two or three years a few of the older stems can be cut out to encourage some new

Rosa banksiae 'Lutea'

replacement growth. R. banksiae was named in honour of Lady Banks, wife of Sir Joseph Banks (1743–1820), one time President of the Royal Society and first Director of the Royal Botanic Gardens, Kew. China (garden origin)
☼ -5°C (23°F) ✃

Var. banksiae ('Albo Plena'): flowers double, white, smelling of violets. ✔ **'Lutea'** YELLOW BANKSIAN ROSE: ♀ flowers double, clear yellow, similar to the type, although not as fragrant. This is the form most often seen in gardens, being slightly more hardy than the others and flowering more freely. **'Lutescens'**: flowers single, yellow, strongly fragrant. **Var. normalis**: flowers single, creamy-white; this is the wild form of the species.

R. beggeriana

A dense-growing bush 2–3m (6½–10ft) high eventually, with stems armed with hooked prickles which are usually in pairs. Leaves grey-green with 5–9 oval leaflets. Flowers white or sometimes pink,

single, 2.5–3cm (1–1¼in) across, usually in small clusters; summer. Hips globose, red turning purplish, 5–10mm (¼–½in) long. The flowers have an unpleasant scent but the attractive leaves smell of sweet briars. SW and central Asia
☼ -20°C (-5°F) ✿

✓ *R. bracteata*
MACARTNEY ROSE
An evergreen or semi-evergreen scrambling shrub with stout stems up to 6m (20ft), bearing paired prickles and covered with dense brownish down. Leaflets 5–11, shiny. Flowers white, single, 5–8cm (2–3¼in) across, with a fruity fragrance, usually solitary, each surrounded by the leaf-like bracts which give the plant its name; summer to autumn. Hips globose, orange-red, 2.5–3.8cm (1–1½in) long. *R. bracteata* is really hardy only in warmer areas of temperate latitudes – it grows well in the Mediterranean area. It is a lovely rose with a long flowering season and is said to be resistant to black spot. Like *R. laevigata*, it has become naturalized in the southeastern United States. The English name commemorates its introduction to Britain by Lord Macartney in 1793. *R. bracteata* is one of the parents of the beautiful and well-known 'Mermaid' rose. Some plants sold in nurseries as *R. bracteata* are misnamed and generally turn out to be *R. wichuraiana*.

SE China, Taiwan
☼ -5°C (23°F) ✿

R. brunonii
(*R. moschata* var. *napaulensis*)
HIMALAYAN MUSK ROSE
A rampant deciduous or semi-evergreen rose with stems up to 12m (40ft). Stems with hooked thorns. Leaflets 5–9, elliptic, grey-green. Flowers white, opening from pale yellow buds, single, very fragrant, 2.5–5cm (1–2in) across, borne in tight clusters up to 30cm (12in) across; summer. Hips up to 1.8cm (¾in) long, egg-shaped, red-brown. *R. brunonii* is reasonably hardy once established, but young plants or young shoots may be cut back by frost. However, it is a fine plant for a lofty south- or west facing wall or for scrambling up a suitable tree in a warm sheltered nook. The leaves have a characteristic rather drooping appearance. At the end of the last century

R.osa brunonii

R. brunonii was thought to be synonymous with *R. moschata*, and even now many plants sold as *R. moschata* turn out to be *R. brunonii*. Himalaya, SW China
☼ -5°C (23°F) ✿

'La Mortola': a very vigorous cultivar, raised at La Mortola in Italy, which is slightly more hardy that the species itself.

✓ *R. filipes*
A striking, vigorous shrubby climber, reaching 10m (33ft). Stems armed with hooked thorns. Leaflets 5–7, coppery when young. Flowers white, opening from cream buds, silky on the back of the petals, single, fragrant, 2–2.5cm (¾–1in) across, borne in enormous loose clusters of up to 100; summer. Hips scarlet, globose, 8–15mm (¼–½in) long. This is one of E.H. Wilson's introductions (1908) and a spectacular plant. *R. filipes* is an ideal plant to grow up through a large tree, as is *R. longicuspis*. They both take time to establish, usually forming a tangled mound below the tree before starting to climb. *R. filipes* is probably the slower, being apparently the least tolerant of shade, but it is well worth waiting for. These species are a wonderful sight when in flower, with their great cascades of white flowers. They are unsuitable for lower walls or fences because they grow too tall. W China, E Tibet
☼ ◗ -15°C (5°F) ✿

'Kiftsgate': ♛ a particularly vigorous cultivar which has

generally replaced the species in nursery catalogues. It produces even larger flower clusters.

R. × *fortuniana*
Possibly *R. banksiae* × *R. laevigata*. Similar to *R. banksiae* but with 3 or 5 leaflets and solitary, cream, double flowers, 5–10cm (2–4in) across; late spring to summer. This attractive rose needs a south-facing sunny wall. It does not produce many flowers in cooler latitudes: it does much better in warmer areas and is probably the best rootstock for roses grown in the subtropics. It was first introduced into cultivation in the West by Robert Fortune in 1850, and named after him. China (garden origin)
☼ -5°C (23°F) ✿

R. gigantea
(*R.* × *odorata* var. *gigantea*)
A vigorous deciduous or semi-evergreen rose with strong stems reaching up to 15m (50ft), or even 25m (82ft) in warmer latitudes. Leaflets 5–7, lance-shaped to oval. Flowers creamy-white, single, slightly fragrant, 8–14cm (3¼–5½in) across, solitary or 2 or 3 together; early summer. Hips globose to lemon-shaped, 20–25mm (¾–1in) long, yellowish or orange-red. Perhaps the most vigorous of all the species, it also has the largest flowers. It is not hardy in higher latitudes and may be killed in a cold winter. SW China, Burma, NE India
☼ 0°C (32°F) ✿

R. helenae

A vigorous, rambling species reaching 6m (20ft) or more, the strong stems armed with hooked thorns. Leaves with 7 or 9, lance-shaped or oval leaflets. Flowers white, single, 2–4cm (¼–1½in).across, in many-flowered, flat-topped clusters; summer. Hips egg-shaped, 1–1.5cm (½in) long, scarlet when ripe, in drooping clusters. This species is suitable for a tall wall or trellis, and looks particularly effective when left to scramble into a tree. It was introduced by E.H. Wilson in 1907 and named after his wife, Helen. Central and W China.

☼ -5ºC (23ºF) ❧

R. laevigata

CHEROKEE ROSE

A semi-evergreen, fairly vigorous climber, reaching 4.5m (15ft). Stems with numerous hooked prickles. Leaflets dark and glossy, usually 3, occasionally 5. Flowers white, single, 5–8cm (2–3¼in) across, solitary; early summer. Hips large and bristly, orange-red, 3.5–4cm (1¼–1½in) long. A beautiful rose, but rather tender and suitable only for milder regions, where it prefers a sunny sheltered position. It is widely naturalized in the southeastern USA; it is the state flower of Georgia. Any pruning should be carried out as soon as the plants cease flowering. Burma, S China

☼ -5ºC (23ºF) ❧

✓ **'Cooperi'** COOPER'S BURMA

ROSE: stems up to 12m (40ft). Leaflets glossy green. Flowers large, pure white, sometimes flushed with pink. A delightful rose, hardier than *R. laevigata* and thought to be a hybrid between it and *R. gigantea*. It is often listed in catalogues as *R. gigantea* 'Cooperi'.

✓ R. longicuspis

A handsome vigorous semi-evergreen rambler growing to 6m (20ft). Stems armed with hooked thorns. Leaflets dark glossy green, leathery, 5 or 7, lance-shaped to oval. Flowers white, opening from cream, long-pointed buds, single, smelling of bananas, 3–5cm (1¼–2in) across, the petals densely silky on the back, borne in loose clusters; mid to late summer. Hips egg-shaped, scarlet, 13–18mm (½–¾in) long. NE India, W China, E Tibet

☼ ● -15ºC (5ºF) ❧

Var. *sinowilsonii (R. sinowilsonii)*: differs in having rounded flower-buds and sepals which are not silky.

R. moschata

MUSK ROSE

A strong-growing, rather loose shrub up to 4m (13ft) tall. Stems with hooked prickles. Leaflets dark shiny green, 5 or 7, oval. Flowers white or cream, single, sweetly musk-scented, 3–5cm (1¼–2in) across, carried in loose clusters, the pointed petals quickly reflexing at the tip; late summer to autumn. Hips small, egg-shaped, orange-red. This lovely rose has today been

largely superseded by some of its hybrids. It is an ancestor of the modern Large-flowered (Hybrid Tea) group of roses. Himalaya, Iran; naturalized in the Mediterranean region

☼ -15ºC (5ºF) ❧

R. mulliganii ♈

A vigorous rambling shrub to 6m (20ft). Stems with wide-based reddish prickles. Leaflets 5 or 7, elliptic. Flowers white, single, fragrant, 4–5cm (1½–2in) across, in loose clusters; summer. Hips orange-red, egg-shaped, 1–1.3cm (½in) long. The young growth is prettily flushed with purple and plants usually flower profusely. It was one of the many introductions of the plant collector George Forrest, who found it on his 1917–19 Chinese expedition. W China

☼ -15ºC (5ºF) ❧

✓ R. multiflora

Stems long and arching, 3–5m (10–16ft), clothed in small prickles. Leaves with 7 or 9, obovate to lance-shaped leaflets, often downy beneath. Flowers white, occasionally pinkish, single, fragrant, 2–3cm (¼–1¼in) across, in many-flowered trusses; summer. Hips globose, bright red, 5mm(¼in) long. This rose is one of the most beautiful of all the species roses and one of the most vigorous in cultivatión. Propagation is made easy by the self-layering habit of branches that touch the soil. It has been widely planted

along highways in the United States and is frequently used as a stock on to which garden roses, especially ramblers, are grafted; many ramblers have it in their parentage. E Asia

☼ -15ºC (5ºF) ❧

'Carnea': flowers double, light pink. It is a rare plant in cultivation, although it was the first form of *R. multiflora* to be introduced to the West from China where it had long been cultivated. **Var.** *cathayensis*: flowers larger, 2–4cm (¼–1½in) across. **'Grevillei'** ('Platyphylla') SEVEN SISTERS ROSE: a very vigorous rose with larger leaves than the species, and flowers which vary in colour from white to pink, red or purplish. This cultivar needs a sheltered position as the new growth can be cut back by frost or winds. Its common name refers to an early description which recorded flowers of seven shades.

R. × odorata

TEA ROSE

The name covers a group of variable hybrids between *R. chinensis* and *R. gigantea*. They are more or less evergreen, reaching 3–6m (10–20ft) tall, or more under favourable conditions. Stems with scattered hooked prickles. Leaflets 5 or 7, oval. Flowers white, pink or yellow, single or double, 5–7.5cm (2–3in) across, solitary or several together; summer to early autumn. This tender group of rose needs the protection of sunny sheltered walls, except in subtropical regions. They require pruning in early spring, cutting out part of the old wood and weak growth to encourage strong new shoots. *R.* × *odorata* was of great historical importance in the development of modern garden roses. W China (garden origin)

☼ -5°C (23°F) ⅄⌀s

'Pseudindica' ('Fortune's Double Yellow'): a vigorous climber with semi-double pinkish-yellow flowers flushed with copper. Introduced to Europe by Robert Fortune in 1845.

R. setigera

PRAIRIE ROSE

A vigorous scrambling shrub with long slender stems reaching 4–5m (13–16ft), covered with straight prickles. Leaves deep green with 3 oval leaflets. Flowers deep rosy-pink fading to whitish, single, almost scentless, 5–6cm (2–2½in) across, in few flowered clusters; summer. Hips globose, red or brownish, 1cm (½in) long. Perhaps the finest North American wild rose, this species is a wonderful sight when left to scramble over a tree or trellis. One of its advantages is its late-flowering character. It is a parent of the famous rambler 'American Pillar', often seen in gardens. Central and eastern N America

☼ ◐ -15°C (5°F) ⌀

R. wichuraiana

A semi-evergreen shrub with trailing stems that can be trained to 6m (20ft). Leaves dark glossy green with 7 or 9 leaflets. Flowers white, single, 3–5cm (1¼–2in) across, borne in few-flowered clusters; mid to late summer. Hips red, egg-shaped 1–1.5cm (½in) long. This rose is more or less evergreen in milder districts. It is increasingly rare in our gardens, having been largely superseded by more flamboyant hybrids and selected cultivars, but is suitable for the larger garden and can be trained against a sunny wall or over a large tree stump. Shoots that rest on the ground often root, so propagation is easy. Its resistance to mildew has made it popular amongst rose breeders. It is a parent of a number of ramblers – 'Albéric Barbier', 'Dorothy Perkins' and 'Albertine' for instance. In the United States it is known as the Memorial Rose because it is often planted in cemeteries. E Asia

☼ -15°C (5°F) ⌀

GARDEN HYBRIDS AND CULTIVARS

RAMBLERS

These are strong-growing roses, mostly derived from *R. moschata*, *R. multiflora*, *R. sempervirens*, *R. wichuraiana*. Their supple stems are easy to train and the small flowers (less than 5cm/2in across) are carried in dense clusters. Most flower around midsummer; a few cultivars are repeat-flowering. The majority require sun.

Ramblers are excellent for growing on fences, trellises and arches, climbing into hedges or rambling into trees. They mix well with small-flowered clematis, like *C. viticella* and its cultivars, which are pruned to ground level in winter or early spring. The stems of ramblers can be pruned when they reach the height required. Because many are susceptible to mildew, growing them against a wall, where air circulation is often restricted, is not advisable, although cultivars such as 'Albertine' will succeed on an airy sunny wall.

Ramblers are best pruned immediately after flowering. Old, dead or diseased wood should be cut out and stems cut back close to ground level or to a strong young growth. This does not apply to the repeat-flowerers such as 'Albéric Barbier' which is should be pruned in winter.

Rosa 'Albéric Barbier'

'Adélaide d'Orléans'. ♛ Semi-evergreen to 5m (16ft). Flowers creamy-pink in bud, opening to whitish, loosely double, scented; summer.

'Aimée Vibert'. Grows to 5.5m (18ft). Flowers double, opening white from pink-tipped buds, in small clusters, faintly scented; midsummer to autumn. The longest-flowering rambler.

'Albéric Barbier'. ♛ Stems to 6m (20ft), practically evergreen in a favourable position. Flowers double, pale yellow fading to creamy-white, sweetly scented, flat and often quartered; summer, repeating at intervals until autumn.

✓ **'Albertine'**. ♛ A vigorous, thorny rose reaching 6m (20ft). Flowers loosely double, red in bud, opening coppery-pink, richly fragrant; midsummer.

'Alexandre Girault'. Stems up to 6m (20ft), with few thorns. Flowers double, carmine-red with a yellowish-salmon base, ageing to lilac-carmine, fragrant; midsummer.

'American Pillar'. A very vigorous rambler, sometimes growing to 7m (23ft) tall. Flowers single, carmine with a large white 'eye', borne in large clusters; midsummer with a few flowers later on. This popular rambler needs careful placing in the garden in relation to other colours, because its flowers are a strident shocking pink. Susceptible to mildew.

'Baltimore Belle'. The double flowers open from red buds and turn pale blush-pink fading to creamy-white; summer.

'Bloomfield Courage'. Stems to 6m (20ft) with almost no thorns. Flowers single, dark velvety red with a white centre and prominent yellow stamens; summer. A good rose for training up a pillar.

'Blush Rambler'. Stems almost thornless, reaching 3–4.5m (10–15ft). Flowers semi-double, pale pink, fragrant; mid- to late summer.

'Bobbie James'. ♥ Grows to 7.5m (24½ft), vigorous with attractive glossy green leaves. Flowers freely borne in large clusters, single or with a few extra petals, creamy-white; midsummer.

'Chevy Chase'. Stems to 4.5m (15ft). Flowers abundant, double, deep crimson-red, scarcely scented, in clusters of 10–35; summer. A disease-resistant rose.

✓ **'Crimson Shower'**. ♥ Stems 3–4.5m (10–15ft). Flowers semi-double, crimson, in large clusters; late summer to autumn. A popular rambler because it flowers late in the season and the colour does not fade, but it has no scent.

'Débutante'. Stems 2.5–4.5m (8–15ft). Flowers double, mid-pink, cupped at first but petals reflexing with age and quilled, slightly fragrant; summer. Similar to 'Dorothy Perkins' but unaffected by mildew.

'Dorothy Perkins'. Stems up to 5.5m (18ft). Flowers double, pink, in large and small clusters, almost scentless; late summer. One of the most commonly grown ramblers, popular since its introduction in the USA in 1901. Subject to mildew: best grown in an airy place such as a trellis or arch.

'Evangeline'. Up to 5.5m (18ft). Flowers single, bright pink, sweetly scented; summer.

✓ **'Félicité et Perpétue'**. ♥ An almost evergreen rambler, especially in mild winters, reaching 4.5m (15ft). Flowers double, white, stained with crimson in bud, delicately perfumed, borne in clusters; midsummer. An attractive rose

Rosa 'Dorothy Perkins'

which is both easy to grow and extremely hardy; it will succeed even when planted on a shady north-facing wall. 'Félicité et Perpétue' flowers most prolifically when left unpruned.

✓ **'Francis E. Lester'**. ♥ Stems to about 4.5m (15ft), with reddish young growth. Flowers single in clusters of up to 30, pink in bud, opening white with a fruity scent; midsummer. A hardy rambler which is not overly vigorous and is easily controlled.

'Goldfinch'. Stems almost thornless, reaching 4.5m (15ft). Flowers semi-double, yellow in bud, gradually changing to white as the flowers open, with dark yellow stamens and a fruity fragrance; mid- to late summer.

'Hiawatha' grows to 4.5–6m (15–20ft) tall. Flowers single, deep crimson with a white centre, scentless; late summer.

✓ **'Kew Rambler'**. Stems 4.5–5.5m (15–18ft) tall, bearing greyish-green leaves. Flowers single, pale pink with a white centre, fragrant; summer to early autumn. Effective when allowed to ramble in a tree.

'Lykkefund'. A thornless rambler to 6m (20ft) tall. Flowers semi-double, creamy-yellow tinged with salmon, fading with age; midsummer.

'Madame Alice Garnier'. Stems up to 3m (10ft) tall. Flowers double, bright pink with a yellow centre, flattening with age and fading to pale pink, quartered, sweetly scented; summer. Free-blooming.

✓ **'Paul Transon'**. ♛ Stems 3–4.5m (10–15ft) tall. Flowers double, coppery-orange in bud, opening salmon-orange, fading in turn to yellowish salmon-cream, fragrant, freely borne; summer with some later flowers.

✓ **'Paul's Himalayan Musk'**. ♛ A vigorous rose growing to 9m (30ft). Flowers small, double, lilac-pink, scented, borne on slender stems; midsummer. Delightful when rown up an old tree.

'Phyllis Bide'. ♛ Grows to 3.5m (11½ft) tall. Flowers double, yellow flushed salmon-pink, sweetly scented; summer to early autumn.

'Rambling Rector'. ♛ A very thorny rose growing to 6m (20ft). Flowers semi-double, cream fading to white, borne in large trusses, fragrant, very free-flowering; summer.

'Russelliana'. Stems densely thorny reaching 3–6m (10–20ft). Flowers small, double, magenta-crimson, fading to mauve, fragrant; midsummer.

✓ **'Sander's White Rambler'**. ♛ Stems almost thornless, reaching 5.5m (18ft). Flowers double, white, sweetly scented; late summer to early autumn. Attractive, closely related to 'Dorothy Perkins' but with white flowers and unaffected by mildew.

'Seagull'. ♛ Grows to 4.5m (15ft). Flowers single or semi-double, white with bright yellow stamens, borne in large clusters, scented; summer.

'Splendens' ('Ayrshire Splendens'). A vigorous rose 5–7.5m (16–24½ft) high. Flowers semi-double, cream, tinged with red along the petal margins, solitary or in small groups, smelling of myrrh; mid summer. Happy in a shady position, particularly if left to scramble into a tree.

'Tausendschön'. Stems 2.5–3m (8–10ft) with few

Rosa 'Francis E. Lester'

Rosa 'Sander's White Rambler'

thorns. Flowers double, deep rose-pink with a white centre, fading to mid-pink, carried in profuse clusters, slightly fragrant; summer.

✓ **'The Garland'**. ♛ Stems up to 4.5m (15ft), green with purplish thorns. Flowers semi-double, salmon in bud, opening cream, flat with quilled petals and a scent of oranges; midsummer.

'Trier'. Stems 2–3m (6½–10ft). Flowers semi-double, the petals creamy white with a yellow base and a pinkish tinge, very fragrant; summer.

'Veilchenblau'. ♛ Stems almost thornless, 3.5–4.5m (11½–15ft) tall. Flowers semi-double, violet with white streaks on the petals and a white centre, darkening later

Rosa 'Veilchenblau'

to maroon and then fading to lilac-grey, sweetly scented; early to midsummer. An early-flowering rambler. The flowers fade less if plants are grown in partial, but not full, shade.

✓ **'Wedding Day'**. A very vigorous rambler attaining 11.5m (38ft). Flowers single, yellow in bud, opening to creamy-white with orange stamens and rather pointed petals; scent reminiscent of oranges; summer. A fine rambler for a high wall or tree, it is somewhat tender and needs a sheltered south-facing aspect. The flowers are long-lasting but the petals are prone to blemishing with pink spots after rain.

LARGE-FLOWERED CLIMBERS

These roses have stems which are stiffer than those of the ramblers and they produce larger flowers (usually more than 5cm–2in across). The flowers can be borne singly or in loose clusters. This group includes climbing 'large-flowered' roses (formerly known as hybrid tea roses) and climbing 'cluster-flowered' roses (formerly called floribundas). Many of these have the advantage of being continuous or repeat-flowerers so that blooms are produced from summer right through to autumn – or even Christmas in a mild winter.

Pruning is best done in late winter, to shorten back and control strong healthy growth and to establish a framework on which the flowers will be borne, as well as to remove excess, dead or diseased wood. However, excessive pruning will result in less flowers, produced later than normal. Having said that, old specimens sometimes require severe pruning to renovate the plant by encouraging new basal growth.

For convenience the following cultivars are divided into groups according to their colour.

(*r*) = repeat flowering.
(*nr*) = non-repeat, or once-flowering.

WHITE OR CREAM

✓ **'City of York'**. (*r*) A vigorous rose growing to 2.5m (8ft) with semi-double, creamy-white, fragrant flowers, borne in clusters of 7–15.

'Climbing Mrs. Herbert Stevens'. (*r*) Flowers double, white tinged with lemon or pale green, fragrant. A vigorous rose growing to 6m (20ft) tall, performing well even on poor soils. A disadvantage is that its flowers tend to suffer in extreme wet weather.

'Swan Lake'. (*r*) Stems 2.5–3m (8–10ft) tall. Flowers double, white tinged with pink in the centre, fragrant. The flowers stand up well to wet weather but plants need protecting from black spot by regular spraying with a suitable fungicide.

'White Cockade'. (*r*) ♇ Grows to 2.5m (8ft) tall. Flowers double, white, slightly fragrant. Free-flowering.

YELLOW

✓ **'Casino'**. (*r*) Grows 2.5–3m (8–10ft) tall. Flowers double, soft yellow, fragrant. A free-flowering and disease-resistant cultivar.

✓ **'Easlea's Golden Rambler'**. (*r*) Stems 4m (13ft). Flowers double, yellow with red marks on the outer petals, sweetly

Rosa 'Gloire de Dijon'

Rosa 'Guinée'

fragrant. Often classified as a rambler in catalogues and, despite its non-repeat status, a few flowers are usually produced late in the season.

✓ **'Compassion'**. (*r*) ♛ Grows to 2.5–3m (8–10ft). Flowers double, pale salmon, shaded orange, very fragrant.

✓ **'Meg'**. (*r*) Stems 3–4m (10–13ft). Flowers almost single, salmon-apricot with red-gold stamens, fragrant.

✓ **'Schoolgirl'**. (*r*) Stems 3–4.5m (10–15ft) tall. Flowers double, orange-apricot with a pinkish reverse, fragrant. A good cultivar in cooler regions where the colour will fade less than in warmer areas.

SCARLET OR CRIMSON

'Altissimo'. (*r*) ♛ Stems 3–4.5m (10–15ft) tall. Flowers single, blood-red, slightly clove-scented. The flowers are not adversely affected by either sun or rain.

'Blaze'. (*r*) Stems to 4.5m (15ft). Flowers semi-double, bright scarlet fading to a bluish tone, slightly fragrant, carried in large clusters. Does not generally flower in the first year, but then blooms profusely.

'Climbing Crimson Glory'. (*r*) Grows 3.5m (11½ft) tall. Flowers double, deep velvety

crimson, very fragrant. In strong sunlight the flowers turn purplish.

✓ **'Climbing Ena Harkness'**. (*r*) Grows 2.5–3.5m (8–11½ft) tall. Flowers double, crimson-scarlet, moderately scented.

'Climbing Etoile de Hollande'. (*r*) ♛ Stems 4–6m (13–20ft) tall. Flowers double, dark red, very fragrant.

✓ **'Danse du Feu'** ('Spectacular'). (*r*) Stems 2.5–3m (8–10ft) tall. Flowers double or semi-double, fiery scarlet, fragrant. A free-lowering rose which will grow well on a north-facing wall.

'Guinée'. (*nr*) but a few blooms later. Reaches 3–6m (10–20ft) tall with double, dark red-maroon flowers, fragrant.

✓ **'Red Fountain'**. (*r*) Very vigorous. Flowers double, velvety scarlet, very fragrant, opening from a pointed bud. A profuse flowerer and disease-resistant.

scented. In catalogues this is often listed as a rambler.

'Emily Gray'. (*nr*) A semi-evergreen, vigorous rose to 6m (20ft). Flowers double, buff-yellow, fragrant. Often slow to establish, but it is worth waiting for the freely produced flowers. Sometimes put with the rambler roses in catalogues.

'Gloire de Dijon'. (*r*) ♛ Grows to 5.5m (18ft) with large double, buff-yellow flowers suffused with pink and apricot, fragrant. Will grow in sunny or shady aspects.

✓ **'Golden Showers'**. (*r*) ♛ Stems only 2.5–3m (8–10ft)

tall. Flowers semi-double, daffodil-yellow, fading to cream, fragrant. A profuse bloomer, weather-resistant and suitable even for a north-facing wall.

'Royal Gold'. (*r*) Stems 2.5–3m (8–10ft) tall. Flowers double, golden-yellow, fragrant. This rose does best on a south- or west-facing wall.

ORANGE, APRICOT OR COPPER

'Auguste Gervais'. (*nr*) Stems up to 6m (20ft). Flowers semi-double, pale apricot with a coppery-salmon reverse, borne in large clusters,

'Souvenir de Claudius Denoyel'. (*r*) ♀ Stems up to 5.5m (18ft). Flowers double, rich crimson, very fragrant; do not fade in strong sunshine.

'Thor'. (*nr*) Stems 3.5–4.5m (11½–15ft). Flowers double, crimson, 10–12.5cm (4–5in) across, slightly fragrant. A hardy rose, suitable for colder areas.

PINK

✓ **'Aloha'**. (*r*) Stems 2.5–3m (8–10ft) tall. Flowers double, pink suffused with orange in the centre when young, fragrant. Will flower on a north-facing wall.

'Bantry Bay'. (*r*) Stems up to 3m (10ft). Flowers semi-double, pale pink, tinged with salmon, only slightly scented.

'Christine Wright'. (*nr*) although there may be a few blooms in the autumn. Stems 3.5–4.5m (11½–15ft). Flowers semi-double, a beautiful pale pink. Early blooming.

'Climbing Madame Butterfly'. (*r*) Reaches 3–6m (10–20ft) tall. Flowers double, pale pink, tinged with yellowish, very fragrant.

✓ **'Climbing Shot Silk'**. (*r*) ♀ Grows 2.5–3.5m (8–11½ft) tall. Flowers double, cherry-pink, yellow at the base, very fragrant.

Rosa 'Aloha'

'Cupid'. (*nr*) Grows to 4.5m (15ft). Flowers single, flesh-pink, with pretty crinkly petals. The flowers are followed by large orange hips which persist into the winter.

'Dream Girl'. (*r*) ♀ Stems to 4m (13ft). Flowers double, salmon-pink overlaid with apricot, with a spicy fragrance. This rose may take 2–4 years to develop a climbing habit.

'Dr. W. van Fleet'. (*nr*) Reaches 3.5–6m (11½–20ft). Flowers double, soft pink, fading with age, fragrant.

'Inspiration'. (*r*) Stems up to 2.5m (8ft). Flowers semi-double, pink becoming paler towards the centre, fragrant. Disease-resistant.

'Madame Grégoire Staechelin'. (*nr*) ♀ Grows to 6m (20ft). Flowers semi-double, pink with darker reverse, fragrant. An early flowerer, producing blooms on a north-facing wall.

'Morning Jewel'. (*r*) ♀ Reaches only 3m (10ft). Flowers semi-double, pink, fragrant. A free-flowering cultivar.

✓ **'New Dawn'**. (*r*) Stems 4.5–6m (15–20ft) tall. Flowers double, silvery-pink, slightly fragrant. This rose is a sport of 'Dr. W. van Fleet'. The flowers withstand rain well.

✓ **'Parade'**. (*r*) ♀ Stems to 2.5m (8ft). Flowers double, deep rose-pink, fragrant. A free-blooming rose which will tolerate a north aspect.

Rosa 'New Dawn'

'Pink Perpétue'. (*r*) Stems to 2.5–3.5m (8–11½ft). Flowers double, bright pink, deeper on the reverse, fragrant.

BI- OR MULTI-COLOURED

'Climbing Masquerade'. (*nr*) but with a few flowers in late summer. Stems to 6m (20ft) tall. Flowers semi-double, yellow in bud opening bright yellow, changing to salmon-pink and later dark red, slightly fragrant, borne in large clusters. A well-known, though somewhat gaudy, rose.

'Climbing Peace'. (*r*) A strong grower reaching 6m (20ft) tall. Flowers large, double, golden-yellow, the petals edged with pale pink, slightly fragrant. A very fine rose which is a shy flowerer until well established.

✓ **'Handel'**. (*r*) ♀ Stems 2.5–3.5m (8–11½ft). Flowers double, cream, the petals edged with deep pink, slightly fragrant. The flowers withstand rain well.

Rosa 'Handel'

'Joseph's Coat'. (*r*) Grows to 3m (10ft). Flowers double, yellow and orange, the petals edged with cherry-red.

CLIMBING TEA

A rather tender group of repeat-flowering roses which grow best in warmer areas and need a sunny position. Their soft wood is susceptible to frost damage, so pruning (to cut out weak, diseased or frost-damaged growth) should be delayed for as long as possible. The climbing tea roses grow best on a rich loamy soil, which ensures a good crop of flowers. Flowers are produced from midsummer until the autumn.

'Climbing Devonensis'. (*r*) Stems to 3.5m (11½ft) tall. Flowers double, the buds tinged with deep pink but opening cream, often pinkish-apricot in the centre, fragrant.

✓ **'Climbing Lady Hillingdon'**. (*r*) ♥ A vigorous rose to 6m (20ft) tall. Flowers nodding, semi-double, apricot-yellow, fragrant. This cultivar will bloom even on rather poor soils.

✓ **'Marie van Houtte'**. (*r*) Stems only 2m (6½ft) high. Flowers double, the petals deep pink tinged with cream towards the edge, fragrant.

'Sombreuil'. (*r*) Grows 4–6m (13–20ft) tall. Flowers large, double but rather flat, creamy-

white tinged with pink in the centre, quartered, with quilled petals, fragrant.

NOISETTE

A group of shrubby, mainly repeat-flowering roses originating from a cross between *R. moschata* and a pink form of *R. × odorata*. The early cultivars in this group bore whitish or pink flowers, but yellow was later introduced into the group by further crosses with a yellow form of *R. × odorata*. Noisette roses are best pruned in late winter. Pruning should be limited to removing old, weak or diseased growths or to shortening back excessively long shoots. The majority are not completely hardy and thrive best on a sunny sheltered south- or west-facing wall.

✓ **'Alister Stella Gray'**. (*r*) ♥ Grows up to 4m (13ft) against a wall. Long-pointed buds open to yellow flowers with orange centres, sweetly scented. A very fine noisette blooming freely from midsummer to autumn.

✓ **'Blush Noisette'**. (*r*) Stems 3–5m (10–16ft), almost thornless. Flowers almost double, deep pink fading with age to lilac-pink, clove-scented, borne in small or large clusters. A well-known old cultivar with good disease resistance.

Rosa 'Claire Jacquier'

'Céline Forestier'. (*r*) ♥ Less vigorous than the previous two cultivars, rarely exceeding 3m (10ft) in height. Flowers double, pale yellow becoming whitish towards the margin, quartered, fragrant. This is a slightly tender rose which requires a warm, sunny wall. It often takes time to become established but, once it is settled, it usually flowers freely.

'Claire Jacquier'. (*nr*) Similar to 'Alister Stella Gray' but much more vigorous, attaining as much as 9m (30ft). Flowers double, yellow, scented, fading somewhat with age. Flowers produced mainly in summer, with a few appearing later.

'Desprez à Fleur Jaune' ('Jaune Desprez'). (*r*) Grows to 5.5m (18ft). Flowers double, rather flat, very pale yellowish shaded peach, with a powerful scent, borne in clusters. An historic hybrid (probably the earliest yellow climbing rose to be produced) formed when 'Blush Noisette' was crossed with 'Park's Yellow Tea-scented China'. Needs a sunny, sheltered position.

✓ **'Madame Alfred Carrière'**. (*r*) ♀ A vigorous rose 6–7.5m (20–24½ft) tall. Flowers globular, creamy pink fading to whitish, fragrant, often with a quartered centre, borne singly or in small clusters. This rose will flower successfully on a north-facing wall.

'Maréchal Niel'. (*nr*) but with a few flowers later. Stems 3–4m (10–13ft). Flowers double, large (10–12cm (4–5in) across), clear yellow, quartered, richly fragrant, nodding on rather weak stems. It is slightly tender and requires the protection of a sunny south-facing wall.

'Reve d'Or'. (*r*) A vigorous rose up to 6m (20ft) tall. Flowers double or semi-double, buff-yellow fading with age, fragrant. A rose for a warm, sheltered niche.

BOURBON

A rather mixed group of roses derived from a cross made in 1817 between the Autumn Damask Rose (*R.× bifera*) and a pink form of *R.× odorata*, made on the island of Réunion, then known as the Ile de Bourbon.

'Blairii Number Two'. ♀ A vigorous climber up to 4.5m (15ft) tall, with young leaves the colour of mahogany. Flowers double, pale pink, deeper in the centre, sweetly fragrant; early to midsummer.

'Climbing Souvenir de la Malmaison'. Stems 3–4.5m (10–13ft) tall. Flowers large, double, creamy-pink, flat and quartered, fragrant; early to midsummer with a few later blooms in autumn. Suitable for sunny or shady walls. Plants can be pruned after the first crop of flowers, if desired.

'Coupe d'Hébé'. (*r*) Flowers very double, deep pink, fragrant; early summer. A useful rose for training up a pillar or along a fence.

'Paul Ricaut'. (*nr*) Flowers very double, mauve-pink, quartered, fragrant, heavy.

Rosa 'Zéphirine Drouhin'

✓ **'Zéphirine Drouhin'**. (*r*) ♀ Stems thornless, 1.5–4.5m (5–15ft) tall bearing brownish-purple young leaves. Flowers semi-double, cerise-pink, fading with age, solitary or in small clusters, fragrant; early summer to autumn. A lovely rose that is widely grown: it is completely thornless. **'Kathleen Harrop'** is a shell-pink sport, less vigorous but well worth growing.

KORDESII HYBRIDS

'Rosa kordesii' was raised by the German breeder Wilhelm Kordes from a hybrid between *R. rugosa* and *R. wichuraiana* called 'Max Graf'. This hybrid is normally sterile, but a chance seedling was found to be fertile and given the name *'R. kordesii'*. This plant was then used in a breeding programme which resulted in the Kordesii hybrids. These roses bear their flowers in clusters and are repeat-flowering. The glossy foliage is disease-resistant. Best pruned in late winter.

✓ **'Dortmund'**. Stems up to 3m (10ft). Flowers single, bright crimson-red with a white eye, borne in large clusters. A fine free-flowering rose for a pillar or trellis; it does equally well on a wall.

'Goldbusch'. Stems to 3.7m (12ft). Flowers semi-double, yellow, becoming paler as they age, with a light fragrance, in clusters of up to 20. Leaves are scented when crushed.

'Hamburger Phoenix'. Reaches 2.5–3m (8–10ft) tall. Flowers semi-double, rich crimson, slightly fragrant. Repeat-flowering depends on the hips from the first flowering being removed.

'John Cabot'. Stems to 3.7m (12ft). Flowers double, cherry-red, fragrant. Often takes 3 or 4 years to climb.

✓ **'Leverkusen'**. Stems 2.5–3m (8–10ft) tall. Flowers double, pale yellow with a lemon fragrance.

✓ **'Morgengruss'**. A fairly vigorous reaching 4m (13ft) high. Flowers double, pale pink suffused with yellow, scented, profusely borne.

✓ **'Parkdirektor Riggers'**. Stems strong, up to 4m (13ft) tall. Flowers semi-double, velvety crimson, borne in large clusters, scarcely scented.

'Sympathie'. Stems up to 3.5m (11½ft). Flowers double, dark velvety red, fragrant.

SHRUBS

A rather mixed group of roses, considered together here for convenience and containing all those roses not covered in the previous groupings. They are best pruned in late winter.

Rosa 'Lawrence Johnston'

✓ **'Anemone'.**
('Anemonoides', *R.×
anemonoides*). A vigorous
climber to 4m (13ft) tall.
Flowers single, pale pink with
deeper pink veins, 8–10cm
(3¼–4in) across, fragrant; late
spring to midsummer. Thought
to be an hybrid between *R.
laevigata* and a Tea rose. In most
areas it requires a warm sunny
wall, where it will continue to
flower for several weeks.

'Climbing Cécile Brunner'. ♕
A strong rose climbing to
about 6m (20ft). Flowers
double, clear pink, fragrant;
late spring to early autumn.

Rosa 'Complicata'

✓ **'Complicata'.** ♕ A beautiful
shrub with arching stems up to
3m (10ft) long. Flowers single,
pink, paler in the centre and
with golden stamens, 10–12cm
(4–5in) across, fragrant;
midsummer. Thought to be an
hybrid of *R. gallica* or *R.
macrantha*. Especially pretty
when trained into a tree or
over a trellis.

✓ **'Constance Spry'.** ♕ A
shrubby rose reaching 2m
(6½ft) against a wall. Flowers
globular, soft pink, 7.5–12cm
(3–5in) across, smelling of
myrrh, borne singly or a few
together on stems produced
the previous year; midsummer.

'Gruss an Teplitz'. (*r*) Grows
to 2m (6½ft). Flowers double,
crimson, in small clusters,
fragrant.

✓ **'Lawrence Johnston'.** (*r*)
A vigorous climber reaching as
much as 9m (30ft) tall. Flowers
semi-double, canary-yellow,
fragrant; early summer and
intermittently into autumn.

'Maigold'. (*r*) ♕ An extremely
prickly rose growing to 3.5m
(11½ft), with glossy leaves.
Flowers semi-double, reddish-
orange in bud opening bronze-
yellow, very fragrant.

✓ **'Mermaid'.** (*r*) ♕ A
vigorous rose to 6m (20ft) tall,
the stems with large hooked
thorns. Leaves almost
evergreen, glossy. Flowers
single, clear yellow with
orange stamens which persist
after the petals have fallen,
9–10cm (3½–4in) across,
fragrant; summer to autumn.
This beautiful and well-known
rose is a cross between *R.
bracteata* and a yellow Tea rose.
It is not very hardy so it is best
grown on a sunny sheltered
west- or south-facing wall: it
does well in Mediterranean
regions. Older plants develop
thick woody stems and greatly
resent harsh pruning; pruning
should therefore be limited to
the removal of dead or diseased
wood or shortening back a few
stems to encourage new shoots.

'Ramona'. (*nr*) Stems 4–5m
(13–16ft). Flowers single,
crimson, paler on the reverse,
8–10cm (3¼–4in) across;
summer. A sport of 'Anemone'.

✓ **'Souvenir du Docteur
Jamain'.** (*r*) This cultivar will
reach 3m (10ft) on a suitable
wall. The large double flowers
are plum-coloured shaded with
crimson; fragrant; midsummer
and again in autumn. Avoid a
south-facing wall as too much
sun turns the flowers brownish.
Plants appreciate a rich soil.

✓ **'William Lobb'.** (*nr*) ♕
Grows to 2.5m (8ft) against a
wall. The flowers are dark
crimson-purple, the petals
with a lighter pink reverse and
tending to fade to a greyish
colour with age; semi-double
with a 'muddled' centre,
fragrant; midsummer. This
lovely moss rose can be grown
as a free-standing shrub but is
beautiful against a wall. The
'mossy' outgrowths of calyx
and flower stalks are pale green.

Rosa 'Souvenir du Docteur Jamain'

Annual and Herbaceous Climbers

Introduction

This group of climbers differs from all the others in this book, except a few of the herbaceous clematis, in that they are not permanent: they die down at the end of the season. These plants are either annuals, which have to be regrown from seed each season, or herbaceous perennials which die down to a rootstock from which fresh shoots grow each year, the shoots in effect behaving as annuals. Because of this they are ideal for less permanent sites in the garden or for temporary cover. At the same time many of them mix well with more permanent climbers and wall shrubs.

Annual and herbaceous climbers are excellent for clothing temporary screens or trellises, or for walls and fences where a permanent cover is undesirable, including walls which need to be painted regularly

and wooden fences that may need treating with wood preservatives. However, it is wise to point out that many preservatives will harm plants if they seep into the soil.

(Above) Herbaceous climbers like this golden hop make quick and effective cover for fences and walls.

(Left) Tropaeolum speciosum is ideal in a cool, moist climate and visually rewarding with its spectacular display of flowers and contrasting fruit.

Most of the climbers mentioned in this section require only a lightweight support. Strong pea sticks, canes or strings may be quite sufficient and these can be removed

at the end of the season. Annual species are useful for masking the lower half of other wall plants or for temporarily filling in gaps, such as where a wall shrub has been removed. Away from the wall or fence, clusters of sticks or a tripod of canes of a suitable height will prove useful temporary supports.

Many of these climbers are readily grown from seed and most are best planted out in the spring, provided you protect the less hardy species from frosts or cold winds at first. Diligent collection of seeds each year will ensure future generations of these rewarding plants, which flower so quickly from seed. All the frost-tender species described in this chapter are excellent for growing in conservatories in temperate climates; a symbol indicates their suitability for this type of culture.

(Above left) The popular everlasting pea (here, *Lathyrus latifolius* 'Albus') is one of the hardiest and easiest of herbaceous climbers.

(Above right) *Cobaea scandens* fascinates with its subtle changes in flower colour.

(Right) The use of pea sticks or canes against a wall allow annual climbers such as the sweet pea easy access for quick growing.

ABOBRA
(Cucurbitaceae)

There is only one species in this genus which, although perennial, is not frost-hardy and is best treated as a half-hardy annual in temperate gardens. Although the flowers are rather insignificant, the foliage is handsome and the red fruits appealing, especially when produced in quantity. Plants raised under glass from seed should be planted outside in early summer. In frosty areas the tuberous roots may be lifted in the autumn and stored in a frost-free place until the following season. Like most members of the family the flowers are either male or female and are borne on separate plants.

✓ ▦ *A. tenuifolia*

To 3–4m (10–13ft), climbing with forked tendrils. Leaves alternate, glossy green, broadly oval with 3 or 5 deep lobes, each cut into narrow segments. Flowers scented, pale green, 5-lobed, hairy inside; male flowers in racemes with 3 stamens, female usually solitary; mid- to late summer. Fruits egg-shaped, berry-like, to 12.5mm (½in), bright red when ripe. Temperate South America
☀ 0°C (32°F) ✿

ACONITUM
(Ranunculaceae)

A genus of about 60 species which contain the well-known

Aconitum hemsleyanum

monkshoods and wolfsbanes, a few of which have climbing stems. They are tuberous perennials native to the temperate northern hemisphere including the Himalaya. The climbing species have attractive neatly dissected leaves and racemes of hooded flowers, produced mainly in late summer and autumn. The fruit consists of 3 or 5 follicles, similar to those of *Delphinium* and *Aquilegia*.

Plants are easily grown in most garden soils and can be increased by division or by seed sown as soon as it is ripe. All the species are poisonous, containing either the alkaloid aconitine or pseudaconitine.

✓ *A. hemsleyanum*
(*A. volubile* of hort.)
Stems slender, twining to 5m (16ft), often less. Leaves deep shiny green, with 5 or 7 segments, each wedge-shaped or lance-shaped and further lobed and toothed. Flowers violet-blue, 3–3.8cm

(1¼–1½in) long, borne in loose, rather drooping racemes; late summer and autumn. Central and W China
☀ -30°C (-22°F) ✿

The recently introduced *A. epsicopale* from western China is similar but with paler flowers. Both species look excellent when trained up pillars or a pergola.

ASPARAGUS
(Liliaceae)

A familiar genus grown for its foliage and edible young stems. The small, 6-parted flowers are followed by colourful berries on female plants.

▦ *A. scandens*

Stems herbaceous, smooth or slightly ridged, to 2.5m (8ft). Leaves scarcely projecting. Leaf-like cladophylls flat, narrowly lance-shaped, in whorls of 2 or 3. Flowers usually solitary. Berry red, containing 1 seed. South Africa
☀ 10°C (50°F) ✿

BENINCASA
(Cucurbitaceae)

There is only one species in this genus – an annual which bears such huge fruits that it is often grown as a ground cover. If cultivated as a climbing plant, care must be taken to support the fruit, which can be boiled as a vegetable, or pickled or candied. It can be grown in temperate gardens in

a hot, sheltered place. For cultivation, see *Cucurbita* (*page 128*). Propagation is by seed.

B. hispida
WAX GOURD, CHINESE WATER MELON
Annual with downy stems, climbing by branched tendrils. Leaves palmately 5–7-lobed, 10–25cm (4–10in) long. Yellow flowers solitary in leaf axils, saucer-shaped to bell-shaped, 5-lobed; stamens 3. Fleshy fruit very large, globose to oblong, at first hairy but becoming hairless and waxy. Very fast-growing. Tropical SE Asia; widely cultivated in the Old World tropics
☀ 10°C (50°F) ✿

BOMAREA
(Alstroemeriaceae)

A genus of over 100 South American species of perennials with tuberous roots. *Bomarea* differs from the better known genus *Alstroemeria* in its climbing habit. The plants are herbaceous, climbing by twining stems which bear usually lance-shaped leaves and terminal clusters of flowers. The flowers are usually narrowly bell-shaped and often beautifully marked.

A fertile sandy soil suits bomareas best, with plenty of water when the plants are in growth. If grown in pots, canes should be provided for support. Propagation is by seed or division of the roots.

⊞ *B. caldasii* ♀

(*B. caldasiana, B. kalbreyeri*)
Stem up to 4m (13ft). Leaves
up to 15cm (6in). Flowers in an
umbel of 20–60, the outer
segments 2–2.5cm ($\frac{3}{4}$–1in)
long, reddish-orange to
brownish, inner segments
2.5–3.5cm (1–1$\frac{1}{2}$in) long,
yellow or orange, sometimes
spotted; summer. Northern S
America
☼ ◑ 0°C (32°F) ✿

⊞ *B. multiflora*

Stems up to 3m (10ft). Leaves
up to 10cm (4in). Flowers in an
umbel of 20–40, all segments
about 2.5cm (1in) long, outer
reddish, inner orange with
brown spots; late summer.
Northern S America
◑ 0°C (32°F) ✿

BOWIEA
(Liliaceae)

An unusual genus containing 3
species with herbaceous
twining stems growing from a
large, globose bulb; the leaves
are small and short-lived. The
flowers are 6-parted and borne
in terminal racemes.
Propagation is by seed and
offsets.

One species is cultivated
both in the tropics and in
temperate gardens, where a
sunny place beneath a wall
should be provided – and
winter protection given. It is a
plant grown more for its
curiousity than for its beauty.
The soil should be light and
well-drained.

⊞ *B. volubilis*

CLIMBING ONION
Plant with a shiny green bulb,
growing mainly above soil level
and becoming very large (to
20cm/8 in across) when
mature. Stems twining to
3–4m (10–13ft); lower shoots
much branched and flowerless,
upper shoots little branched
and bearing flowers. Leaves
short, linear, soon falling,
leaving the stems bare. Flowers
greenish-white or yellowish,
1–1.5cm ($\frac{1}{2}$in) across;
summer to autumn. Fruit
green, globose, containing
many seeds.

In temperate areas the bulbs
should be half or fully buried
and kept dry until growth is
seen to begin. In the autumn,
as the stems begin to die back,
water should be gradually
withheld. In areas prone to
frost it may be best to lift the
bulbs and store them over
winter in a dry, frostproof
place. South Africa
☼ 0°C (32°F) ✿

CALYSTEGIA
(Convolvulaceae)

The giant bindweeds are
familiar enough plants with
their large and fleeting funnel-
shaped flowers that open by
day and have withered by the
late afternoon. Although they
can become aggressive weeds,
the heart-shaped foliage and
attractive flowers, produced
over a long season, always
attract attention. Though not a
plant for the refined flower

border, it is certainly an
effective one for the wild
garden or for covering wire or
chain link fences.

This genus of mostly
rampant twinning perennials
with heart- or arrow-shaped
leaves have a far-ranging
stoloniferous rootstock and
can prove invasive. They are
easily propagated, either by
division of the rootstock, or
from seed.

C. hederacea

(*C. japonica*)
To 5m (16ft). Leaves narrowly
arrow-shaped, to 10cm (4in)
across. Flowers borne on
winged stalks, rose-pink,
3–4cm (1$\frac{1}{4}$–1$\frac{1}{2}$in) long,
solitary; summer to autumn.
E Asia
☼ -25°C (-13°F) ✿
   'Flore Pleno': flowers pink,
   double; this is the common form,
   seen in cultivation, which is
   sterile.

C. macrostegia

To 4m (13ft), often less; stems
rather woody at the base.
Leaves triangular to arrow-
shaped, slightly fleshy and
hairy. Flowers mostly solitary,
white changing to pale pink,
5–6cm (2–2$\frac{1}{2}$in) across;
summer to early autumn.
USA (California including
coastal islands)
☼ -10°C (14°F) ✿

C. sepium

BINDWEED, WILD MORNING
GLORY
To 4m (13ft). Leaves arrow-
shaped to heart-shaped,

5–10cm (2–4in) long. Flowers
solitary, white, 5–7.5cm
(2–3in) long; calyx not
concealed by bract pair;
summer to autumn.
Europe
☼ -30°C (-22°F) ✿
   subsp. *spectabilis*: has a rounded,
   not triangular, gap at the leaf base
   and pink flowers.
   Russia (Siberia)

C. silvatica

Similar to *C. sepium* but calyx
concealed by bract pairs and
flowers rather larger, white
and sometimes banded pale
pink on the outside; summer to
autumn. S Europe, N Africa
☼ -30°C (-22°F) ✿

C. tuguriorum

Stems slender to 2.5m (8ft).
Leaves heart-shaped, 1–4cm
($\frac{1}{2}$–1$\frac{1}{2}$in) long. Flowers
solitary, white or pink,
2.5–5cm (1–2in) across;
summer to autumn. New
Zealand, S Chile
☼ -25°C (-13°F) ✿

CANARINA
(Campanulaceae)

A genus of 3 tuberous,
herbaceous perennials with
flowers similar to those of the
bellflowers (*Campanula*)
except that they have 6 rather
than 5 corolla-lobes and the
fruit is a berry, not a capsule.
They climb by curling their
leaf stalks round a support.
Propagation is by seed or basal
cuttings, or the plants may be
divided.

Canarina eminii

⊞ *C. canariensis* ♀
CANARY BELLFLOWER
Stems semi-scandent to 2m
(6½ft). Leaves opposite,
narrowly oval to linear, toothed.
Flowers 2.5–5cm (1–2in)
long, hanging from the tips of
side branches, bell-shaped with
spreading to recurved lobes,
orange with red-brown veins;
autumn to early spring. This
species needs a fertile soil with
water during the growing
season; when the stems die
down after flowering, much
less water is needed. In
temperate regions, it makes an
unusual conservatory plant and
can be planted out of doors in a
warm position during the
summer. Canary Islands
☼ ☀ 7°C (45°F) ✿

⊞ *C. eminii*
Smilar to *C. canariensis*,
perhaps even more beautiful,
but the stems are not quite as
tall. Flowers 7.5cm (3in) long,
solitary, lateral, orange with
red veins. Rare in cultivation.
E Africa
☀ 13°C (55°F) ✿

CAYRATIA
(Vitaceae)

A genus of 16 or so species of
climbing, rather shrubby vines
which are grown primarily for
their luxuriant foliage. The
genus is closely related to *Vitis*,
except that its flowers have
their parts in fours rather than
fives. Cultivation for the
Cayratia family is the same as
for *Cissus* (*see page 150*).

C. japonica
(*Cissus*, *Columella* or *Vitis
japonica*)
A herbaceous tendrilled vine
to 4m (13ft), with slender,
ridged stems. Leaves digitate
with 5 oval, toothed, leaflets.
Flowers small, greenish, in
forked lateral clusters; mid- to
late summer. Berries pea-
sized, whitish when ripe.
Hardy in some cooler regions
provided the roots are
protected during the winter
months. Japan to Malaysia,
Australia
☀ 0°C (32°F) ✿
    var. *marmorata*: leaves blotched
    with yellow.

CLEMATIS
(Ranunculaceae)

Some of the herbaceous
climbing species of clematis,
especially the *C. viticella*
types, fit within this chapter in
that they die down in winter,
but they are described along
with the other members of the
family clematis in a separate
chapter (*see page 66*).

CLITORIA
(Leguminosae)

Beautiful members of the pea
family grown for their relative
large and brightly coloured
flowers, produced over a long
season. *Clitoria* is a tropical
and subtropical genus of about
70 perennials, many of which
are climbers. The alternate
leaves are pinnate and the
curious pea-flowers are
carried upside-down, one to a
few in the leaf axils. The
standard is large and notched
at the apex.
    Propagation is by seed or by
separating suckers. In
temperate gardens clitorias
have to be grown as annuals
and raised from seed each year,
planting them out when all
danger of frost has passed.

⊞ *C. mariana*
Stems twining to 1m (3ft 3in).
Leaves with 3 oval leaflets,
2.5–7.5cm (1–3in) long.
Flowers lilac, about 5cm (2in)
long, borne 1–3 together;
summer. Fruit a narrow pod to
5cm (2in). E and S USA and
Mexico
☼ 5°C (41°F) ✿

✓ ⊞ *C. ternatea*
BLUE PEA, BUTTERFLY PEA,
PIGEON WINGS
Stems trailing or climbing to
6m (20ft), although less in
temperate regions. Leaves with
5–9 elliptic leaflets, 1–6cm
(½–2½in) long. Flowers blue
with a white and yellow centre,
3–5cm (1¼–2in) long, 1 or 2
in the leaf axils; summer to

early autumn. Fruit a downy
pod 6–12.5cm (2½–5in) long.
Evergreen in frost-free
regions. Tropical Asia,
naturalized throughout the
tropics and subtropics.
☼ ☀ 5°C (41°F) ✿s
    'Blue Sails': flowers semi-double,
    deep blue. **'Semi-double'**: flowers
    semi-double, rich blue.

COBAEA
(Polemoniaceae)

One of the loveliest of all
climbers, vigorous and free-
flowering at its best, and
producing a long-lasting
display of large, bell-shaped
flowers which fascinate by
changing colour as they age.
These shrubby climbers have
alternate pinnate leaves which
end in a branched tendril. The
flowers are usually solitary and
borne in the leaf axils; they
have a large 5-lobed calyx,
with leaf-like lobes, and a bell-
shaped, 5-lobed corolla. The
fruit is a capsule containing
numerous winged seeds.

✓ ⊞ *C. scandens*
CUP AND SAUCER VINE
Stems angled, to 7.5m (25ft),
much less if treated as an
annual. Leaves pinnate with
4–6 oblong or oval leaflets,
each up to 10cm (4in) long.
Flowers solitary on long stalks,
the calyx about 2.5cm (1in)
long, the corolla twice the
length, with roundish lobes,
white or greenish at first but
aging to a striking violet;
midsummer to autumn.

Codonopsis vinciflora

Codonopsis grey-wilsonii 'Himal Snow'

To encourage a plant to branch and produce plenty of flowers, the tips of the growing shoots should be regularly pinched out. In tropical and subtropical gardens plants can live for five or more years. In cooler regions plants take a long time to come into flower, often just flowering at the end of summer; can be grown in a large conservatory in such areas. Mexico
☼ 4°C (39°F) ⚘ (when grown as a perennial)
'Alba': flowers plain white.
'Variegata': cream-variegated leaves.

CODONOPSIS (Campanulaceae)

A delightful genus of mostly climbing harebells noted for their bell or salver-shaped flowers in a variety of colours, sometimes beautifully marked within. Many have an unpleasant foxy odour but this should not deter their cultivation. The genus includes 30–40 tuberous-rooted species native to central and eastern Asia, the Himalaya and Malaysia. The climbing members have twining stems that die back each winter to ground level. The 5-parted flowers are usually solitary. The fruit is a dry, or occasionally fleshy, capsule containing numerous small seeds.

Codonopsis are easily raised from seed, generally flowering in the second or third year, and will thrive in a moist, light soil. They can be trained on a wall but are at their best when allowed to scramble over a suitable shrub. They also make excellent plants for large tubs and can be trained up branched sticks or wire netting.

C. convolvulacea
To 1.5m (5ft); stems slender. Leaves oval to narrowly lance-shaped, 2.5–6cm (1–2½in) long, untoothed or slightly toothed. Flowers salver-shaped, blue or violet-blue, 2.5–4.5cm (1–1¾in) across; sepals enlosing the corolla in bud; late summer to mid-autumn. Fruit pear-shaped. Plants sold under this name are likely to be *C. forrestii* or *C. grey-wilsonii*. N Burma, extreme SW China
☼ -15°C (5°F) ⚘

✓ C. forrestii
Like a large version of *C. convolvulacea*. To 3.5m (11½ft). Leaves oval to lance-shaped, generally untoothed, 6–10cm (2½–4in) long. Flowers salver-shaped, blue to lavender-blue, 5–10cm (2–4in) across; late summer to autumn. Fruit pear-shaped. The finest and most vigorous of the climbing species. W China
☼ -25°C (-13°F) ⚘

✓ C. grey-wilsonii
(*C. nepalensis* of hort.)
To 2.5m (8ft). Leaves pale green, oval, toothed, 1.5–5.5cm (½–2¼in) long. Flowers salver-shaped, 5–8cm (2–3¼in) across, blue with a crimson or purple hairy ring in the centre; late summer to autumn. Fruit top-shaped. Often sold under the name *C. forrestii*.
W and central Nepal.
☼ -25°C (-13°F) ⚘
✓ **'Himal Snow'** (*C. convolvulacea* 'Alba'): ♔ flowers pure white.

C. lanceolata
Stems purplish, to 1m (3ft 3in). Leaves crowded at ends of lateral branches, narrowly oval, 2.5–6cm (1–2½in) long, untoothed or with rounded teeth. Flowers pendent, bell-shaped, to 4cm (1½in) long, pale bluish or lilac with violet spots or lines inside; late summer to autumn.
China, Japan
☼ -15°C (5°F) ⚘

C. tangshen
To 2m (6½ft). Leaves oval, 2.5–6cm (1–2½in) long. Flowers pendent, bell-shaped, 3–4cm (1¼–1½in) long, greenish, flushed with purple, with purple spots and stripes inside; late summer to early autumn. W China
☼ -25°C (-13°F) ⚘

✓ C. vinciflora
To 1.5m (5ft), with very slender stems. Leaves oval, toothed, pale green, 1–3.5cm (½–1½in) long. Flowers salver-shaped, 3–4cm (1¼–1½in) across, blue to violet-blue; sepals spreading in bud; midsummer to autumn. Fruit pear-shaped. Confused with *C. convolvulacea* but readily distinguished by the characteristics of its buds.
S and SE Tibet to W China
☼ -25°C (-13°F) ⚘

Codonopsis viridis

▦ *C. viridis*

Vigorous, tuberous-rooted twiner to 3m (10ft). Leaves heart-shaped to lanceolate, alternate. Flowers green, banded and edged with purple or red inside, broadly bell-shaped, 2.5–4cm (1–1½in) long; summer to early autumn. One of the largest species but rather scarce in cultivation. Central and E Himalaya; mainly in subtropical areas.
☀◗ 5°C (41°F) ✿

CONVOLVULUS (Convolvulaceae)

A large and familiar genus that contains the bindweeds, with their familiar funnel-shaped flowers. However, only a few are troublesome weeds and some are very fine garden plants. Of the climbing species only one species is generally available. It is a wholly delightful plant and, given a warm niche in the garden, will flower over much of the summer.

Convolvulus althaeoides

C. althaeoides

Twining perennial to 1.5m (5ft) with numerous slender stems, suckering. Leaves grey-green, the lower oval but the upper usually deeply lobed. Flowers pink to purple-pink, often with a dark eye, 2.5–4cm (1–1½in) across, usually 2 or 3 together; summer. Excellent climber for the base of sunny walls and fences, especially as a mask for the lower bare bases of shrubs and other climbers such as clematis. S Europe, Turkey
☀ -10°C (14°F) ⌥s

subsp. *tenuissimus* (*C. elegantissimus*): foliage more deeply lobed and silvery, flowers solitary. More widely available.

CUCURBITA (Cucurbitaceae)

Although the bright yellow flowers of this genus are attractive, it is the diversity of fruit sizes and shapes that most appeal to the gardener. This genus contains the vegetable marrows and some of the gourds, with their extraordinary fruit shapes. They are trailing or climbing annuals or perennials native to America, with alternate lobed leaves and yellow 5-parted flowers. Male and female flowers are borne separately but on the same plant, the female generally larger than the male. The fruit is often large and contains many seeds which germinate readily in a warm greenhouse or frame. In temperate regions the young plants need to be hardened off with care. They thrive on moist, humus-rich soils with plenty of water throughout the summer.

Most of these cucurbits are rampant and rather coarse plants which are difficult to mix with other climbers. However, they can cover a large screen or fence boldly and effectively, especially when the ornamental fruits develop. The fruits can be dried and used for winter decoration and the seeds from them collected later and used for the next season.

The main stems need to be trained to some extent, tying them in loosely to supports to direct the growth; they can be pinched out at the tip if they become too invasive.

C. argyrosperma
SILVER-SEED GOURD
To 6m (20ft); stems smooth, tendrilled. Leaves heart- to kidney-shaped, shallowly lobed. Flowers yellow, 5–6cm (2–2½in) across; summer. Fruit rounded to egg-shaped, greyish-white striped green, 15–20cm (6–8in). Mexico.
☀ 0°C (32°F) ✿ -

✓ *C. ficifolia*
CIDRA, FRENCH MELON, MALABAR GOURD, FIG-LEAVED GOURD
Perennial to 9m (30ft), sometime more. Leaves pale green, sometimes marbled, oval or roundish with a heart-shaped base and 5 rounded lobes, resembling the leaves of the common fig. Flowers yellow or pale orange, 7–12cm (2¾–4¾in) across; mid- to late summer. Fruit up to 30cm (12in) long, roundish or egg-shaped, green-speckled or striped with white, containing black or brown seeds. Central and South America
☀ 5°C (41°F), ✿

✓ *C. pepo*
AUTUMN AND SUMMER PUMPKIN, SUMMER SQUASH, VEGETABLE MARROW
Annual with rough, running or climbing stems, to 3–4m (10–13ft); tendrilled. Leaves equally rough, heart-shaped, with 5 blunt-toothed lobes. Flowers deep yellow 7.5–10cm (3–4in) across, with pointed lobes; summer. Fruit extremely variable in size, shape and colouring, smooth or warty. The ornamental gourds, grown for their fruit which can be dried and preserved for decoration, are forms of *C. pepo*. S USA, N Central America
☀ 5°C (41°F) ✿

CYNANCHUM
(Asclepiadaceae)

Climbers with twining stems related to *Hoya*, with paired leaves and clusters of small 5-lobed flowers with a cup-like corona in the centre. The fruit is a pair of fleshy, pointed, pod-like follicles. This pretty and unusual plant deserves to be more widely grown in gardens; it looks very effective clambering up shrubs.

C. acutum
STRANGLEWORT
To 3.5m (11½ft). Leaves lance-shaped, to 15cm (6in) long, heart-shaped at the base. Flowers scented, white or pink, 8–12mm (¼–½in) across, in lateral clusters, the corolla hairless; midsummer. Follicles about 7.5cm (3in) long when mature. S Europe
☼ -5°C (23°F)

DICENTRA
(Fumariaceae)

Every gardener knows the bleeding heart (*Dicentra spectabilis*) but few realise that the genus also contains some attractive herbaceous climbers. These usually climb by means of fine-branched tendrils at the leaf tips. The heart-shaped flowers are 4-petalled, the outer two petals rather flat with a pouched base. Dicentras like moist, loamy, though well-drained, soils and are readily raised from seed or by careful

division of old clumps. They are seen at their best when allowed to climb up shrubs.

D. chrysantha
(*Dielytra chrysantha*)
GOLDEN EARDROPS
To 1.5m (5ft) tall; stems woody at base, scrambling, without climbing tendrils. Leaves pale bluish-green, divided into numerous linear or wedge-shaped leaflets, 1.5–4cm (½–1½in) long. Flowers bright yellow, 1.2–2.5cm (½–1in) long, in erect clusters at the stem tips; summer to early autumn. This species was discovered by David Douglas and first introduced to cultivation in 1852. Plants are not long-lived in cultivation and have to be propagated regularly from seed. In the wild this species grows on dry, sunny hill slopes, so in cultivation a light loamy soil at the base of a sunny south-facing wall is ideal. USA (California)
☼ -10°C (14°F)

✓ D. scandens
(*D. macrocapnos*, *D. thalictrifolia*)
Graceful tendrilled climber to 4m (13ft), though often less; stems succulent, pale green. Leaves pale bluish-green; leaflets oval to lance-shaped, 5mm–3cm (¼–1¼in). Flowers pendent, yellow, 2–2.5cm (¾–1in) long, borne in drooping clusters; late summer and autumn. Fruit elliptic, pendent, pale green, to 2.5cm (1in) long. C and E Himalaya
☾ -20°C (-4°F)

D. torulosa
Slender tendrilled climber with a tuberous rootstock, to 3m (10ft). Leaves grey-green with numerous narrow elliptic leaflets 5–20mm (¼–¾in) long. Flowers yellow, 13–15mm (½in) long, borne in drooping clusters; late summer to early autumn. The plant gets its name from the slender fruit pods, 4.5–6cm (1¾–2½in) long, which are constricted between each seed. SW China, India (Assam)
☼ -15°C (5°F)

DIOSCOREA
(Dioscoreaceae)

Although many yams are grown for their edible tubers in tropical and subtropical regions of the world, a number of the herbaceous species are grown for decoration.

Dioscorea is a genus of some 200, mostly tropical, twining climbers with handsome, usually heart-shaped, or digitate leaves. Most have large tuberous roots, the 'yams'; the common yam (*Dioscorea batatas*) is grown and eaten in many tropical countries. Only three species are suitable for outdoor culture in temperate regions; the tubers are best over-wintered in sand in a cool, frostproof place and planted outdoors when the danger of frost has passed. They need a sunny, sheltered position and a light, well-drained soil with the addition of well-rotted farmyard

manure. During the growing season yams need plenty of water, but this should be withdrawn gradually as the herbaceous shoots begin to die down in the autumn. The flowers are small, male and female usually being borne separately but on the same plant – the female in small clusters, the male in long slender racemes or spikes. These are useful and luxuriant climbers for both pergolas and fences.

D. balcanica
BALCAN YAM
Tubers small, rounded, 2cm (¾in). Stems to 1.5m (5ft). Leaves oval to heart-shaped, alternate or paired, 9-veined. Flowers small, greenish; summer. Fruit in drooping spikes, 2.5cm (1in). SW former Yugoslavian States, Albania
☼ ☾ -20°C (-4°F)

D. batatas
COMMON OR CHINESE YAM
Tubers large, elongated, 60–90cm (2–3ft) long when fully grown, reaching down deep into the soil. Stems smooth, 2–3.5m (6–11ft), green or purplish. Leaves paired, large, glossy, deep green, heart- or lyre-shaped, with 7–9 prominent veins; lower leaves generally bear small tubers in their axils. Flowers small, white, with a pleasant cinnamon fragrance; mid- to late summer. Philippines
☾ -25°C (-13°F)

D. caucasica

Rootstock thick, horizontal and rhizome-like. Stems 1–3m (3ft 3in–10ft). Leaves heart-shaped with wavy, sometimes lobed, margins; lower leaves in whorls of 3–5, the others usually paired. Flowers small, greenish, in slender sparse racemes at the upper leaves, mid- to late summer. Fruits with 3 broad, rounded, papery wings, 1.5–2.5cm (½–1in) across. Caucasus Mountains
☼ -20°C (-4°F) ✿

ECCREMOCARPUS (Bignoniaceae)

An attractive small group of South American subshrubby climbers. One species, *Eccremocarpus scaber*, is widely cultivated, being treated generally as an annual, although it will over-winter in mild areas. It is noted for its finely cut foliage and abundance of brightly coloured tubular flowers, generally in shades of yellow, orange or red: An excellent climber to combine with other climbers such as clematis, honeysuckles or roses, as well as shrubs, as the delicate cut foliage and clusters of tubular flowers can add colour when the host climbers have finished flowering. Readily grown from seed sown in the early spring at about 15°C (59°F). Pinching out the shoot tips of young plants encourages a bushier habit. Even in subtropical gardens they are not long-lived

climbers but in most gardens they can be relied upon to set copious amounts of seed.

⊞ E. longiflorus

Like the more familiar *E. scaber* but stems red with hairs. Flowers borne on pendent stalks, yellow with green lobes, tubular but somewhat curved, 2.5–3.5cm (1–1½in) long, with a contrasting red calyx; summer. Peru
☼ ☀ -5°C (23°F) ⑂ₛ

✓ ⊞ E. scaber ♔
GLORY VINE
Semi-woody climber with slender ribbed stems to 4m (13ft). Leaves paired, each twice pinnate and terminating in a fine branched tendril. Flowers in long-stalked racemes, nodding, orange-red, tubular, 2–2.5cm (¾–1in) long with a narrow mouth surrounded by 5 small rounded lobes; summer to mid-autumn. Fruit pods inflated, about 3.5cm (1½in), containing numerous small papery winged seeds. Among the most handsome of climbers for a sheltered semi-shaded or sunny corner of the garden. In temperate regions, even if the stems are killed back by frost as low as -5°C (23°F), plants will often sprout again from the base. Few climbers flower for such a long season. Chile
☼ ☀ -5°C (23°F) ⑂ₛ
  'Aureus': flowers golden-yellow.
  'Carmineus': flowers carmine-red.
  'Roseus': flowers bright pink.
  Anglia hybrids occur in yellows, reds, pinks, scarlet and crimson.

Eccremocarpus scaber

ECHINOCYSTIS (Cucurbitaceae)

An American genus of 15 annual species which produce male and female flowers on the same plant. They climb by branched tendrils and the flowers have 5 or 6 corolla-lobes. The fruit is dry and prickly.

E. lobata
WILD CUCUMBER, PRICKLY CUCUMBER
Rapid growing to 8m (26ft); stems more or less hairless. Leaves alternate, about 5cm (2in) long, with 3–7 deep triangular, toothed lobes. Flowers greenish-white, 10–15mm (½in): female solitary in the leaf axils, male borne in panicles, midsummer to early autumn. Fruit egg-shaped, 3–5cm (1¼–2in) long, covered with long slender prickles. An unusual plant to grow on wall wires or on a trellis. It needs a rich soil and plenty of water. It is

naturalized in parts of central and south-eastern Europe. E North America
☼ -5°C (23°F) ✿

GLORIOSA (Liliaceae)

The genus contains one variable species – a tuberous perennial which produces 1–4 stems from each tuber. The climbing lily is renowned for its brightly coloured, elegant flowers with their swept-back segments and prominent diverging stamens. The plant is poisonous in all parts. Gloriosas should be planted in a sunny position in a well-drained soil: although it tolerates poor soils, it appreciates fertilizer when actively growing. In cooler areas the tubers can be grown under glass in pots and moved outside for the summer. Water should be withheld in the autumn as the stems die down, and the tubers should be overwintered in a frost-free place. If grown in a conservatory, the tubers may be left in place during the winter, provided the soil is kept dry. Propagation is by seed (which is slow) or by division of the tubers.

⊞ G. superba ♔
CLIMBING LILY, FLAME LILY, GLORY LILY
Stems slender, twining up to 2.5m (8ft). Leaves stalkless, narrowly oval to oblong, ending in a clinging tendril.

Gloriosa superba

Flowers solitary in the leaf axils, on long stalks, with 6 reflexed segments 4—10cm (1½—4in) long, yellow, red, purplish or bicolored, margins often wavy or crisped; summer to autumn. Stamens 6, spreading. Style bent at a right angle at the base. The colour of the flower often changes as the flower ages. Old World tropics ☼ ☽ 8°C (46°F) ✿

'**Rothschildiana**'(*G. rothschildiana*): scarlet segments which darken with age and have a central yellow stripe; '**Superba**': narrow, yellowish-green segments which turn orange and red, with margins strongly wavy or crisped.

HUMULUS
(Cannabaceae)

Most people know this genus as the hop or beer plant, although there are a number of species. They are twining perennial herbs with paired, rather rough leaves, with male and female flowers are produced on separate plants; male flowers are borne in loose clusters while the female are borne in short, bracted spikes which, at maturity, look rather like a greenish fir-cone. They grow readily on most average garden soils, and provide quick and effective cover for walls, pergolas and fences, being grown primarily for their handsome leaves. They are excellent plants for producing a rapid cover of handsome foliage and in late summer and autumn the female plants carry attractive clusters of papery fruits.

H. japonicus
(*H. scandens*)
JAPANESE HOP
Vigorous vine to 10m (33ft). Leaves 5- or 7-lobed, deeply toothed. Flowers greenish; midsummer to early autumn. 'Cones' of female flowers, to 2cm (¾in), green flushed purple, not enlarging in fruit. Often grown as an annual, it is rapid growing and will make a lush green screen against which to place brightly coloured flowers. It rarely survives sub-zero temperatures for long. Temperate E Asia ☼ ☽ -5°C (23°F) ✿

'**Lutescens**': leaves pale gold to lime-green. '**Variegatus**': leaves mottled with white streaks.

H. lupulus
COMMON HOP
To 6m (20ft), with rough stems. Leaves usually 3- or 5-lobed, coarsely toothed. Flowers greenish; male about 5mm (¼in) across, female flower spikes 15—20mm (¾in) long; midsummer to early autumn. Mature drooping 'cones' 3—5cm (1¼—2in) long. The fruiting 'cones' are the hops used in brewing beer and this species is grown as a crop in many of the world's temperate regions. In the garden it is a rather coarse plant, although attractive at the fruiting stage. Can run extensively underground once established. Europe, W Asia ☼ ☽ -20°C (-4°F) ✿

✓ '**Aureus**': ♀ handsome golden leaves; needs a sunny aspect.

IPOMOEA
(Convolvulaceae)

Popular and showy plants related to the bindweed genus, *Convolvulus*, these are native to the subtropics of both hemispheres. They are grown for their profusion of flowers which, although individually not long-lived, are large and

Humulus lupulus 'Aureus'

brightly coloured, being produced throughout the summer. Quick growing, they are ideal for making a screen.

There are over 500 species of morning glory, although only a relatively small number are cultivated; in temperate gardens only a few succeed outdoors, and then only in warm, sheltered niches. They are predominantly evergreen or deciduous twining climbers with alternate heart-shaped, or variously lobed, leaves. The showy funnel-shaped or tubular flowers open in sunshine; they usually last only a day) but are produced in abundance over a long season.

In cultivation most require plenty of room and love to romp up trellis against walls or pillars. They are ideal for mixing with other climbers (clematis for instance), especially to continue the colour after the companion plant has ceased blooming. They need warm conditions, sheltered in the open garden, with a rich, moist loam and plenty of water during the growing season. Dig well-rotted farmyard manure into the soil before planting or use as a mulch. Plants are easily propagated from seed but resent disturbance once germinated: pot them on with great care. Most make fine plants for conservatory walls.

✓ ▦ *I. alba*
(*I. bona-nox, Calonyction acuminatum*)
MOON FLOWER, BELLE DE NUIT
Vigorous perennial herbaceous climber to 5m (16ft); stems often with small, tuber-like outgrowths. Leaves rounded to heart-shaped with a long-pointed apex. Flowers salver-shaped, white, greenish on the outside, 7.5–14cm (3–4½in) across; summer. A weed in the tropics. Pantropical
☼ -5°C (23°F)

  'Giant White': flowers pure white.

✓ ▦ *I. coccinea*
(*Quamoclit coccinea*)
RED MORNING GLORY, STAR IPOMOEA
Perennial to 3m (10ft). Leaves variable, generally heart- or arrowhead-shaped, with a slender pointed apex, angled, toothed or untoothed. Flowers fragrant, brilliant scarlet, 1.8–3.6cm (½–1½in) long, with yellow throats; late summer to mid-autumn in abundance. E, S and central USA, Central America
☼ 10°C (50°F) ✍

  var. *hederifolia* (*I. hederifolia,*

Ipomoea coccinea

Mina sanguinea): leaves 3- or 5-lobed. **'Luteola'**: flowers yellow or orange.

I. hederacea
(*Pharbitis hederacea*)
Annual to 3–5m (10–16ft). Leaves heart-shaped, entire or 3-lobed, pointed. Flowers solitary or paired, funnel-shaped, pale blue, pink, red or purple, 2.5–5cm (1–2in)

Ipomoea hederacea

across; midsummer to early autumn. Often confused with *I. nil* but with smaller flowers and narrower spreading or recurved sepals. S USA to Argentina
☼ 0°C (32°F) ✍

▦ *I. × imperialis*
IMPERIAL JAPANESE MORNING GLORY
Probably a form of *I. nil.* Flowers double, fluted, blue to purple-blue. Garden origin.
☼ -5°C (23°F) ✍

▦ *I. indica* ♀
(*I. acuminata, I. congesta*)
BLUE DAWN FLOWER
Fast-growing herbaceous perennial twiner, to 6m (20ft). Leaves heart-shaped, entire or 3-lobed. Flowers funnel-shaped, blue or bluish-purple, 6–8cm (2½–3¼in) across, in

clusters, only one or two opening at a time; late summer to autumn. Frequently confused with *I. purpurea*; it can be easily distinguished by its finely hairy, not bristly, sepals. Pantropical (where it is sometimes a pernicious weed)
☼ 0°C (32°F) ✍

  'Leari' (*I. leari, Pharbitis leari*): leaves silvery-haired, especially underneath.

I. jalapa
(*Batatas jalapa*)
To 5–8m (16–26ft), with a stout woody tuberous rootstock. Leaves rather membranous, triangular to heart-shaped, entire or 3-lobed, pointed. Flowers narrowly funnel-shaped, in pairs, red to pinkish-purple or white, 5–6.5cm (2–2½in) long; summer. The tubers,

which have purgative properties can grow large and heavy. S USA, Mexico

☼ 5°C (41°F) ✎

I. × *multifida*
(*I.* × *sloteri*)

CARDINAL CLIMBER, HEARTS AND HONEY VINE

An annual hybrid between *I. coccinea* and *I. quamoclit* with deeply 3- to 7-lobed leaves and deep red flowers, 2–2.5cm (³⁄₄–1in) across; summer. Garden origin.

☼ -10°C (14°F) ✎

I. *nil*
(*I. imperialis, Pharbitis nil*)

Annual or herbaceous perennial twiner to 5m (16ft); stems hairy. Leaves heart shaped, entire or 3-lobed. Flowers funnel-shaped, pale to bright blue, usually aging to red or reddish-purple, with a white tube, 4–5cm (1¹⁄₂–2in) across; summer to early autumn. It is grown in many tropical and subtropical countries and has become a weed in some. *I. nil* is sometimes found under the name *I. acuminata*, although this name is a synonym of *I. indica*. North America

☼ -10°C (14°F) ✎

'Chocolate': flowers pale chocolate-brown. **'Early Call'**: flowers scarlet with a white tube, 7cm (2¹⁄₄in). **'Flying Saucers'**: flowers marbled blue and white. ✓ **'Limbata'**; flowers violet-purple edged with white. ✓ **'Scarlet O'Hara'**; flowers deep red. **'Scarlet Star'**: flowers cerise with a white star centre.

Ipomoea purpurea colour forms

I. *pandurata*
(*Convolvulus panduratus*)

WILD SWEET POTATO VINE, MAN OF THE EARTH

Herbaceous perennial twiner growing to 4m (13ft) tall, with long tuberous roots. Leaves heart-shaped, entire, fiddle-shaped or 3-lobed, finely downy beneath. Flowers broadly funnel-shaped, 7.5–10cm (3–4in) across, in small lateral clusters, white with a dark purple throat; summer. Widely cultivated and attractive, this is probably the hardiest perennial species. It has unfortunately become a troublesome weed in a number of warm countries, being extremely difficult to eradicate because of its long tuberous roots. USA

☼ -10°C (14°F) ✎

I. *purpurea*
(*Convolvulus purpurea, Pharbitis purpurea*)

COMMON MORNING GLORY

Annual or herbaceous perennial twiner with hairy stems, 3–5m (10–16ft). Leaves heart-shaped, entire or 3-lobed. Flowers borne one or several together, 5–7.5cm (2–3in) across, ranging from dark purple to purple-blue or reddish, with a white tube; midsummer to early autumn. This widely grown species has been cultivated since 1629. Often confused with *I. indica* and *I. nil*, it can be distinguished by the sepals which are covered in bristly hairs; it is also hardier. Central America, but now pantropical, often as a weed.

☼ ◑ -15°C (5°F) ✎

'Alba': flowers white.

'Dickensonii': flowers blue. **'Flore-pleno'**: flowers double, bluish-white streaked with purple; later-flowering. ✓ **'Huberi'**: flowers pink to purple, edged white; leaves edged silver. ✓ **'Kermesiana'**: flowers scarlet. ✓ **'Rosea'**: flowers blush-rose. **'Tricolor'**: flowers blue, striped with red and white; not to be confused with *I. tricolor*. **'Violacea'**: flowers double, deep violet.

✓ I. *quamoclit*
(*Quamoclit pinnata*)

CYPRESS VINE, INDIAN PINK

Annual to 5–7m (16–23ft); stems smooth. Leaves ferny looking, short-stalked or stalkless, finely pinnately cut, with numerous linear lobes. Flowers scarlet, 1–5 together, 1.8–2cm (¹⁄₂–³⁄₄in) across, with a narrow tube that broadens into a flattened 5-lobed limb; midsummer to autumn. A beautiful and unusual-looking species with finely cut foliage and brilliant flowers. Tropical America

☼ -5°C (23°F) ✎

'Alba': flowers white.

I. *tricolor*
(*I. rubrocaerulea, Pharbitis rubrocaerulea, P. tricolor*)

MORNING GLORY

Short-lived perennial, generally best treated as an annual, to 7m (23ft), generally far less. Leaves heart-shaped, pale to mid-green. Flowers funnel-shaped, whitish in bud but unfurling reddish-purple, azure or china blue, 7.5–10cm (3–4in) across; midsummer to autumn. A beautiful plant most

Ipomoea tricolor 'Heavenly Blue'

commonly seen in conservatories but it will succeed on a sunny sheltered wall. This species gained notoriety a few years ago because it was discovered that the seeds contain small amounts of the hallucinogen, LSD. Mexico

☼ 0°C (32°F) ⚘

'Blue Star': flowers sky-blue with darker stripes. ✓ **'Crimson Rambler'**: flowers crimson with a white tube. ✓ **'Heavenly Blue'**: to 3m (10ft) with large china-blue flowers. ✓ **'Heavenly Blue Improved'**: ⚘ flowers even larger, bright blue with a white throat. **'Pearly Gates'**: flowers blue marbled white. **'Summer Skies'**: flowers sky-blue. ✓ **'Wedding Bells'**: flowers lavender-pink.

JACQUEMONTIA
(Convolvulaceae)

Similar to *Ipomoea* but the flowers have two stigmas rather than one. The species described below is grown for its charming blue flowers,

produced over many months. Propagation is from seeds or cuttings.

J. pentantha
LITTLE BLUE HAT

Perennial with slender, herbaceous stems up to 3m (10ft). Leaves heart-shaped. Flowers bell-shaped, blue with a white centre, about 2.5cm (1in) across, in lax clusters of 5–12; spring to summer. The flowers begin to close in mid-afternoon but this species blooms prolifically throughout most of the year.
USA (Florida), West Indies
☼ 16°C (61°F) ⅄S

LABLAB
(Leguminosae)

An attractive twining bean grown primarily for its showy flowers, which are followed by a sumptuous display of colourful fruits. It can be used as an effective and fast growing screener, and its fruits are as attractive as its flowers. It is particularly impressive when grown up a tripod of long canes or over net fencing.

L. purpureus
(*Dolichos lablab*)
DOLICHOS BEAN, HYACINTH BEAN,
LUBIA BEAN

A vigorous twiner to 6m (20ft). Leaves alternate, trifoliate, leaflets oval to triangular. Pea-flowers in long-stalked racemes, purple to mauve; midsummer to mid-autumn. Pods oblong, to 15cm

Lablab purpureus

(6in), shiny crimson-purple. In cooler regions it is often grown as an annual; seeds germinate best at a temperature of about 18°C (65°F). The pods are edible. Plants require copious water during the summer months. Asia
☼ ◑ 0°C (32°F) ⅄S

LAGENARIA
(Cucurbitaceae)

These gourds are grown for their spectacular and intriguing fruits. The genus contains both annuals and perennials which climb by

tendrils. The leaves are alternate and the leaf stalks have a pair of glands at the top. Male and female flowers are produced on the same plant. For cultivation see *Cucurbita*. Propagation is by seed.

L. siceraria
(*L. vulgaris*)
BOTTLE GOURD, CALABASH GOURD,
WHITE-FLOWERED GOURD

Annual with stems climbing to 10m (33ft). Leaves oval to heart-shaped, toothed, downy, the stalks with 2 glands at the top. Male flowers solitary, white, petals 5, stamens 3. Female flowers solitary, white,

bell-shaped, smaller than male. Fruit varying enormously in size (7.5–90cm/3–36in), almost globose to 'gourd-shaped', green or yellowish, downy. Grown primarily for its highly ornamental and decorative fruits and long used for domestic utensils in tropical countries. There are many cultivated variants which produce fruits of various shapes. The bottle gourd can be grown in a warm spot in temperate gardens.
Pantropical
☼ 10°C (50°F) ✿

LATHYRUS
(Leguminosae)

This delightful genus contains the popular sweet pea and the everlasting pea, with their tendrilled leaves and showy racemes of flowers. There are some 130 species in all, native to northern temperate regions as well as the mountains of South America and tropical Africa. They are annual or perennial herbs, many of which climb by leaf tendrils. They have the typical pea-flowers characteristic of the family. The fruit is an oblong compressed pea pod which splits into two to release seeds.

Easily propagated from seed; some gardeners advocate chitting the hard-coated seeds or soaking them for 24 hours before sowing. Tips of seedlings can be pinched out to encourage lateral shoots. Perennial species can be sown

in a similar way, but they are best started off in pots. Once established, self-sown seedlings often occur; these should be transplanted while still fairly young.

The climbing species, especially the everlasting pea (*L. latifolius*) are good plants for scrambling through shrubs or over old walls, fences or up a trellis. Fine pea sticks make ideal supports or 2–3m (6½–10ft) long canes may be used for growing high quality sweet peas. Most species like a moist, loamy soil with plenty of well-rotted manure or compost. All those listed below have tendrils, unless otherwise indicated.

✓ *L. grandiflorus*
TWO-FLOWERED PEA
Herbaceous perennial with unwinged stems to 1.5m (5ft) tall. Leaves usually with 2

Lathyrus grandiflorus

(occasionally 3) oval leaflets. Flowers 1–4, purple with a violet standard and pink keel, 2.5–3cm (1–1¼in) long; summer. Pods hairless, 6–9cm (2½–3¾in). Makes an effective and floriferous low screen, particularly useful for masking the base of other climbers such as clematis. The plants run underground and may be difficult to control.
S Europe
☼ ◐ -20°C (-4°F) ✿

L. heterophyllus
Like *L. latifolius* but leaves with 2 or 3 pairs of leaflets and smaller flowers; summer.
Central and W Europe
☼ -25°C (-13°F) ⑂s

L. laetiflorus
Like *L. violaceus* but flowers larger, to 2.5cm (1in) long, borne in longer racemes, white or white flushed pink,

Lathyrus latifolius

with pink or purplish veins on the standard, early to midsummer.
USA (California)
☼ -5°C (23°F) ✿

L. latifolius ♀
EVERLASTING PEA
Robust herbaceous perennial with strongly winged stems to 3m (10ft), often less. Leaves with a pair of bluish-green lance-shaped to almost round leaflets, 4–10cm (1½–4in) long. Flowers purplish-pink, 2–3cm (¾–1¼in) across, borne in a raceme of 5–15; midsummer to early autumn. Pods hairless, 5–11cm (2–4½in). This beautiful plant has a long flowering season. It dislikes being moved and may take a year or two to settle down. It is superb for masking the lower parts of climbing roses or clematis, and very effective if allowed to tumble down a bank.
Central and S Europe
☼ -25°C (-13°F) ⑂s
  'Albus': flowers white with a hint of green. ✓ **'Blushing Bride'**:

Lathyrus odoratus

flowers white flushed pink.
✓ **'Pink Beauty'**: flowers dark purple and red. **'Pink Pearl'**: flowers pink. **'Red Pearl'**: flowers carmine-red. ✓ **'Snow Queen'**: flowers pure white in long stalked racemes. ✓ **'Splendens'**: flowers deep pink. **'White Pearl'** ('Weisse Perle'): ♀ flowers pure white.

⊞ *L. nervosus*
(*L. magellanicus*)
LORD ANSON'S BLUE PEA
Short-lived perennial to 2m (6½ft), often less. Leaves blue-green, rather fleshy, with a pair of oval to oblong leaflets. Flowers purplish-blue, 1.8–2.2cm (½–¾in), borne in many-flowered, long-stalked racemes; summer to early autumn. A beautiful pea introduced into cultivation in 1744 by Admiral Lord Anson. It is rare in gardens and deserves to be grown more widely; plants require a sheltered position and plenty of moisture during the growing season.
S Chile
☼ -5°C (23°F) ⎮ℓₛ

✓ *L. odoratus* ♀
SWEET PEA
Annual climber with winged stems up to 3m (10ft). Leaves with a pair of oval to elliptic leaflets, 2–6cm (¾–2½in) long. Flowers, 2–3.5cm (¾–1½in) across, are purple-blue with a deep crimson-purple standard, very fragrant; summer. Pods downy, 5–7.5cm (2–3in), brown when ripe.

Lathyrus odoratus is the ancestor of the modern sweet peas which can have white, cream, pink, lilac, mauve, purple, red, crimson-red, or even bicoloured flowers, some of which are almost scentless. There are many named cultivars on the market: select favourites from catalogues or at garden centres. Sweet peas can be sown in pots in frames during early winter or sown directly outdoors in spring. Mice are very partial to both seeds and young plants. The flowers are excellent for cutting. A first rate cottage garden plant. Italy, Sicily
☼ -20°C (-4°F) ⊗ℓ

✓ *L. pubescens*
Vigorous herbaceous or partly evergreen perennial with hairy winged stems to 3m (10ft). Leaves with 1, occasionally 2, pairs of oval leaflets. Flowers lilac or violet-blue, 2.5cm (1in), in clusters on the ends of stiff stalks; summer to early autumn. In cooler regions this pea needs to be grown on a south-facing wall or fence where it will produce abundant seed in a hot summer; it may take three years to flower from seed. A fine plant to mix with wall roses, such as 'Maréchal Niel'. There is a fine white form which is rare but well worth obtaining. Chile, Argentina
☼ -5°C (23°F) ⎮ℓₛ

L. rotundifolius
PERSIAN EVERLASTING PEA
Hairless herbaceous perennial with winged stems to 1.5m (5ft). Leaves with a pair of oval to rounded leaflets. Flowers bright pink to purplish-pink, 1.5–2cm (½–¾in) long, in racemes of 3–8; summer. Pods hairless, 4–7cm (1½–2¾in). E Europe, W Asia
☼ -20°C (-4°F) ⊗ℓ

L. tuberosus
EARTH CHESTNUT, TUBEROUS PEA
Herbaceous perennial; stems hairless, 4-angled, to 1.2m (4ft); rootstock creeping, with small tubers. Leaves with a pair of oblong-oval leaflets. Flowers rose-pink, 1.2–2cm (½–¾in) long, 2 to 7 in a raceme; early to midsummer. Pods hairless, 2–4cm (¾–1½in) long. This plant spreads by its creeping roots and new stems often emerge at some distance from the parent. It can be propagated by division of the tuberous roots as well as by seed. It will tolerate more shade than the other species. Europe, W Asia
☼ ◑ -25°C (-13°F) ⊗ℓ

L. violaceus
Herbaceous perennial with unwinged stems, to 2.7m (9ft). Leaves with 4–6 pairs of linear to oval leaflets. Flowers violet-blue, 1.5cm (½in), with darker veins on the standard, 10 to 14 in a raceme; early to midsummer. USA (California)
☼ -5°C (23°F) ⊗ℓ

LITTONIA
(Liliaceae)

A genus of 7 or 8 perennial herbaceous climbers which grow from tubers. Only *L. modesta* is at all common in cultivation, grown for its attractive bell-shaped flowers. The flowers have 6 perianth segments (tepals) which are free almost to the base and the fruit is a capsule. Cultivation as in *Gloriosa*.

⊞ *L. modesta*
CLIMBING BELLFLOWER
Stems branched, reaching 1.8m (6ft). Leaves stalkless, the lower ones scattered on the stem, the upper in whorls, linear to narrowly oval, hairless, each with a tendril at the tip. Flowers deep yellow to

orange, bell-shaped, 1.5–4cm (³/₅–1³/₅in) long, nodding, with pointed segments, borne singly in the leaf axils; summer. South Africa

☼ ◑ 8°C (46°F) ✿

LUFFA
(Cucurbitaceae)

A genus with 6 species of annual climbers, grown mainly for their fruits which have a fibrous skeleton. The large flowers have petals which are free from one another and usually golden-yellow. Male flowers are carried in a raceme and female flowers are solitary. Cultivation as in *Cucurbita*. Propagation is by seed.

L. cylindrica
(*L. aegyptiaca*)
LOOFAH

Annual climber or trailer with downy stems to 15m (50ft). Tendrils with 3–6 branches. Leaves oval to heart-shaped, 3–7-lobed. Male flowers in a 12.5–35cm (5–14in) raceme of 4–20 flowers; female flowers solitary; all flowers with 5 yellow petals; summer. Fruit cylindric to ellipsoid, sometimes curved or bent, downy, up to 60cm (2ft) long. Seeds with narrow wings. Probably best known as the source of the bathroom loofah which is the skeleton of the fruit. This species can be grown in temperate gardens in a hot, sheltered position. Tropical Asia, Africa

☼ ◑ 5°C (41°F) ✿

MARAH
(Cucurbitaceae)

A genus of about six tuberous-rooted herbaceous perennials, native to the western USA, which are best raised from seed. They are grown primarily for their handsome foliage and intriguing spiny fruits. Male and female flowers are borne on the same plant and a single plant will set fruit readily.

M. fabaceus
(*Echinocystis fabacea*, *Megarrhiza californica*)
BIGROOT

Tendrilled climber to 6m (20ft), or more. Leaves silvery-green, alternate, palmately lobed. Flowers yellow, rather small, the male flowers in racemes with solitary female ones at their base; midsummer to early autumn. Fruit rounded or oblong, about 5cm (2in) long, densely spiny. USA (California)

☼ -5°C (23°F) ✿

M. macrocarpus
(*Echinocystis macrocarpus*)

Tendrilled climber 3–6m (10–20ft). Leaves deep green, alternate, deeply lobed, up to 20cm (8in) wide. Flowers like those of *M. fabaceus*; midsummer to early autumn. Fruit broadly oblong, 7.5–10cm (3–4in) long, densely spiny, the spines of varying lengths. USA (S California)

☼ -5°C (23°F) ✿

MAURANDYA
(Scrophulariaceae)

A small Central American genus (sometimes wrongly listed in catalogues as *Maurandia*) of charming perennial herbs and climbers, grown for their showy snapdragon- or foxglove-like flowers borne over a long season. Today they are often included in *Asarina*. The climbing species, being fast-growing, are excellent for walls and fences, in warm sheltered positions where they prefer a well-drained fairly light soil.

In cold regions they are best dug up in the autumn and over-wintered in a cool, frostproof place. Alternatively, cuttings can be taken at the end of summer and placed in gentle heat, to produce new plants for the following season. Seed is easily germinated and young plants flower readily in their first season.

The climbing species have opposite or alternate, more or less heart-shaped leaves. The flowers broaden at the apex into 2 lips, the upper 2-lobed and the lower 3-lobed. The plants climb by means of twisting leaf and flower stalks which wrap themselves around supports.

✓ ⊞ *M. barclaiana*
(often spelt *barclayana*; *Asarina barclaiana*)

To 2m (6½ft); stems slender, greenish. Leaves rather thin,

Maurandya barclaiana

heart-shaped and rather angular, pointed, with long twining stalks. Flowers funnel-shaped, pale to deep purple with a whitish throat, downy outside, 4–5cm (1½–2in) long, with an open mouth; midsummer to mid-autumn. Flowers are variable in colour and a number of cultivars have been recognized most of which were previously thought to be species. The best colour forms should be increased from cuttings. Mexico

☼ ◑ -5°C (23°F) ⚘s

'Alba' (*M. alba*): flowers white. **'Rosea'** (*M. rosea*): flowers rose-pink. **'Purpurea Grandiflora'** (*M. purpurea-grandiflora*): flowers purple, larger than the type.

✓ ⊞ *M. erubescens* ♔
(*Asarina* and *Lophospermum erubescens*)
CREEPING GLOXINIA

Slightly woody climber to 3m (10ft) tall; stems and leaves covered in soft sticky hairs. Leaves triangular to heart-shaped, sharply toothed, the lower ones opposite, upper

alternate. Flowers rose-pink,
7–7.5cm (2¼–3in) long, the
tube swollen on one side;
midsummer to mid-autumn.
Mexico

☼ -5°C (23°F) ⅄ℓ**s**

'Alba': flowers white.

M. filipes

(*Antirrhinum* and *Asarina*
filipes)

YELLOW TWINING SNAPDRAGON
Twining perennial to 2m
(6½ft); stems much branched.
Leaves lance-shaped,
untoothed, the lower smaller
and more oval. Flowers
golden-yellow with black
spots, 1–1.3cm (½in) long;
late spring to midsummer.
W USA from Oregon
southwards

☼ -5°C (23°F) ⅄ℓ**s**

✓ ▦ M. lophospermum

(*Asarina lophospermum*,
Lophospermum scandens)
Very like *M. erubescens* and
often regarded as a variety of
it. Stems and somewhat lobed
leaves less hairy or almost
hairless. Flowers rosy-purple
with a whitish, non-swollen
tube, faintly dotted;
midsummer to early autumn.
A handsome plant, certainly
better in gardens than *M.
erubescens* and, like *M.
barclaiana*, quick to flower
from seed. It is often found
under the name *M. scandens*,
but the latter is a quite distinct
species, rarely seen in our
gardens, with smaller flowers
ranging in colour from pale
violet to lavender or reddish-
purple. Mexico

☼ -5°C (23°F) ⅄ℓ**s**

'Victoria Falls': A particularly fine
selection.

MINA
(Convolvulaceae)

An interesting genus closely
related to, and once included
in, *Ipomoea*. It is easily
distinguished by its 1-sided
racemes of tubular, pouched
flowers that are not expanded
into a broad limb. A useful
and quick growing climber
for fences and pergolas;
particularly effective in the
autumn.

▦ M. lobata

(*Ipomoea versicolor*,
Quamoclit lobata)
SPANISH FLAG
Vigorous, twining perennial to
6m (20ft), often less. Leaves 3-
lobed with a heart-shaped
base. Flowers pouched and
slightly curved, crimson fading
to orange, then pale yellow,
1.3–2.5cm (½–1in) long, in
paired, 1-sided racemes,
borne in profusion;
midsummer to mid-autumn.
A beautiful, rapidly growing
twiner. In temperate gardens
plants can be cut back and
over-wintered in a frostproof
place, then planted out in early
summer, once the danger of
frost has passed. They are
readily raised from seed and
flower in the first season if
started off in warmth early in
the year.
S Mexico

☼ -5°C (23°F) ⅄ℓ**s**

Mina lobata

PASSIFLORA
(Passifloraceae)

For general notes on *Passiflora*
see page 153.

✓ ▦ P. amethystina

(*P.* 'Lavender Lady')
Herbaceous climber with
slender stems and 3-lobed
leaves which have 3–5 glands
on the stalks. Flowers 9–11cm
(3½–4½in) across;
intermittently all year. Sepals
and petals purple or purple-
blue. Corona banded with
purple, white and violet-blue;
filaments in 5 rows, up to
2.5cm (1in) long. Fruit orange,
5–6cm (2–2½in) long. The
plant which is sold in the UK as
P. amethystina and in continental
Europe as *P. violacea* is not
thought to be the true *P.
amethystina*, which has bluer
flowers only 6–8cm
(2½–3¼in) across. It is able to
tolerate light frost provided the
soil is not wet, and new stems

will grow when the weather
warms up. In temperate
regions, grows best under glass.
E Brazil

☼ -2°C (28°F) ⅍ℓ

▦ P. incarnata

MAYPOPS
Stems herbaceous, up to 6m
(20ft), sometimes more.
Leaves with 3 lobes, the
margin with tiny teeth and the
stalks with 2 glands. Flowers
7–9cm (2¾–3½in) across,
fragrant; sepals green outside
but white or mauve within,
petals white or mauve; corona
pink or mauve; filaments
1.5–2cm (½–¾in) long, the
inner ones very short, in
several rows. Fruit egg-shaped,
yellow-green, about 6cm
(2½in) long. Probably the most
hardy passion flower, it needs a
very well-drained, rather poor
soil to grow and flower well; it
should be given a sunny,
protected south-facing wall in
the garden. It often produces
suckers which appear some
distance from the parent plant.
If grown under glass, hand-
pollination may be needed to
produce fruit. Propagation is
from seeds or from stem or
root cuttings. Eastern USA

☼ -15°C (5°F) ⅍ℓ

PUERARIA
(Leguminosae)

A genus of some 35 Old World
twiners or sub-shrubs. The
leaves are alternate, with 3
leaflets and the pea flowers are
borne in lateral racemes. The
fruit is a narrow pod.

P. lobata
(*P. hirsuta, P. thunbergiana*)
JAPANESE ARROWROOT,
KUDZU VINE
Hairy twiner to 5m (16ft).
Leaflets broadly oval,
sometimes with shallow
marginal lobes, to 15cm (6in)
long. Racemes erect, to 30cm
(12in) long, with fragrant
reddish-purple flowers, each
2–2.5cm (¾–1in); mid- to late
summer. Pods hairy, to 7.5cm
(3in). Useful rapid-growing
climber for screens or as a
temporary cover. In warmer
regions the roots will over-
winter, sending up new stems
in the spring, but in colder
gardens the plant is best
treated as an annual. In the
south-eastern United States it
is grown both as a fodder plant
and to control erosion; in some
parts it has escaped and become
a terrible weed. Its invasive
nature makes it a bad choice for
gardens in the subtropics and
tropics. China, Japan
☀ -15°C (5°F) ⸙ s

RHODOCHITON
(Scrophulariaceae)

This genus contains only one
species. In temperate latitudes
it is normally grown under
glass as a perennial, but it may
be planted outside in the
summer and treated as an
annual. It has unusual flowers
which always attract attention
and even when the flowers
have faded, the fruits, with
their large, expanded
persistent calyces, continue its

decorative appeal. Plants are
best trained up thin canes or
pea sticks. A humus-rich,
well-drained soil is preferable;
plants dislike dry conditions,
especially round the roots. It is
readily propagated from seed
sown in a peaty compost in
gentle heat in the early spring.
The seedlings are slow to
develop at first.

✓ ▦ R. atrosanguineus ♀
(*R. volubile*)
Slender stems to 3m (10ft)
climb by means of twining leaf
and flower stalks. Leaves
alternate, heart-shaped, 6–8cm
(2½–3¼in) long, somewhat
toothed, often flushed with red
or purple. Flowers pendulous,
solitary, blackish-purple,
tubular with 5 flaring lobes,
5cm (2in) long, surrounded at
the base by a large-lobed, bell-
shaped, reddish-purple calyx;
midsummer to mid-autumn.
Fruit a papery capsule with
numerous winged seeds. A
splendid plant, though often
rather short-lived, even when
grown under glass; pinching
out the shoot tips regularly
encourages a bushier plant.
Mexico
☀ ◖ -5°C (23°F) ⸙ s

SANDERSONIA
(Liliaceae)

There is only one species in
this genus which is related to
Gloriosa. It is a herbaceous
perennial with a tuberous
rhizome, grown for its
attractive, drooping urn-

shaped flowers. Cultivation as
for *Gloriosa*.

▦ S. aurantiaca
CHINESE LANTERN LILY,
CHRISTMAS BELLS
Stems twining to about 75cm
(2½ft). Leaves scattered up the
stems, stalkless, often ending
in a tendril. Flowers orange,
urn-shaped, about 2.5cm (1in)
long with 6 tepals which are
fused except at the curved tips,
solitary on slender stalks in the
upper leaf axils; summer. Fruit
a capsule. In South Africa, this
species produces its flowers,
reminiscent of Chinese
lanterns, at Christmas, hence
its vernacular names.
South Africa
☀ ◖ 0°C (32°F) ⸙

SICYOS
(Cucurbitaceae)

A genus of 15 tendril-bearing
annual climbers mainly from
tropical America and the
Pacific Islands. *Sicyos
angulatus*, the only species that
is widely cultivated, has
become naturalized in
southern Europe and America,
where it is grown for its
handsome foliage and its
curious fruits.

▦ S. angulatus
BUR CUCUMBER, STAR CUCUMBER
To 6m (20ft); stems glandular-
hairy, with branched tendrils.
Leaves alternate, broadly oval,
about 7.5cm (3in), with 5
shallow lobes. Flowers whitish,
1–2cm (½–¾in) across, in

Rhodochiton atrosanguineus

clusters, male and female on
the same plant; midsummer to
early autumn. Fruit spiny, egg-
shaped, 1.2–1.5cm (⅓in) long.
A useful rapid-growing
screening plant. Fruit will be
set, even with a single plant.
E North America
☀ -5°C (23°F) ⸙

THLADIANTHA
(Cucurbitaceae)

A genus of 15 perennial
climbers with tuberous roots,
native from eastern Asia to
Malaysia. In cooler regions
they are usually grown under
glass, but *Thladiantha dubia* is
hardy enough to grow outside.

▦ T. dubia
To 2.5m (8ft); stems softly
hairy, climbing by means of
simple tendrils. Leaves
alternate, oval with a heart-
shaped base, 5–10cm (2–4in).
Flowers golden-yellow, 5-

Thladiantha dubia

lobed, bell-shaped, the male in crowded racemes 5–7.5cm (2–3in) long, the female solitary, borne on separate plants; midsummer to mid-autumn. Fruit red, hairless, oblong or egg-shaped, 3.5–5cm (1½–2in) long, with 10 longitudinal grooves. Has become naturalized in Central and SE Europe and in some subtropical regions of the world is viewed as a pernicious weed. Fruits are only produced if male and female plants are present. N China, Korea
☼ ☽ -15°C (5°F) ⌇⃰s

T. nudiflora
Similar but tendrils forked and fruit more rounded, 3–4cm (1¼–1½in). Flowers somewhat larger; midsummer to early autumn. E China
☼ -5°C (23°F) ⌇⃰s

THUNBERGIA
(Acanthaceae)

For a general description, see pages 157–8.

▦ *T. alata*
BLACK-EYED SUSAN
Perennial with herbaceous, twining stems up to 2m (6½ft). Leaves elliptic to arrow-shaped, toothed, with winged stalks. Flowers solitary in leaf axils on long stalks, each with 2 leafy, slightly inflated bracts at the base. Corolla about 4.5cm (2in) long with a short curved tube and 5 spreading lobes, cream, yellow or orange, with a usually purple-brown or blackish throat; summer to early autumn. Can be grown as an annual, especially in temperate regions. If grown in a conservatory, it will live as a perennial.
Tropical Africa
☼ ☽ 7°C (45°F) ⌇⃰s

▦ *T. gregorii*
(*T. gibsonii*)
Similar to *T. alata* but has triangular-oval leaves and larger orange flowers which lack the dark throat; summer. It is somewhat less hardy.
Tropical Africa.
☼ ☽ 10°C (50°F) ⌇⃰s

TRICHOSANTHES
(Cucurbitaceae)

A rampant habit with handsome foliage and large fringed flowers characterize this genus of tropical climbers. The 15 herbaceous species are native to Australia and Indo-Malaysia. The variety described below is an annual, raised from seed each year.

✓ *T. cucumerina* var. *anguina*
COMMON SNAKE GOURD,
SNAKE CUCUMBER
Stems to 4m (13ft) or more, downy, somewhat twining, with branched tendrils. Leaves alternate, broadly oval, to 22.5cm (9in), sometimes with 3–7 shallow lobes. Flowers white, 5-parted, 4–5cm (1½–2in), with deeply fringed lobes; male and female flowers borne on the same plant, the male in racemes, the female solitary; midsummer to early autumn. Fruit often curved or coiled, 30–200cm (12–80in), striped green and white. Seed needs a temperature of about 20°C (68°F) for optimum germination. India to Pakistan
☼ 15°C (59°F) ⊗⃰

TROPAEOLUM
(Tropaeolaceae)

Few herbaceous climbers can rival the tropaeolums for their splendour and profusion of flowers when they are well grown. The smaller climbing species make fine plants for pots and tubs while the more vigorous and flamboyant can enhance screens, trellis and hedges. They mix well with other climbers or shrubs; for example, *T. peregrinum* can be grown on *Clematis montana*, to bloom when the clematis has finished flowering. In addition many make fine conservatory plants, while the annual *T. majus* is not only decorative but its young leaves and fruits, as well as its flowers, make an interesting addition to salads.

There are about 90 species of *Tropaeolum* native to Mexico and the Andes of South America. The climbing types generally have coiling leaf-stalks and the spurred 5-petalled flowers vary in shape from almost flat to deeply cupped. Propagation is by seed, or by tubers in the case of the tuber-bearing species. The annual species germinate readily from seed, but the perennial ones can be far more tricky; the reasons for this are unclear. Regularly pinching out the shoot tips of young plants encourages branching.

The caterpillars of cabbage white butterflies can be a nuisance. The butterflies lay their eggs on the underside of the leaves and the caterpillars can do considerable damage if not controlled. Aphis can also infest plants but beware – some systemic insecticides can damage the plants and it is safer to use organic sprays such as derris or biological controls.

Species such as *T. azureum*, *T. hookeriana*, *T. pentaphyllum* and *T. tricolorum*, which are best grown in pots in a cool greenhouse, should be gradually dried off as the leaves turn yellow in the late spring and the plants kept barely moist until the new shoots appear in the autumn.

✓ ▦ **T. azureum**

Perennial to 1.2m (4ft) with small rounded underground tubers. Leaves to 5cm (2in), with 5–6 narrow-elliptic or lance-shaped grey-green lobes. Flowers purplish-blue, about 1–2cm (½–¾in) across, with notched petals; spur conical, about 4mm (⅙in) long; spring to early summer. A lovely species with flowers of a colour rarely seen in *Tropaeolum*. It is still a rare plant in cultivation,

Tropaeolum azureum

but well worth acquiring. Chile
☼ -5°C (23°F) ✣

▦ **T. brachyceras**

Perennial to 1m (3ft 3in), with small rounded or oblong underground tubers; stems threadlike. Leaves with 5–7 oval to linear, pale green lobes. Flowers yellow, often marked with purplish lines, about 12.5mm (½in) across, the petals somewhat notched; spur blunt, about 6mm (¼in) long; late spring to early summer. Chile
☼ -5°C (23°F) ✣

T. ciliatum

Vigorous perennial to 3m (10ft) with 'strings' of small rounded tubers. Leaves rather pale green, with 5–7 oval

Tropaeolum brachyceras

lobes. Flowers small, yellow or orange-yellow with deeper veining, 1–2cm (½–¾in); spur short, conical; midsummer to early autumn. Plants tend to be more or less evergreen but respond well to pruning back in the spring; during cold weather the stems will be cut back by frost. A highly stoloniferous plant that can become invasive in time. Chile
☼ ☽ -15°C (5°F) ✣ s

▦ **T. hookerianum**

Herbaceous perennial to 1.5m (5ft), with oblong underground tubers. Leaves usually with 7 elliptic lobes. Flowers yellow with a pale green calyx, 2cm (¾in) long, borne on long slender stalks; spur conical; spring to early summer. Chile
☼ -5°C (23°F) ✣

▦ **T. leptophyllum**

Perennial to 1.5m (5ft), with large underground tubers. Leaves with 6 or 7 elliptic lobes. Flowers pinkish-white

to yellow or orange, 2–3cm (¾–1¼in) long, with notched petals; spur straight, about 1.8cm (½in) long; early to midsummer. Chile, Bolivia
☼ -5°C (23°F) ✣

✓ **T. majus**

GARDEN NASTURTIUM, INDIAN CRESS

Rather succulent, vigorous annual 2–3m (6½–10ft) high, hairless. Leaves almost round, 5–17.5cm (2–7in) across, with the stalk attached to the centre. Flowers fragrant, 5–7.5cm (2–3in) across, yellow, orange or red, often darker marked; spur straight to 2.5cm (1in) long; summer to mid-autumn. Semi-double and double-flowered forms are available, as well as dwarf non-climbing forms. The garden nasturtium is best grown in a soil that is not too rich, otherwise lots of large leaves and few flowers will result; a shady position will have the same effect. A good plant for training up strings or wires or left to scramble over a trellis or fence.

Plants are prone to attack from blackfly, which needs to be controlled once spotted. Plants can be badly damaged by moderate frosts but seed may survive in the soil even after prolonged winter freezing. It can be grown in those areas of the tropics that have a dry season.
Peru (Andes)
☼ -3°C (37°F) ✿

T. peltophorum
(*T. lobbianum*)
Hairy annual climber to 2m (6½ft). Leaves roundish with a wavy margin, hairy beneath. Flowers red or orange-red, about 2.5cm (1in) long, with the 3 lower petals fringed; spur curved, about 3cm (1¼in) long; early to midsummer.
Ecuador, Colombia
☼ 3°C (37°F) ✿

'Spitfire': flowers deep orange-red.

✓ ▦ T. pentaphyllum
Perennial to 1.5m (5ft), with long underground tubers and hairless purplish stems. Leaves with 5 oval lobes and purplish stalks. Flowers red, 2.5–3cm (1–1¼in), with rounded petals and protruding stamens; spur green and red, about 2.5cm (1in) long. Late spring to midsummer.
South America
☼ -10°C (14°F) ✿

✓ T. peregrinum
(*T. canariense*)
CANARY CREEPER
Rather pale green annual to 2.5m (8ft). Leaves usually with 5 oval lobes. Flowers bright

Tropaeolum peregrinum

yellow, 2–2.5cm (¾–1in) across, with upper 2 petals much larger and fringed; spur greenish, curved, 1.2cm (½in) long; summer to early autumn. A fine plant for an effective, quick-growing screen. Like *T. majus*, it is readily raised from seed. The flowers and young leaves and fruits can also be used in salads.
Peru, Ecuador
☼ ◐ 3°C (37°F) ✿

✓ T. speciosum
SCOTTISH FLAME FLOWER,
FLAME NASTURTIUM
Spreading stoloniferous perennial with slender stems to 3m (10ft). Leaves with 5 or 6 oval leaflets. Flowers bright scarlet, 2–3cm (¾–1¼in) long, with notched petals; spur 2.5–3cm (1–1¼in) long; summer to early autumn. Fruits are bright blue when ripe, set in the persistent, deep

red calyx. One of the gems of the genus, it is a wonderful sight in full flower. It will grow on a north- or east-facing wall and in any position, being happiest with its roots in the shade. It is unpredictable in its needs but seems to appreciate a cool, leafy soil. It can be grown on trellis or netting on a wall and looks especially good growing up an evergreen hedge such as yew or box, or over low shrubs. The eye-catching fruits are unique and an added bonus at the end of the year. Chile
☼ ◐ -15°C (5°F) ✿

✓ ▦ T. tricolorum
(*T. tricolor*)
Perennial, to 1m (3ft 3in) rounded or oblong underground tubers and thread-like reddish or purplish stems. Leaves with 5–7 oval or obovate lobes. Flowers glowing orange-red tipped with violet-black and with small yellow petals, 1.8–2.5cm (½–1in) long overall, including the long slightly curved spur; late spring to early summer. One of the finest and most elegant species. Chile, Bolivia
☼ -10°C (14°F) ✿

✓ ▦ T. tuberosum
Perennial to 2.5m (8ft), producing a cluster of oblong, crimson-streaked, yellow tubers. Leaves with 3–6 oval lobes. Flowers about 2cm (¾in) long, red with orange-yellow to orange-red untoothed petals, borne on long slender stalks; summer to

Tropaeolum speciosum

early autumn. The tubers, produced at the soil surface around the base of the plant, will survive moderate frosts but are best dug up and over-wintered in a frost-free place over winter. They can be planted out again when the danger of frosts is over. In its native countries, *T. tuberosum* is grown as a crop for its edible tubers.

Andes of Peru, Bolivia

☼ ◐ -10°C (14°F) ✂

'Ken Aslett': ♀ a free-flowering clone which is widely available, with orange flowers. Generally considered to belong to var. *lineamaculatum*.

TWEEDIA (OXYPETALUM)
(Asclepiadaceae)

A genus of about 150 species related to *Hoya* and native mainly to Mexico, the West Indies and Brazil. The one species commonly grown is noted for its clusters of beautiful, eye-catching, blue flowers. They have paired leaves and bear their 5-parted flowers in loose lateral clusters. Like *Hoya*, the flowers have a distinctive corona in the centre, concealing the stamens.

✓ *T. caerulea* ♀
(*Oxypetalum caeruleum*)
Weakly twining sub-shrub to 2m (6½ft); stems densely white-downy. Leaves narrowly oblong with a heart-shaped base, to 10cm (4in) long, hairy. Flowers rather fleshy, pale blue, to 2.5cm (1in) across,

Tweedia caerulea (in fruit)

darker and somewhat purplish with age; corona scales deep blue; midsummer. Fruit spindle-shaped, to 15cm (6in) long. In cooler regions this plant is usually treated as an annual and raised each year from seed, although it can be lifted and over-wintered in a frost-free place. Plants thrive best with a minimum temperature of 5°C (41°F).

Brazil, Uruguay

☼ 3°C (39°F) ✂ᵴ

VIGNA
(Leguminosae)

A genus of about 150 herbaceous species which contains the edible aduki bean (*V. angularis*), black-eyed pea (*V. unguiculata* subsp. *unguiculata*) and the asparagus bean (*V. unguiculata* subsp. *sesquipedalis*). The alternate leaves have 3 leaflets and the pea flowers have a round standard and an incurved keel, which may be twisted. The pod is narrow. Propagation is by seed.

V. caracalla
(*Phaseolus caracalla*)
CORKSCREW FLOWER,
SNAIL BEAN
Perennial with stems twining to 6m (20ft). Leaflets oval, pointed, downy. Flowers up to 5cm (2in) long, white, yellow or lavender, the wings pinkish-purple and the keel coiled; spring to summer. Fruit a linear pod up to 18cm (7in) long. Grown for its curious

'snaily' flowers which always provoke comment.

Tropical S America

☼ ◐ 10°C (50°F) ✂ᵴ

VINCETOXICUM
(Asclepiadaceae)

Very similar to *Cynanchum*, but differing in the flowers having a single corona with 5 lobes. They are grown primarily for their rapid growth and clusters of flowers, although the fruits are decorative when they split to reveal a mass of silky seeds that are wafted away by the slightest breeze.

V. ascyrifolium
(*Cynanchum acuminatifolium*)
CRUEL PLANT, MOSQUITO PLANT
Herbaceous perennial about 1m (3ft 3in); stems greyish, angled, twining at tips. Leaves opposite, broadly oval, untoothed. Flowers white, 0.8–1cm (⅓–½in) across, in lateral clusters; summer. Fruit a pair of spindle-shaped pods; seeds with silky hairs. Like the related *Araujia* (also known as cruel plant) the common name refers to the fact that the flowers trap visiting insects.

Japan

☼ ◐ -25°C (-13°F) ✂

V. nigrum
DARK SWALLOW-WORT
Similar but with longer-pointed leaves and dark purple flowers; summer.

S Europe

☼ ◐ -20°C (-4°F) ✂

Conservatory
Climbers

Introduction

(Above) Many tropical climbers, such as this *Allamanda cathartica*, make excellent, if vigorous, climbers for heated conservatories.

(Right) *Hoya carnosa* is one of the most popular conservatory climbers, with its fragrant flower clusters.

(Left) *Mandevilla × amabilis* 'Alice du Pont' is a luxuriant tropical climber producing a mass of blooms.

Whereas a south-facing wall in your garden will enable you to grow some of the more tender plants, a conservatory or greenhouse will enormously expand the range of plants that can be cultivated. There is a wonderful diversity of climbers suitable for cultivation in conservatories and they can create a lush, tropical effect. However, it must be borne in mind that some of these plants can grown very large and, unless the proportions of the conservatory or the greenhouse are extremely generous, they will need to be kept under control by pruning. Provided the conservatory is kept frost-free, it will be possible to cultivate many plants which would not survive out of doors without protection, and investment in heating which raises the minimum winter temperature to 10°C (50°F) will allow many tropical and subtropical plants to be grown.

Modern conservatories and greenhouses are usually constructed of metal or wood (or a combination of the two) and the glazing can be glass or plastic. It is essential to clean the glazing regularly, to allow optimum light through. If plastic is chosen, it is important to select a material which has optical properties similar to glass.

The aspect of the conservatory or greenhouse must be considered when selecting plants. A freestanding structure will receive all-round sunlight, whereas one which is attached to a building will do so only if it faces south. A north-facing conservatory will provide the right growing conditions only for plants with low light requirements. Conversely, if the conservatory faces south, it may be necessary to use shading, such as a coating on the glass or movable external or internal blinds or screens, to prevent the temperature from rising too high. Both temperature and humidity can also be controlled by ventilation: methods of ventilating vary from manually operated openings in the roof or walls to automatically controlled motor-driven vents, or extractor fans. What you choose will depend on factors such as whether you will be there to open manual vents (not a good idea if you are working or on vacation) and the cost.

Within the conservatory, plants can be grown in specially constructed beds, or in containers. If you are using beds it many be worth considering heating the soil by means of buried heating pipes or electric cables, and at the same time installing some sort of irrigation system. Again, what you do will depend on how much time you have to devote to the plants and the price of heating and watering (of both their installation and their operation). An advantage of growing plants in pots is that they can be moved, either within the conservatory or outside on warmer days.

Many countries now impose minimum standards of construction on all new greenhouses, whether they are built of wood or metal and have glazing of glass or plastic. Compliance with these standards is compulsory, and especially sensible in areas which may be subject to high winds or snow loading.

All dual-purpose climbers, those suitable for conservatories or warm sites in the open garden, are listed on page 158 and cross-referenced to their appropriate section in the book.

(Right) Conservatories add another room to the house, making an ideal place to relax among the lush growth of flowers and climbers. Here, plumbago, bougainvillea and hoya introduce height and colour.

Allamanda cathartica

ALLAMANDA
(Apocynaceae)

Shrubby, evergreen species from the American tropics with large, eye-catching flowers produced at the branch tips. The most often seen is *A. cathartica*, grown for its golden flowers. If plants become too vigorous they can be tied into their support and the previous season's growth pruned back to 1 or 2 nodes. Propagation is by cuttings.

✓ *A. cathartica*
COMMON ALLAMANDA,
GOLDEN TRUMPET
Stems very vigorous, climbing to 16m (55ft). Leaves in whorls of 3 or 4, narrowly obovate, leathery, shiny. Flowers 6–10cm (2¼–4in) across, funnel-shaped with a narrow tube and 5 rounded lobes, golden yellow; summer to autumn. It demands no care and is virtually free of pests and diseases. This species is poisonous. Tropical S America
☼ ☽ 13°C (55°F) ⋎ℓs

'**Hendersonii**': flowers 9–12cm (3½–4¾in) across, deeper yellow, tinted bronze outside and opening from brown buds, throat with white spots at the base of the lobes. '**Williamsii**': flowers yellow with a brown throat.

ARISTOLOCHIA
(Aristolochiaceae)

A genus of about 300 species, most of which are climbers. They are grown for their handsome leaves and their curious flowers. The flowers have no petals, just a calyx with a swollen base (utricle) contracted into a tube which flares at the top into a flat or funnel-shaped structure (limb). The flowers of most species have a foul smell; this attracts insects which enter the flower and are held there by downward-pointing hairs. They pollinate the flower and escape only when the flower ages and changes shape or the downward-pointing hairs wither. Aristolochias like rich well-drained soil with plenty of water in the growing season. Pruning may be necessary to control their growth. They should be sited with care because of their unpleasant-smelling flowers; in a conservatory they are best grown close to a door or window with a through draught. Propagation is best from cuttings. Many species are cultivated and only a selection is given below.

A. californica and *A. chrysops* (see page 40)

A. gigantea
Stems herbaceous, up to 4m (13ft). Leaves broadly triangular, 10–15cm (4–6in) long, white-hairy beneath. Flowers purple and white, tube about 4cm (1½in) long, limb broadly heart-shaped, about 14cm (5½in) across; summer. Panama
☼ ☽ 15°C (59°F) ⋎ℓs

A. grandiflora
PELICAN FLOWER, SWAN FLOWER
Stems herbaceous, up to 3m (10ft). Leaves triangular to heart-shaped. Flowers solitary in leaf axils, variable in size, blotched with white, yellow, red, purple and green, utricle 6–16cm (2½–6½in) long, tube bent at mid-point, 7–15cm (6in) long, limb heart-shaped with a straplike appendage, 20–50cm (8–20in) across; summer. Central America, the Caribbean
☼ ☽ 15°C (59°F) ⋎ℓs

A. littoralis ♛
(*A. elegans*)
CALICO FLOWER
Leaves heart-shaped, grey-green beneath, foetid when crushed. Flowers solitary, on long stalks, with a bent greenish-yellow tube about 3.5cm (1½in) long and a purple-brown, irregularly white-marked limb about 10cm (4in) across; summer. Brazil
☼ ☽ -5°C (23°F) ⋎ℓs

BEAUMONTIA
(Apocynaceae)

Evergreen climbers with large, showy, highly fragrant flowers, borne in axillary and terminal clusters. Propagation is by seed, semi-ripe cuttings or root cuttings.

✓ *B. grandiflora*
(*B. jerdoniana*)
EASTER LILY VINE, MOONVINE,
HERALD'S TRUMPET
Stems woody, twining to 5m

Beaumontia grandiflora

(16ft) or more, with milky sap. Leaves broadly oblong, shiny, 10–30cm (4–12in) long. Flowers funnel- to bell-shaped, 12–18cm (4¾–7¼in) long, with 5 spreading lobes, white, greenish inside; spring to summer. A good conservatory plant but one that can grow vigorously and may need to be kept in check by pruning after flowering: this also promotes more lateral shoots. If allowed to grow unchecked, ensure that it has a strong support to carry its weight. India to Vietnam

☼ 7°C (45°F) ⚘⌀

BOUGAINVILLEA
(Nyctaginaceae)

Probably the best-known of all tropical climbers, cultivated outside in all the warmer regions of the world and under glass (often in pots) in temperate latitudes. They are grown for their often dazzling (some might say vulgar!) bracts: usually 3 bracts surround 1–3 tubular flowers and they are produced over a long time-span.

Bougainvilleas are not fussy about soil, although they grow and flower best in a fairly rich medium. They should be given water and fertilizer when actively growing. Pruning is best done after flowering, to encourage the new growth which will bear the next crop of flowers. To reduce the size of a plant, it should be cut back by about a third and all spindly growth removed. Propagation is by cuttings.

The species *B. glabra*, *B. peruviana* and *B. spectabilis* are all in cultivation, as is the hybrid *B.* × *buttiana*. However, these have now largely been replaced in gardens by cultivars which are available in a range of colours. The naming of cultivars is in a state of considerable confusion. Descriptions, especially of bract colour, may be different in a number of sources, including nurserymen's catalogues. The allocation of synonyms is also often inconsistent, with examples of the same synonym being assigned to up to three different cultivars. The following list contains names which (it is hoped) are not controversial. The colours refer to the bracts.

✔ **'Alba'**: white. **'Afterglow'**: deep orange aging to orange pink. **'Asia'**: red-purple. ✔ **'Barbara Karst'**: bright red. **'Bois de Rose'**: dusty pink. ✔ **'Camarillo Fiesta'** ('Orange Glow'): burnt orange, fading to coppery-red. **'Elizabeth Angus'**: bright purple. **'Formosa'**: light purple. ✔ **'Lateritia'** (Brasiliensis'): brick-red. **'Miss Manila'** ('Tango'): apricot fading to rose. **'Mrs Butt'**: ♀ crimson. **'Mrs H.C. Buck'**: rich magenta. **'Poultonii Special'**: ♀ red-purple. **'Rosa Catalina'**: rosy pink. ✔ **'Sanderiana'**: deep purple. ✔ **'Scarlett O'Hara'** ('San Diego Red'): dark red. **'Shubra'** ('Mary Palmer's Enchantment'): white. **'Texas Dawn'**: pale purple-pink. **'Thomasii'**: bright carmine.

Bougainvillea 'Pride of Singapor'

Double cultivars (with several bracts surrounding the flowers). ✔ **'Mahara'** ('Carmencita'): purple-red. **'Mahara Orange'** ('Thai Gold'): orange. **'Mahara Pink'** ('Pagoda Pink'): light cerise. ✔ **'Roseville's Delight'**: orange-red fading to orange-pink and red-purple.

Cultivars with variegated foliage. ✔ **'Golden Summers'**: white. ✔ **'Orange Stripe'**: light orange. **'Pride of Singapor'**: purple-pink, veined bracts. **'Raspberry Ice'** ('Brilliant'): crimson-red. **'Red Fantasy'**: deep red. ✔ **'Sanderiana Variegata'**: deep purple. **'Thimma'** ('Harlequin'): bicolored pink and white.

Cultivars with bicolored bracts. **'Begum Sikander'**: rosy purple and white. **'Chitra'**: white, mauve and red-purple. **'Makris'**: pink and white. ✔ **'Mary Palmer'** ('Surprise'): pink and white. **'Wajid Ali Shah'**: magenta-red and white. **'Thimma'** ('Harlequin'): pink and white, leaves variegated.

Cissus
(Vitaceae)

A genus of some 350 perennial, often woody, species from tropical and subtropical regions which are grown primarily for the bold, sometimes beautifully marked leaves. The flowers are tiny, 4-petalled, greenish-white and carried in clusters. Most species have tendrils. The fruit is a berry. Propagation is by seed or cuttings.

Cissus discolor

C. antarctica ♈
KANGAROO VINE
Evergreen with woody stems to 5m (16ft) or more, climbing by forked tendrils which are borne opposite the leaves. Leaves glossy, oval to oblong with entire or toothed margins. A popular and easy conservatory or house plant. Australasia
☀ 7°C (45°F) ⑂ℓs

✓ C. discolor
(*Vitis discolor*)
REX BEGONIA VINE
Stems dark red, slender, woody, up to 3m (10ft). Leaves oval-oblong to lance-shaped, toothed, deep green with silver-white or pink blotches between the veins above, dark red beneath. One of the glories of the genus, which requires both high temperature and humidity to perform at its best. It is a spectacular conservatory foliage plant. SE Asia to Australia
☀ 18°C (64°F) ⑂ℓs

C. rhombifolia ♈
GRAPE IVY, VENEZUELA TREEBINE
Evergreen with stems to 3m (10ft) or more, red-brown hairy when young, climbing by forked tendrils. Leaves with 3 toothed leaflets, red-brown hairy when young. Widely grown as a conservatory and house plant. Sometimes sold under the name *Rhoicissus rhomboidea*, a similar-looking South African species which is not in general cultivation. Mexico to Brazil, West Indies
☀ 7°C (45°F) ⑂ℓs
> **'Ellen Danica'**: ♈ vigorous, with large deeply lobed leaves.

C. striata (see page 89)

Epipremnum
(Araceae)

A genus of about 12 species from SE Asia and the Pacific Islands. They are evergreen, with juvenile and adult phases, climbing by means of stem-roots. Plants grow best in a

Epipremnum aureum

rich soil and in semi-shade. Propagation is by cuttings or layering.

E. aureum ♈
(*Pothos aureus, Scindapsus aureus, Rhaphidophora aurea*)
DEVIL'S IVY, GOLDEN POTHOS, HUNTER'S ROBE, MONEY PLANT
Adult stems up to 15m (50ft). Juvenile leaves up to 15cm (6in) long, broadly heart-shaped, green with irregular variegations of white or yellow; adult leaves up to 80cm (32in) long, oval to oblong, irregularly pinnatisect. Flower spikes up to 15cm (6in) long. A fast-growing climber which is a popular conservatory or pot plant. Some botanists now call this plant *E. pinnatum* 'Aureum'. Solomon Islands
☀ ☀ 15°C (59°F) ⑧ℓ
> **'Marble Queen'**: less vigorous that the species. Leaves entire, green with darker green and white streaks, leaf stalks white. **'Tricolor'**: leaves entire, variegated with cream and white, leaf stalks whitish. **'Tropic Green'**: leaves green.

FICUS
(Moraceae)

There are some 800 mainly tropical species of fig, most of which are evergreen. They range from small creeping shrubs to giant trees. The alternate leaves vary considerably in shape. Figs have unisexual flowers which characteristically cover the internal walls of a hollow receptacle – in the common fig (*F. carica*) it is this receptacle or 'fig' which is eaten.

F. pumila ♀
(*F. stipulata*)
CREEPING FIG, CLIMBING FIG
Stems cling to a suitable support by aerial roots which are produced at the stem nodes. The plant has two stages in its development – juvenile and adult – but reaches the adult stage (which bears the flowers and fruit) only when grown in warmer areas or under glass and when it reaches a height of 3–4m (10–13ft). Juvenile leaves heart-shaped, 1.8–3cm (¾–1¼in) long. Adult leaves 3–8cm (1¼–3¼in) long, very leathery. Fruits obovoid, about 6cm (2½in) long, green at first, becoming bright orange, eventually suffused with purplish-red. A delightful species which is often grown in conservatories or as a trailing house plant. However, it is hardier than generally supposed and will survive on a warm, sheltered wall or tree trunk in warmer temperate regions, although it normally remains in the juvenile state. It dislikes drought and cold winds. To promote branching, the stem tips can be pinched out. China, Taiwan, Japan
☼ ◐ ● 5°C (41°F) ✿
'Minima': a slender, slow-growing cultivar with leaves only about 1cm (½in) long. **'Quercifolia'**: leaves lobed. **'Variegata'**: leaves with a white or cream margin.

HOYA
(Asclepiadaceae)

Hoyas are grown for their rather unusual, waxy flowers. A genus of about 90 species, many of which are climbers. They are evergreen shrubby or succulent plants with 5-lobed flowers produced in clusters in the leaf axils. Each flower has a central 5-lobed corona formed from outgrowths of the stamen bases. The fruit is a more or less cylindric, horn-like follicle containing tufted seeds.

Plants grow best in a well-drained soil which should not be allowed to dry out. Brightly lit positions are preferable but direct hot sunlight can scorch the leaves. The weakly twining stems need support, such as wires or trellis. Propagation is by semi-ripe cuttings.

✓ *H. carnosa*
A slow-growing climber with stems reaching 6m (20ft) or more. Leaves thick, elliptic-obovate, hairless, 5–10cm (2–4in) long. Flowers fragrant, star-shaped, 1.5cm (½in) across, lobes white to pale pink, somewhat recurved, with dense papillae above, corona white with a red centre, borne in hanging, rounded umbels; spring to autumn. Australasia
◐ 5°C (41°F) ✿

JASMINUM
(Oleaceae)

The jasmines are much-loved plants, grown for their often highly fragrant flowers. The genus is described on page 94.

J. angulare
An evergreen climber. Leaves dark green, with 3 oval to lance-shaped leaflets. Flowers fragrant, white, in clusters of 3–7 which make up handsome broad panicles; late summer to early autumn. A lovely plant which makes a fine conservatory subject. It can be grown in temperate gardens if given a warm, sheltered position and protected in winter. South Africa
☼ 0°C (32°F) ✿s

✓ *J. grandiflorum*
CATALONIAN JASMINE, ROYAL JASMINE, SPANISH JASMINE
An evergreen scrambler. Leaves with 7 or 9 leaflets. Flowers fragrant, white, occasionally tinged with red, 3–4cm (1¼–1½in) across, with 5 or 6 lobes, in clusters of up to 50; summer to autumn. A lovely species, sometimes confused with *J. officinale* but with larger flowers. It can be grown in temperate regions if given a very warm, sheltered position; it grows well in the Mediterranean area. It was first introduced into southern Europe by the Arabs, and used for perfume extraction. Today, the area around Grasse in southern France is the main centre for this industry. SW Arabia, NE Africa
☼ 7°C (45°F) ✿s

J. laurifolium forma *nitidum* (*J. nitidum*)
ANGEL WING JASMINE, STAR JASMINE, WINDMILL JASMINE
Evergreen with slender twining stems up to 3m (10ft). Leaves narrowly elliptic, bright shiny green. Flowers star-like, borne in sparse clusters at the ends of branches, fragrant. Calyx hairy, lobes sharply pointed, spreading. Corolla white, sometimes tinged with pink in bud, tube up to 2cm (¾in), lobes narrow, 8–11, about 3cm (1¼in) across; summer. Thought to have originated in India
☼ 7°C (45°F) ✿s

J. mesneyi and *J. officinale*
(*see page 95*)

✓ *J. polyanthum* ♀
Evergreen with twining stems to 3m (10ft) or even to 8m (26ft) in a favourable position. Leaves with 5 or 7 lance-shaped leaflets. Flowers in large clusters, fragrant, white although often flushed with pink or red outside, especially in bud, 1–2cm (½–¾in)

across, with 5 lobes and a corolla-tube 2—2.2cm ($\frac{3}{4}$in) long; late spring to early autumn. A beautiful, free-flowering jasmine which will survive on a warm, sheltered wall in cool temperate latitudes, and may be grown over an arch or pergola where the danger of frost is insignificant. It is more often grown in a conservatory (where plants have been known to reach 7.5m (24½ft) tall against a wall), or used as a house plant, where it will require vigorous pruning to keep it in check. S China

☀ 0°C (32°F) ⊻ₛ

J. rex

KING'S JASMINE
A vigorous climber with slender stems up to 3m (10ft). Leaves broadly oval, long-pointed. Flowers 2 or 3 in the leaf axils on drooping stalks, not scented; summer, or throughout year in warmer areas. Calyx with 6 narrow lobes twice as long as the tube. Corolla white with 6—9 lobes, about 5cm (2in) across. Thailand, Cambodia

☀ 18°C (64°F) ⊻

✓ J. sambac

ARABIAN JASMINE
Evergreen with stems up to 3m (10ft). Leaves oblong to oval. Flowers fragrant, in clusters at the branch tips and in the leaf axils just below; late spring. Calyx lobes tiny. Corolla white, 3—5cm (1¼—2in) across with 5—9 oblong to rounded lobes. India

☀ ◑ 15°C (51°F) ⊻ₛ
'Grand Duke of Tuscany'
('Grand Duke', 'Flore Pleno'): flowers double.

MANDEVILLA
(Apocynaceae)

Mandevillas are popular climbers, grown for their beautiful flowers which, in some species, are fragrant. They are spectacular conservatory plants and flower over a relatively long period. They are tuberous, evergreen perennials with twining stems containing milky sap. The flowers are funnel-shaped with 5 spreading lobes and the stamens are borne within the throat. The fruit is a pair of cylindrical follicles. Mandevillas should be grown in a fertile, humus-rich soil with plenty of water while they are growing. In winter they can be kept almost dry. Propagation is from cuttings. The roots go deep, which makes the plants difficult to transplant.

✓ M. × amabilis ♛
(M. × amoena, Dipladenia × amabilis)
Stems up to 4m (13ft). Leaves oblong, wrinkled. Flowers rose-pink shading to a darker colour at the centre, throat yellow, lobes rounded, each with a short point, 9—13cm (3½—5¼in) across; summer. Garden origin

☀ ◑ 7°C (45°F) ⊻ₛ
'Alice du Pont': flowers smaller,

Mandevilla laxa

bright pink, in larger clusters, produced over many months.

✓ M. laxa
(M. suaveolens)
CHILEAN JASMINE
Stems up to 4m (13ft) or more. Leaves oblong, long-pointed, base heart-shaped. Flowers very fragrant, up to 5cm (2in) across, white to cream, tube downy inside, lobes broad, rounded, often crinkled on the edge, in clusters of 5—15; summer. This species is slightly hardier than the others and can be grown in temperate gardens in a really warm, sheltered position, if given protection in winter. Argentina

◑ 2°C (36°F) ⊻ₛ

✓ M. splendens
(Dipladenia splendens)
PINK ALLAMANDA
Shrub with stems twining to 6m (20ft). Leaves broadly elliptic, pointed, downy, up to 20cm (8in) long. Flowers rose-pink with spreading lobes, tube up to 3.2cm (1¼in) long,

flowers eventually 10 cm (4in) wide, borne in a 3—5-flowered raceme; spring to autumn. As the flowers age they deepen in colour. SE Brazil

☀ ◑ 7°C (45°F) ⊻ₛ

MONSTERA
(Araceae)

A genus of about 22 evergreen species, grown mainly for their handsome foliage. The thick stems often produce aerial roots and the leaves (which have juvenile and adult states) are large and perforated. The spadix bears hermaphrodite flowers and is shorter than the white or cream spathe. The fruit is a spike of white berries, usually sweet and edible. Propagation is by seed or cuttings.

⊞ M. deliciosa ♛
CERIMAN, FRUIT SALAD PLANT, SWISS CHEESE PLANT
Plant climbing to 20m (66ft). Leaves thick and leathery, 25—90cm (10—36in) long, broadly oval, pinnatifid or pinnatisect into curved, oblong, truncate lobes; more mature leaves often have holes. Spathes up to 20cm (8in) or more long; spadix 10—18cm (4—7in) long; summer. Fruits smelling of pineapple. Grows best in a moist but well-drained, humus-rich soil, in semi-shade. As a house or conservatory plant, *M. deliciosa* will tolerate low light and a dryish atmosphere, but will not attain the huge size that it

displays out of doors in tropical regions. Mexico to Panama
☼ ☀ 15°C (59°F) ⌇🖉s

'**Variegata**': ♀ leaves variegated with white.

PANDOREA
(Bignoniaceae)

A genus of 6 species of evergreen, twining climbers from Australasia, grown for their pretty leaves and flowers. The corolla is tubular, ending in 5 spreading, rounded lobes. They grow well in pots under glass and may even be tried out of doors in a very sheltered, warm spot with winter protection. Propagation is by seed or cuttings.

P. jasminoides
(*Bignonia jasminoides, Tecoma jasminoides*)
BOWER OF BEAUTY, BOWER PLANT
Stems woody, up to 5m (16ft). Leaflets 5–9, narrowly oval to lance-shaped, pointed, 2.5–6cm (1 2½in) long. Flowers white, deep pink inside the throat, 3–5cm (1¼–2in) long, in 4–8-flowered clusters; spring to autumn. NE Australia
☼ 5°C (41°F) ⌇🖉

'**Alba**': flowers white with a yellow throat. '**Rosea Superba**': ♀ flowers large, pink with a darker throat. '**Variegata**': cream-variegated leaves.

P. pandorana
WONGA-WONGA VINE
Stems up to 6m (20ft). Leaflets usually 13, oval to lance-

Pandorea jasminoides

shaped. Flowers fragrant, 1–2cm (½–¾in) long, creamy-yellow with red or purple markings in the throat, in many-flowered clusters; winter to spring. Australia, New Guinea, Pacific Islands
☼ 5°C (41°F) ⌇🖉

'**Alba**': flowers white both inside and out. '**Rosea**': flowers pale pink.

PASSIFLORA
(Passifloraceae)

The passion flowers are widely known and grown plants, popular for their exotic blooms and attractive, sometimes edible fruit. In all there are some 350 species. Most are woody climbers, primarily native to Central and South America, although a few come from the Old World tropics. The species most commonly grown in temperate latitudes is *P. caerulea*, the blue passion flower (*see page 98*). The fruits for sale usually come from

P. edulis, the granadilla.

The flowers of passion flowers are beautiful but rather complicated. They have a tubular calyx with 5 sepals, and 5 petals which usually resemble the sepals. Within these there is a ring or several rings of threads or 'filaments', which are usually brightly coloured – these filaments make up the 'corona'. In the centre of the flower are 5 conspicuous stamens carried on an elongated central column which also supports the ovary and 3 stigmas. A characteristic of most species is the presence of nectaries on the leaf stalks. The climbing species have coiling tendrils which cling to any support they can find. The passion flower gets its name from the resemblance which Spanish priests in South America saw between the flower parts and the instruments of Christ's passion. The 10 sepals and petals thus represent the 10 apostles, the corona the crown

of thorns, the 5 stamens the 5 wounds and the 3 stigmas the 3 nails.

Usually the only pruning needed is that required to keep the plant within bounds; this is best done in the spring or while the plant is actively growing. Propagation is by seed or cuttings of semi-mature shoots.

Only a few species can tolerate outdoor conditions in temperate regions, none being completely hardy. They require a sunny, sheltered south- or west-facing wall or a tall protected fence. Species which can be grown in temperate gardens are described on pages 98 and 138.

✓ P. × allardii
A cross between *P. caerulea* 'Constance Elliott' and *P. quadrangularis*. Stems vigorous, up to 5m (16ft), square in cross-section. Leaves 3-lobed with 4 glands on the stalks. Flowers fragrant, 7–11cm (2¾–4½in) across; spring to autumn; almost all year in the tropics. Sepals white edged mauve, petals mauve-pink. Corona violet, banded with white and purple-red towards centre; filaments in 3–5 rows. Fruit about 6cm (2½in) long, orange, lacking seeds. A lovely hybrid which can be grown in temperate regions, especially if frost is rare.
Garden origin
☼ 5°C (41°F) 🍃🖉

✓ P. amethystina
(*see page 138*)

✓ *P. antioquiensis* ♀
(*Tacsonia vanvolxemii*)
RED BANANA PASSION FRUIT
Stems slender, brown-downy, growing to 5m (16ft). Leaves either unlobed and lance-shaped, or deeply 3-lobed, the stalks with up to 8 glands. Flowers pendulous, 10–14cm (4–5½in) across; late summer to autumn. Sepals and petals rose-red. Corona violet; filaments in 3 rows, only 2mm (⅛in) long. Fruit golden-yellow, banana-shaped, edible. A very beautiful species which, although usually grown under glass in temperate latitudes, will succeed out of doors in milder areas. It can stand a slight frost provided the roots are not frozen. Fruits are seldom set in temperate regions. Colombia
☼ 0°C (32°F) ↴ₛ

P. caerulea (*see page 98*)

✓ *P. coccinea*
RED GRANADILLA, RED PASSION FLOWER
Stems grooved, brown-downy, purplish when young. Leaves oblong, heart-shaped at base, margin toothed or scalloped, the stalks with 2 glands or glands lacking. Flowers scarlet, to 12.5cm (5in) wide; summer to autumn. Sepals and petals scarlet. Corona purple and white; filaments 1cm (½in) long, in 3 rows. Fruit edible, yellow or orange, blotched and with 6 stripes. Guyana, Surinam, Venezuela, Brazil, Bolivia, Peru
☼ 15°C (59°F) ✍

✓ *P. edulis*
GRANADILLA, PASSION FRUIT
Stems vigorous, angular, growing to 8m (26ft) or more. Leaves evergreen, 3-lobed (young leaves often unlobed), with 2 glands on the stalks. Flowers 5–8cm (2–3½in) across; year-round. Sepals green outside, white inside, petals white inside and outside. Corona white with a purple centre; filaments crinkled towards the ends; summer to early autumn. Fruits egg-shaped, 4.5–6cm (1¾–2½in) long, yellow or purplish. This attractive plant can be grown in temperate latitudes with frost protection, although it *can* tolerate periods of 5–11°C (10–52°F) for a short time. *P. edulis* is the most widely grown species for fruit production but, outside tropical areas, fruit production is not good. The fruits are eaten and used to make a juice. Brazil, Paraguay, N Argentina
☼ 10°C (50°F) ✍
> ✓ **'Crackerjack'**: fruit very large and abundant, dark purple to black. **'Flavicarpa'**: yellow fruit and larger flowers. **'Perfecta'**: fruit very large.

P. incarnata (*see page 138*)

✓ *P. quadrangularis* ♀
GIANT GRANADILLA
Stems vigorous, up to 15m (50ft) or more, square in cross-section with wings at the corners. Leaves oval with 4 or 6 glands on the stalks. Flowers up to 12cm (4¾cm) across; summer to early autumn.

Passiflora quadrangularis

Sepals green or reddish outside, pale or deep red inside, petals pale to deep red. Corona banded red-purple and white; filaments in 5 rows, 6cm (2½in) long, wavy towards the ends. Fruit oblong to egg-shaped, up to 30cm (12in) long, green or orange. A spectacular species with the largest flowers and fruit in the genus. Central America, West Indies
☼ 10°C (50°F) ✍

✓ *P. vitifolia*
(*P. sanguinea*)
VINE-LEAVED PASSION FLOWER
Stems vigorous, covered in rusty brown hairs. Leaves 3-lobed, with 2 glands at the top of the stalk and sometimes 2 or 3 in the middle. Flowers 10–19cm (4–7½in) across, fragrant; spring to early autumn. Sepals and petals bright red. Corona red to yellow; filaments in 3 rows, 10–20mm (4–8in) long. Fruit egg-shaped, about 6cm (2½in) long, downy, mottled greenish-yellow; they are edible. A spectacular plant in full flower and a wonderful conservatory subject. Very free-flowering.
S Central America, NW South America
☼ 16°C (61°F) ✍

PHILODENDRON
(Araceae)

A tropical American genus of about 500 evergreen perennials many species of which are widely grown for their attractive leaves, both as conservatory and house plants. The stout stems have

Passiflora vitifolia

distinctive leaf-scars and produce aerial roots. The leaf stalk has a sheath and the leaves usually have juvenile and adult states, and can be entire or variously dissected. The inflorescences are produced in the leaf axils. A fleshy spathe surrounds the spadix which is usually white and covered with male and female flowers arranged in adjacent bands. The fruit is a white, orange or red berry. The climbing species grow best in semi-shade in a humus-rich soil; they appreciate regular applications of fertilizer. Philodendrons need no pruning, except to limit their growth; this can be done at any time. Propagation is by cuttings or layering, more rarely by seed.

✓ *P. bipennifolium*
FIDDLE LEAF
Leaves 30–80cm (12–32in), oval to arrow-shaped with 5–7 radiating lobes, reflexed on the stalk. Leaf stalk somewhat shorter than blade. Spathe about 11cm (4½in) long, greenish-cream. SE Brazil
☼ ● 15°C (59°F) ✤

✓ *P. erubescens* ♀
BLUSHING PHILODENDRON, RED-LEAF PHILODENDRON
Young stems red or purple. Leaves up to 40cm (16in) long, reflexed on their stalks, leathery, dark green above, often with a coppery flush, brownish-purple beneath, oval-triangular with short basal lobes. Leaf stalk equal in length to blade, flattened towards top,

purplish. Spathe about 15cm (6in) long, deep purple outside, crimson inside, fragrant. Colombia
☼ ● 15°C (59°F) ✤
'**Burgundy**': ♀ leaves burgundy-red. '**Red Emerald**': more robust, with the stems, leaf stalks and veins on the underside of the leaves reddish-purple. '**Imperial Red**': leaves deep purple to red.

✓ *P. melanochrysum*
BLACK-GOLD PHILODENDRON
Leaves up to 100 × 30cm (40 × 12in), narrowly lance-shaped or narrowly oval, pointed at the tip and with the basal lobes overlapping or with a narrow gap, velvety blackish-green or olive-green with paler veins, variously reflexed on their stalks. Leaf stalk rather scaly. Juvenile leaves are smaller, oval to heart-shaped and with the basal lobes sometimes joined. Spathe about 20cm (8in) long, with a green tube and a white limb. A handsome species, which can provide a different shade of green. Colombia.
☼ ● 15°C (59°F) ✤

✓ *P. scandens* ♀
(*Pothos scandens*)
HEART-LEAF PHILODENDRON, SWEETHEART VINE
Stem climbing up to 4m (13ft) or more with the top part eventually hanging down and producing flowers. Leaves heart-shaped, reflexed on their stalks, juvenile 10–15cm (4–6in) long, adult up to 30cm (12in) long. Leaf stalk shorter than blade, with a channel on the upper side. Spathe up to

Plumbago auriculata

20cm (8in) long, green with a whitish limb. Fast-growing and probably the most commonly cultivated species, often used as a house plant, partly because it can tolerate neglect and low light. Sometimes sold as *P. cordatum*, a name which applies to a different species. Mexico, West Indies to SE Brazil
☼ 15°C (59°F) ✤
Forma *micans*: leaves are brownish above and red to reddish-brown beneath, and the basal leaves overlap slightly. **Subsp. *oxycardium*:** juvenile leaves tinged with brown when young. **Subsp. *scandens*:** juvenile leaves with a metallic or velvety sheen above. **Forma *scandens*:** leaves green above, green or red-purple beneath. '**Lemon Lime**': leaves yellow-green. '**Variegatum**': leaves deep green variegated with grey-green and white.

PLUMBAGO
(Plumbaginaceae)

Of the 10 species of *Plumbago*, only the one described below is commonly cultivated. It is

grown for its freely borne clusters of blue flowers. Heavy pruning is best carried out in late winter or spring, but plants may also be pruned after flowering to prevent them becoming straggly. Propagation is usually by suckers, by division of the roots or by cuttings, as *P. auriculata* is self-sterile and its seed is produced only infrequently.

✓ *P. auriculata* ♀
(*P. capensis*)
CAPE LEADWORT
Evergreen shrub with somewhat scandent, slender stems up to 6m (20ft). Leaves up to 7cm (2¾in) long, oblong to spoon-shaped. Flowers with a tubular, 5-lobed, glandular-hairy calyx and a pale blue 5-lobed corolla 2.5cm (1in) across, the narrow tube 4cm (1½in) long, in many-flowered clusters at the ends of the shoots; spring to autumn. South Africa
☼ ☼ 7°C (45°F) ✤
var. *alba*: flowers white. ✓ '**Royal Cape**': flowers deep blue.

PYROSTEGIA
(Bignoniaceae)

Pyrostegia is an evergreen genus which contains the flame vine, grown for its spectacular display of tubular, 2-lipped orange flowers. The species climb both by their twining, 6–8-ribbed stems and by tendrils. The leaves have 2 leaflets and usually a terminal tendril, or 3 leaflets. The flowers have protruding stamens. Propagation is by semi-ripe cuttings 2 or 3 nodes long.

✓ *P. venusta*
(*P. ignea*)
FLAME VINE, FLAMING TRUMPET, GOLDEN SHOWER

Stems to 25m (82ft), usually less in gardens. Leaflets oval to narrowly so. Flowers bright orange, tubular, curved, 3.5–7cm (1½–2¾in) long, 2-lipped, the upper lip 2-lobed and the lower 3-lobed, lobes downy; flowers borne in clusters of 15–20 at the branch

Pyrostegia venusta

ends; autumn to spring. A fast-growing plant which makes a beautiful conservatory subject It grows best in slightly acid soil. Brazil, Paraguay, Bolivia, Argentina
☼ 13°C (55°F) 🌿

SOLANDRA
(Solanaceae)

About 8 species of tall, evergreen climbing shrubs grown for their enormous flowers; the plant needs lots of room to show them to advantage. The leaves are simple, entire and usually leathery. The broadly funnel-shaped flowers have 5 lobes which become reflexed: they are produced at the branch tips. They make good conservatory plants provided they are given enough space. Flowering is induced by a dry period: plants will not flower well if watered continuously. Propagation is by seed or greenwood cuttings.

✓ *S. grandiflora*
SILVER CHALICE

Stems scrambling to 6m (20ft) or more. Leaves elliptic to obovate, up to 17cm (6¾in) long. Flowers fragrant at night, solitary, up to 23cm (9¼in) long, the corolla-tube equal in length to the calyx, opening white but turning yellow or sometimes pinkish and with purplish lines inside, lobes wavy-margined; autumn to spring. Jamaica, Puerto Rico, Lesser Antilles
☼ ☀ 10°C (50°F) 🌿

S. longiflora
(*S. macrantha*)
GABRIEL'S TRUMPET

Stems up to 2m (6½ft). Leaves elliptic to oblong. Flowers up to 30cm (12in) long with the narrow tubular part of the corolla much longer than calyx. Flowers fragrant at night, white at first with 5 purplish lines in throat, eventually turning yellow and deepening even further with age; winter. Jamaica, Cuba, Hispaniola
☼ ☀ 10°C (50°F) 🌿

✓ *S. maxima*
(*S. hartwegii*)
CUP OF GOLD, GOLDEN CHALICE

Stems up to 6m (20ft) or more. Leaves elliptic, hairless. Flowers fragrant, rich yellow, deepening with age, with 5 dark purplish lines inside, 15–22cm (6–9in) long, abruptly contracted into a narrow tube, the lobes folded back so the scalloped edge is often hidden. Perhaps the most

Solandra maxima

striking species, which is often offered by nurseries under the name *S. guttata*. Mexico, Central America, Colombia, Venezuela
☼ ☀ 10°C (50°F) 🌿

SOLANUM
(Solanaceae)

A large genus of about 1400 species, relatively few of which are climbers. Those described below are grown for their pretty flowers which are often produced in abundance. The flowers have a 5-lobed corolla with a short tube. The 5 stamens' anthers converge around the style to form a cone. Propagation is by seed or cuttings. See page 52 and page 100 for temperate species.

✓ *S. seaforthianum*
BRAZILIAN NIGHTSHADE, TOMATILLO, ST VINCENT LILAC

Stems woody, slender, up to 6m (20ft). Leaves broadly elliptic, entire or pinnately divided into 3–5 or more lobes. Flowers star-like, flattish to bell-shaped, pale blue or sometimes white, pink or purple, about 2cm (¾in) across, borne in drooping clusters; summer. South America

☼ ☽ 🌡 5°C (41°F) ⋎ℓ**s**

S. wendlandii
GIANT POTATO CREEPER, MARRIAGE VINE, PARADISE FLOWER

Differs from *S. seaforthianum* in having stems with hook-like spines, lower leaves usually pinnate with 9–13 leaflets, flowers 4.5–6cm (1¼–2½in) across, lilac-blue and hardly lobed but with a ruffled edge, borne in large terminal clusters; late summer to autumn. A most attractive evergreen climber which is a good conservatory subject. It may need severe pruning to keep it within bounds and to produce new flowering wood. Costa Rica

☼ 🌡 10°C (50°F) ⋎ℓ**s**

STEPHANOTIS
(Asclepiadaceae)

Twining, evergreen shrubs. The waxy flowers have a cylindrical corolla-tube, often inflated at the base, and 5 spreading lobes. There are 5 scales in the throat. The fruit is a fleshy follicle containing numerous flattened seeds, each with a plume of hairs. They are slow-growing plants which do best in an acid soil. Pruning is best carried out in winter before the plant produces new growth.

Propagation is by seed (though this is not produced reliably), layering, or semi-ripe cuttings; the latter are difficult to root and should be treated with a hormone rooting compound.

✓ S. floribunda ♀
BRIDAL WREATH, MADAGASCAR JASMINE, STEPHANOTIS

Stems up to 5m (16ft). Leaves elliptic, thick and leathery, 5–15cm (2–6in) long. Flowers very fragrant, waxy, white or ivory, the corolla-tube 4–6cm (1½–2½in) long with ovate-oblong lobes, in terminal and axillary clusters; spring to autumn. Fruit broadly cylindric, about 15cm (6in) long, often remaining for 2 years. A good conservatory plant whose flowers are long-lasting, both on the plant and when cut; there are usually two flushes of flower with sporadic flowers at other times. It is popular in bridal bouquets and decorations. Madagascar

☽ 🌡 13°C (55°F) ⋎ℓ**s**

Stephanotis floribunda

Tecomaria capensis

TECOMARIA
(Bignoniaceae)

This genus has only one species, a shrubby evergreen climber, much-loved for its bright flowers and its attractive, divided leaves. Propagation is by seed, suckers, semi-ripe cuttings or air-layering.

✓ T. capensis ♀
(*Tecoma capensis*)
CAPE HONEYSUCKLE

Stems twining to 8m (26ft). Leaves divided into 5–9 leaflets with toothed edges. Flowers tubular, curved, orange-red to scarlet, about 5cm (2in) long, with 5 rounded lobes and protruding stamens, in clusters of 6–8 at stem tips; spring to autumn. As well as being a good conservatory plant, Cape honeysuckle can be grown in temperate latitudes in a hot, sunny position against a sheltered south-facing wall. South Africa

☼ 🌡 10°C (50°F) ⋎ℓ**s**

'Aurea': flowers golden-yellow.

THUNBERGIA
(Acanthaceae)

A genus of about 100 annual or perennial herbs and shrubs, many of which are climbers. The leaves are simple and the flowers are produced singly in the leaf axils or in terminal racemes. The small calyx is covered by bracts and the curved, tubular corolla-tube has 5 rounded lobes: there are 4 stamens. Propagation is by seed, cuttings or layering.

T. alata *(see page 140)*

T. fragrans
SWEET CLOCK VINE
Fast-growing perennial evergreen with woody stems. Leaves broadly triangular to oblong, the base heart-shaped to arrow-shaped. Flowers solitary in the leaf axils, on long stalks. Corolla white, about 5cm (2in) across, with a short tube and spreading lobes; summer to autumn. India, Sri Lanka, Australasia
☼ 5°F (41°F) ⋎ℓs

✓ *T. grandiflora* ♀
BLUE TRUMPET VINE, CLOCK VINE, SKY FLOWER
Perennial evergreen with woody, twining stems up to 6m (20ft). Leaves elliptic, rough-hairy. Flowers solitary or in racemes. Corolla blue-mauve, tube up to 5cm (2in) long, with 5 somewhat unequal lobes, the upper 2 erect and the lower 3 spreading, about 7.5cm (3in) across, usually in drooping 8–10-flowered racemes; intermittently through the year but mainly summer to autumn. One of the most beautiful tropical climbers, but too vigorous for any but the largest conservatory.
N India
☼ ☀ 10°C (50°F) ⋎ℓs
✓ **'Alba'**: flowers usually larger, white with a yellow throat.

Thunbergia grandiflora

T. gregorii *(see page 140)*

✓ *T. mysorensis*
Evergreen with woody stems twining to 6m (20ft). Leaves narrowly elliptic. Flowers in hanging racemes, but each flower erect with 2 greenish-purple bracts. Corolla 3.5–5cm (1½–2in) long with a yellow tube and 5 unequal, reflexed lobes usually red-brown or sometimes spotted, borne in pendent racemes up to 45cm (18in) long; spring to autumn. Unusual and attractive, this is a novel plant for a large conservatory.
India
☼ 15°C (59°F) ⋎ℓs